AF527506

MISERY OF LEADERSHIP

A Holistic Approach to Good Leadership

MISERY OF LEADERSHIP

A Holistic Approach to Good Leadership

Irmel V. Marla
Kamal Taori

AUTHORSPRESS
Publishers of Scholarly Books
Under the Auspices of

International Institute for Holistic Research and Voluntary Action (India-Germany) &
Rural Business Hub Foundation India

Worldwide Circulation through Authorspress Global Network

First Published 2011

by

Authorspress

Editorial

Q-2A Hauz Khas Enclave,
New Delhi-110 016
e-mail: authorspress@yahoo.com

Marketing

E-35/103, Jawahar Park
Laxmi Nagar, Delhi-110 092
e-mail: authorspress@yahoo.com

Copyright © 2011 Authors

Misery of Leadership: A Holistic Approach to Good Leadership

ISBN 978-81-7273-597-5

Printed in India at Tarun Offset, Delhi.

Dedication

Dr. V. Sarma Marla

Dr. V. Sarma Marla, eminent social scientist and anthropologist, once said during a lively discussion where most of the people present were of the opinion, that India only would lack the right leaders, then, everything would fall into place: "*The cry for LEADERSHIP or LEADERS only leads to more submissiveness and individual irresponsibility. Why do we not demand "able leaders", "honest leaders", "accountable leaders", or, to say it all: GOOD LEADERS? Why do we accept all these puffed-up jokers?*"

This was sometime in the middle of the 1980s, in one of our frequent get-togethers with friends and acquaintances, when we could spend time in India, during some respite from research work in rural India.

Leadership issues had been of great concern for him, and he especially propagated the issue of preparing in time "second line leadership" to avoid ego-battles and constraints on organisations in all fields.

Sarma Marla is no more with us, but his memories are still lively and inspiring, and a lot of his thoughts have found their place in this book. We feel that by dedicating our second co-authored book to him, too, we can honour him and show that he is still alive in our hearts and minds—inspiring us!

We again present here parts of the dedication from our earlier co-authored book on *Operationalising Holistic Human Development* as it gives the background of his commitment to sustainable development in India:

This book is dedicated to late *Dr. V. Sarma Marla*, a visionary and eminent social scientist and anthropologist whose commitment for the underprivileged found expression in his manifold researches, action plans and activities. Most outstanding is his research and book on *Incidence of Bonded Labour in India* (published 1981), with tremendous effect on the hitherto conveniently hidden existence of these lowest strata of society. His tragic and untimely death deprived India of a Gandhian fighter against the evils of society and also, his friends and acquaintances of a warm-hearted, inspirational companion. With this book, his wife Irmel Marla and also, the co-author Dr. Taori, want to honour him in a way he would have appreciated. We found his unfinished manuscripts, notes, research findings, his visionary action plans embedded in Gandhian thoughts, a legacy which compelled us to take it up for realization.

He was harmoniously living in two different cultures, Germany and India, combining the best of each in his life and work. To promote Gandhian Philosophy in the West, he translated and edited Hind Swaraj, written by Gandhiji in 1908, into German language at a time when almost nobody saw the meaning of these writings as an action plan for a peaceful world.

The world has become poorer without Sarmaji. Let us take up his legacy.

Irmel V. Marla ***Dr. Kamal Taori***

Contents

1

Leadership in the Twenty-first Century

In spite of the fact that we observe a really inflationary increase in numbers of "leaders" in India, we hardly find genuine leaders among them who show key leadership potential in their personality structure.

What are the reasons for this abysmal picture?

We find three main attitudes prevalent in Indian society that are responsible for the present state of condition:

1. As soon as a person occupies a "position of power"—this applies to all levels of 'power'—he/she enjoys full appreciation as "leader", even when everyone knows that the person is basically incompetent, a rascal, an exploiter, corrupt, etc.—it is the *position* which counts, not the man or the woman who occupies it, not competency nor any merit.
2. Positions of power are given to persons not after their suitability, competency, merit, or expertise, but mainly after *seniority*[1], nepotistic influences, politics / party politics, blackmail, or any other pressure on decision makers.
3. A majority of Indian citizens, especially all levels of middle classes, are too ready to accept and pathetically show admiration to anyone who:
   a) shows tendencies to occupy a positions of power in the near future, or
   b) already occupies a position of power, or they
   c) change a basically negative opinion about a person the minute this person comes into power—no hesitation, and no shame attached, or
   d) are falling head over heels for persons in power, even if they cannot expect direct personal advantages.

Thus, the younger generation grows up in an atmosphere of hypocrisy and sycophancy, where the position holders are enjoying all undeserved benefits. The worst of it: our younger generation will repeat these significances exactly as they had the opportunity to observe and emulate it. They know that only this way they can succeed in both, in career and in their striving for a lifestyle they so much admire in all our Bollywood films. Only the Bollywood films have nothing to do with reality, and they always have a happy end. We asked a film producer in Mumbai why there is so much sugar-coating, and why there is always a happy ending. He smiled: "If we would not show a happy ending, people would demolish our cinema halls."

If the two main evils of our society, hypocrisy and sycophancy, are not drastically fought against and done away with, conditions in view of sustainable positive development will stay not only put, but there will be a very dangerous roll back in every aspect. Good leadership can only develop in a sound, open society where civil courage, visions, boldness, merit and commitment to solve societal problems are awarded. Submissiveness, meekness, greed, exploitation, reservation and the like should not have the upper hand like we have it today.

Perception and conduit of leadership in India are mainly an *outdated* concept, and executed as authoritarian as possible, further deepening the rift between those who are 'led' and those who are 'leading, i.e., wielding power in their own interest, not in those who should benefit from good leadership.

Nina Sibal put it this way[2] (on politicians vs. administrators): "Sometimes it's good to keep everyone in a state of hul-chul, never let them rest, keep them on their toes. It's an old, tried technique of administration. ... The British taught it to the civil service, the steel frame of their bureaucracy. Divide and rule, turn even husband against wife. Rule by fear, and uncertainty. We catch you by the balls, you bureaucrats, and twist your anxieties around inside you so that you remain constantly anxious. ... You watch me strut through your corridors, stand in your verandahs and terraces, always on display, a symbol of repository of the will of the people. Next year they will express it again. That's the trouble with democracy, elections come around every few years."

Now, we all are enjoying the freedom of a democratic country but yet, in spite of the fact that our Constitution gives equal rights to every citizen, there are some who are 'more free' than others. It seems that 'leaders' are free to enjoy all rights, and those who are subjects, and are to be 'led', have to perform all the duties. Thus, the required balance between "Rights & Duties" is abysmally perverted.

In this book, we venture into the main areas of leadership, analyse the impact of behavioural patterns of present-day leaders in the hierarchical set-ups, and give suggestions for mitigating the most burning damages, and for improving the overall conditions.

It goes without saying that essentially, we have to strive for a change of mindset and attitudes, the most difficult task as there are too many vested interests involved, too many advantages to be held on to, and too much would be at stake for those in the advantageous positions.

On the other hand, we cannot compete in a globalised world if we still cling to old-fashioned infrastructure and outdated, un-democratic behavioural patterns. After all, we blindly took over all the societal, administrative and political pattern from our colonial masters; we further bureaucratised them instead of positively develop them, and we are now horribly stuck up with leaders who don't have any clue on how to lead us into a promising future. Nor do they have any clue about the shape of our future: at the best, they react to day-to-day challenges, at the worst, they just don't care for the future; they cannot comprehend the tasks anyway, and we are extremely short of personalities with a vision. We dedicated one of the chapters exclusively to the visionary leaders this country would need so badly.

Let us first put some essential questions:

a) How to constructively face the challenges of our time and prepare for a bright future?
b) How to create conditions which would make it possible to determine actions, thus avoiding the usual only reacting to challenges in the first place?
c) How to define success parameters for good leadership valid for the present and for the time to come?
d) How to achieve a future-oriented change of mindset and attitudes in present-day decision makers and also in those who are subject to these decisions?

e) How to bring about an overall atmosphere conducive to change and to people-centred policies?

f) How can we bring about good leaders who are communication with the people instead of the present day telling them what to do, and what is good for them. How to bridge the gap between the rulers and those who are ruled?

g) How to abolish the outdated concept of leader = ruler, and put a future-oriented democratic, egalitarian concept of society in place?

What we have to work for is a drastic change in mindset and attitudes. Albert Einstein once said: "Problems cannot be solved at the same level of awareness that created them."

We have the impression that finding good leaders in our country amounts to the most difficult task that is to search for the needle in a haystack, but finally, in our realistic optimism, we are of the opinion that with all the gigantic hidden and un-used potential in India, the potential of good leadership will be found, the same way a needle in a haystack can be found by using the right tool, in the proverbial case: what about a magnet? This way, we have to find the right and suitable way to assess hidden leadership potential, to encourage developing of key abilities for leadership, and thus build up broader confidence with all the potential at hand.

For this, the existing patterns of leadership and the highly hierarchical structures in all ways of life—worse: the overall acceptance of these—are the main obstacles which have to be overcome.

In spite of the fact that we observe a really inflationary increase in numbers of "leaders" in India, we hardly find genuine leaders among them who show key leadership potential in their personality structure.

The position holders enjoy all undeserved benefits, whereas very often all those who contribute to success and achievement with their ideas, with their work, time, all efforts, don't get any appreciation.

It is not only a stumbling-block in the way of sound motivation and self-motivation, also the motivating impact a motivated colleague yields, it is also a very de-masking picture we get from the respective leader: people who are supposed to do work, would only do it properly and in good quality if they feel appreciated for their good work, and not being lauded for the wrong reasons altogether.

In the context of defining "Good Leadership", we come across many definitions, and very often, the term is defined exactly after what we deplore as contra-productive to good, efficient leadership.

Some authentic an opinions given by persons who are occupying leadership positions; we leave it to the reader to decide if they are up to the expectations:

Case 1

Q: How would you define "Good Leadership"?

A: You see, it is very simple. The leader shows the path, and the others follow (*smiles and laughs*) they have to follow, I mean. As simple as that.

Q: Why do you define leadership in this quite authoritarian way?

A: Well, I would not say authoritarian, I would say leading means that others follow, isn't it? That is logic. If there is no following, there need not be a leader. And for keeping up the rules and regulations, there must be someone who checks, who controls that things are properly done. Just someone who leads the way and decides.

Q: You mean to say that decision making is the task of the leader alone?

A: Oh yes. He is responsible for the outcome, and he has to take the decisions. After all, if something goes wrong, he has to bear the brunt.

Q: Is that really so? We observe very often that the so called inferior is made a scapegoat, and that the leaders always get away.

A: Yes, sometimes it happens. But if an inferior commits mistakes you cannot expect the leader to make them his own. This is would not be fair and true, and the public has the right to know the truth if things go wrong.

Q: *You are serious?*

A: O yes. Leaders have to bear so many burdens, they cannot take over other's mistakes, too.

(End of interview)

Case 2

Q: *How would you define "Good Leadership"?*

A: A leader has to show the path, he has to tell what to do, and he has to control that people are working.

Q: *You mean to say that the people don't know where to go, that they don't know what to do?*

A: Oh yes, they know. Because I tell them. A good leader has to tell, people expect me to tell.

Q: *Then, you consider yourself a good leader?*

A: (*mimicking embarrassment*) I think so, I have to admit. You know, people need a strong hand to guide them. They feel safe, and they take care not to go astray. They appreciate my regime (*he laughs heartily*).

Q: *Would you say that your people like you?*

A: Yes, I think so, I never heard anything else. They would jump out of the window here if I would want them to[3], they would do everything for me.

Q: *Out of liking for you? Or out of fear?*

A: Oh, I know where you are pointing (*chuckles*)! No, no, they don't fear me, but they know that I keep discipline at all costs.

Q: *Discipline?*

A: Yes, keeping up discipline is the most important task of a leader. Many of my colleagues don't understand that, and they have utter chaos in their departments. Here, there is a system for everyone to see and to follow. I am in command, and they know it. I am running a tight ship, and it is in their own interest. They are not paid for amusement, but for work.

Q: [4]*I heard that there are lots of cases pending since years. What about work efficiency?*

A: There might be some long-pending cases, but surely much less than in other departments. Just tell me the names, and I'll get it done immediately.

Q: *No, no, not that. How do you measure work efficiency?*

A: What? What is there to measure? Either they work or they don't work. Thus much is clear.

Q: *Do you have regular meetings with the staff?*

A: Oh yes, I meet my PS every day. Sometimes several times a day!

Q: *No, what I meant was: regular meetings with all employees to listen to them and get important information. Perhaps some good suggestions, too.*

A: If I want to talk with the employees, I talk to them if necessary. I call them personally. I don't believe in this 'leading-through-democracy-nonsense'. People only get funny ideas. They think the leader is not strong enough, and they don't take him serious. This is what happened in other departments. It won't happen here, you can be assured.

Q: *Which other departments?*

A: Practically all. All weak leaders.

Q: *What is your opinion on organisation development?*

A: It is good for departments which are not working properly. Here, we don't need that. Our organisation is perfect.

(End of interview)

The above interviews show very clearly that there is no positive concept of leadership, more so, there is utter mis-perception of 'good leadership', and a display of over-estimation and self-righteousness which fills you with despair.

In the following chapters we categorise the problems, analyse them and evolve suggestions for practical improvement. But we have to state clearly that there has to be the will for change, and also, the will for introducing parameters of good leadership combined with the respective consequences if quality is not delivered.

It is to be seen if all those decision makers who are constantly harping on 'Good Leadership' come up to the expectations and deliver the goods, namely, good leaders!

India would have a bright future on the national and international level, if only the will to mitigate evils in society, and to seriously introduce necessary change at all levels would be seriously developed. Competing in the global market is not only the task of the greedy Indian middle classes alone, it needs the mobilisation of all resources, especially all the hitherto untapped potential and wealth: the so called rural masses and the immensity of the rural potential.

Good leaders would know. Good leaders would act accordingly. Good leaders would propagate change.

Are our present-day leaders even in the vicinity of this change of mindset? We are afraid that our present-day leaders are the biggest stumbling blocks for change and problem solving.

We do not observe any sincere efforts for change with our decision makers, be it in politics, or be it in other influential circles. Too much is at stake for the self-centred individuals, and there is no commitment for the society. The demand for good leaders is drowned in the big muddy waters of pretensions and greed. The following chapters will show facts and reasons for evils in our society (like, reservation policies, abysmal educational system, mushrooming of bureaucracy, etc.), and we will put our fingers right into the wounds by suggesting ways and means out of the misery.

Some of these are definitely decentralisation and creating transparency as pre-conditions and valid parameters for good leadership.

References

1. The principle of promoting people after "seniority" is a completely outdated concept: it appreciates not performance, but just the sitting long enough somewhere and, what is even more destructive for efficiency, it de-motivates all those who really perform because they are not appreciated after their performance. In highly bureaucratised hierarchies, this principle of seniority is necessary to keep the stringent infrastructures intact, and to hold at bay performers who come with the looming danger of bringing about change, and of challenging the comfortably settled non-performers.
2. From: Nina Sibal: *The Dogs of Justice*, Ravi Dayal Publisher, 1998, p.188.
3. The office is situated at the fifth floor!
4. We were informed by several trustworthy people that there are many applications and other cases not being processed for years and years together, and that this department is known for its slow procedures, for corruption, and for lack of decision making from the head of the department.

2

All the Misery of Leadership!

> If you want to know what a man's like, take a good look at how he treats his inferiors, not his equals.[1]

Considering the almost unsurmountable problems in present-day India's spheres of life, we invariably come to the conclusion that they all come down to one single issue: *Good Leadership,* or, more appropriate, the lack of it. In this book, the term and perception of 'leadership' will be viewed from the holistic angles, i.e. from all points of view so that we may gain a whole picture. The demand for good leadership should become a battle-cry all over the country, and it should rattle all self-styled so-called 'leaders' out of their undeserved complacency.

Our initial questions of 'for whom this book is intended', and also, 'who might benefit from it' were satisfactorily answered by many discussions and talks we had with people from all walks of life. We are convinced that there will be lots of individuals, groups, institutions and organisations who will benefit from it and, finally, will join hands with all those who want things to be done and not only talked about or else, put on paper and filed away.

Our basic objective to write this book is to provide a basic framework for the most salient question: What to do to bring about a mindset conducive for continuous change for the better?

How to propagate solutions for those who really want to facilitate change?

How to create an atmosphere of positive change once and for all?

We felt the need to share our ideas and our suggestions for holistic change with all those who are open-minded and willing to act accordingly. This book will be a fundament for advancing in the right direction, and we welcome all suggestions and critique leading to improvement in our abysmal leadership situation.

A sustainable, positive change should be perceived as a continuous development process. In order to achieve this, we have to learn from the past. The lessons of the past are to be kept in mind, without hanging on to them, as this would mean 'living in the past'. We know very well from history the world over and also from our recent history since Independence, that many good, well intentioned leaders, after coming into positions of power developed the same style as their predecessors, not different from earlier self-centred or power-greedy performers. From psychology we know the answer for this phenomenon: they succumbed to the temptations of power, be it their conscious or unconscious personal vanity, the greed for "name and fame", prestige, bathing in admiration, companied by the all-too-willing Indian society to idolise a so-perceived 'leader'.

This aspect has to be taken into serious consideration, as it shows that often leaders with originally good intentions, having a quite non-pretentious attitude and positive communication patterns, quickly transform their original behavioural patterns into something they never expected themselves in the first place. But, what is worse, in this process they don't even realise what is happening, and they are not aware of the retro-change: they mutate into the same as the usual lot of exploitative, self-obsessed creatures we know so well.

Of course, it is extremely difficult to be strong enough a personality to desist the temptations of power with all the accompanying appreciation, admiration, veneration, notwithstanding the many privileges that come with all these. Very few only are self-critical enough to withstand these temptations of power which is invariably connected with access to enormous financial resources.

In a certain sense, they are victims themselves: on the one hand, victims of their own weakness and vulnerability and, on the other hand, victims of their social surroundings who are only too willing to prostrate before their masters.

Thus, it is a double deceit: they deceive themselves, and they are deceived.

Who in his or her senses could believe into the sincerity of the exaggerated veneration people shower on them? Do they not know from own experiences that this behaviour comes and disappears within minutes depending on the attributes of power or no power of a person?

Also, "learning from the past" would prevent repeating the same mistakes over and over, like we observe it in governmental decisions concerning development issues, or the fact that our black market is a much more powerful economy than our "white" economy: we have to ask if the successful 'Leaders' in black market areas are better and more efficient than our official leaders. Or, in case of doubling in both, do our official leaders put all their energy in black market efficiency? Why is our official leadership either not able nor willing to clamp down on the black-marketers? What are the reasons, the vested interests? What type of leadership would deprive the real owners of the wealth of a country—the people, in a democratic set-up—for selfish interests instead of using it for sustainable development?

Our questions in the context of holistic leadership are oriented on results: do our leaders, self-styled or otherwise, really *know* what to do (meaning: what they want to achieve)? Do they have clear aims and objectives? And if so, do they really know how to do what they want to do? Are they aware of the opportunities and the right timings: when to do what, and also, if and when to put a stop?

Do they really know how to bring about change and make it people-centric? And finally, the most important question of all: *Do they genuinely want change, and do they genuinely want to initiate a continuous change process?*

The system is too complicated and subjugated to powerful vested interests; thus, the system itself is victim of its inherent machinations, and thus, it cannot heal itself—there is no inbuilt self-healing mechanism. Not only policies, but the whole set-up is infested with vested interests inbuilt, inherent, and self-perpetuating.

We have to deal with lack of Good Leadership on all fronts:

1. Government
2. Political parties/politicians
3. Administration
4. Education
5. Judiciary
6. Media
7. Public and private enterprises (the latter somewhat better off, due to pressure from competitors)
8. Within families (the most submissive clerk mutates into the authoritarian 'leader' as soon as he steps in his home after work: here, he can wield power, compensating for all frustrations at work)

The following will show the main deficiencies. We will put the fingers into the wounds of the society to stir up complacency, and to de-tabooise issues which are conveniently shoved under the carpet. We are dealing with the "Misery of Leadership" in our country, and we emphasize the fact that only good leadership on all fronts will lead us into a bright future. One of the main features characterising a 'good leader' is speaking out what is wrong, and what is to be done, calling a spade a spade and not something vague like, perhaps, an 'unspecified agricultural tool'.

Openness, courage, civil courage for that matter on the side of the Indian people, all these attributes are wanting, and we all have to take up the challenges and help in building up a strong, competitive nation where everyone can be happy and realise the dreams according to the abilities.

Here, we venture into a compilation of activities we undertook within the last five years. We approached governmental, political, administrative, educational, judicial, media, and all sorts of public and private enterprises to show that there is an un-conventional way for sustainable development—welfare for all, and not welfare for a few. We were not really successful, as we observed one very strong attitude: avoid changes at all costs (literally!). Now, exactly this attitude is characteristic for weak leadership, for non-performance as leaders, and exactly this is the malady of our present-day stalemate in all walks of life.

Of course, there are no convenient shortcuts to sustainable development, but a drastic change of mindset and attitudes towards holistic approach is necessary. We have to adopt ways and means for development on a *subha-labha-basis*, intended to mitigate and finally remove economic and social dependencies, building up an atmosphere for overall vibrancy as opposed to the present-day lethargic climate. The necessary food for thought and action is there on a platter; it needs a holistic approach to the problems and also, learning from those who are positive performers in the same system, i.e. on the fundament of our democratic constitution.

Analysing failures and successes in the past, we came to the firm conclusion that in order to bring about and to manage change, the holistic approach is the only solution. It is one of the most convincing lessons of the past, and the learning process requires a continuous activity of learning, unlearning and visionary, future-oriented planning, as against the bureaucratic mock-planning,[2] dealing only with what is already there as data and statistics, and interpret it, in the same way, over and over again—the same data, similar outcome, reports and paper to be filed, wholly futile exercises! If we want to avoid making the same mistakes over and over, like in the past six decades, we have to adopt a holistic and unconventional approach to development. Also, we have to re-define 'development' and also, introduce accountability and transparency at all levels of leadership.

Not only the stereotyped way of dealing with data, conventionally evaluating them, and finally filing them for eternity, are futile actions keeping people occupied, but leading to nowhere—even worse is the fact that the data themselves are highly suspicious. Not only the way they are collected, often by untrained persons, or else, by people who are negligent of importance of data, or are just too lazy to do the necessary for collecting reliable data, but time-wise, the gap is too vast to make the officially collected data viable at all. Reality mows them over, and our planners are dealing with out-'dated' data—it seems to be all the same for them.

The manifold duplications within the existing systems and mechanisms, the wastage of all resources, the overall squandering and negligent mindset and attitudes, all these have to be tackled with good leadership and, as pre-condition, logically, by good leaders; leaders who would pay attention to the real problems, encourage transparency and awareness, who are sincere, and who act for the implementation of practicable tools for change.

Our leaders lack the wisdom, the visions, and the basic skills for good leadership, like Antoine de Saint-Exupery said: "If you want to build a ship, don't drum up people together to collect wood and don't assign them tasks and work, but rather teach them to long for the endless immensity of the sea." From this viewpoint, we are rather abysmally short of good leaders!

In the following chapters, and also, in our various papers we sent to the decision makers for better planning and performance, we show practical suggestions for sustainable improvement, enhancing quality consciousness, and entrepreneurship at grassroot level which will bring out the best of people and society.

Above, we mentioned the necessity to re-define the term 'development', which we will render here. At present 'development' is perceived as almost everything which is characterised by 'change', like:

a) The coming up of settlements consisting of huge high-rise buildings around the cities, housing hundreds of thousands of people, mostly middle classes. These buildings are mostly designed on business lines, i.e. stuffing as much people as possible into them, very often of low quality concerning fittings, appliances, building material, etc. It goes without saying that a process of 'slumming' is unavoidable in the future as is clearly to be seen in comparatively new settlements where maintenance is poor. Also, building material is mostly concrete which creates bad climatisation and insulation, so that installation of AC is almost a must, another reason for increase of energy consumption and global warming. Huge previously agricultural or forested areas were converted into concrete deserts, and consequently, the groundwater level is dramatically decreasing. Concerning the middle class population, we are confronted with a traffic breakdown in the cities where there is hardly any remedy. Again, we have to put the question after holistic leadership: what were the decision makers for these settlements deciding about? Usually, they decide with the compartmentalised tunnel view about settlements which promised to bring good revenues from consumers and/or, the so-called developers helped with appropriate finances to take decisions in their interests. This is one of the many examples of lack of good leadership, leading to disastrous consequences.

b) The 'cleaning' of urban areas from slum dwellings: again, the city leaders decide about the fate of human beings through their compartmentalised tunnel view. Usually, all our cities and townships have their slum dwellings, or settlements of very poor people; these people are catering to the needs of the better-off strata of society; they are servants, rickshaw-pullers, small hawkers, or follow some odd occupation. Basically, they provide basic amenities for the higher strata of society, lower middle classes mainly who cannot afford to employ permanent servants. Nevertheless, they are an eyesore for the municipalities, and the city leaders decide to get rid of them. Where is the good leadership to find a humane solution for—undoubtedly—squalor-prone living conditions which have to be mitigated? Just flush them out, or else, hide them behind some walls, but let them be invisible.

c) The all-pervading plastic bottles and –cups, -bags and similar goods: the city leaders are not much concerned with these problems, otherwise, why should they let places of human habitation degrade like they do? There are laudable exceptions, but the majority of decision makers in our cities are seemingly unaware of the dire consequences of their negligence, they just go on doing business as usual, sticking to old (fashioned) ways of administration and, if need be, do some emergency measures if worse comes to worst, which fizzle out naturally after some time, not having improved anything. Good leadership would learn from past experiences, and would rather think in terms of 'disaster prevention' than in 'disaster management'.

d) Textiles fabricated of synthetic fibres everywhere: in spite of the fact that more and more people in India are supposedly becoming more and more health conscious, plastic good and synthetics are on the increase to the disadvantage of natural products. True, it has become fashionable to 'go ethnic', and to take to 'bio-food' in middle and upper classes, but as yet, it is more a superficial fashionable thing to do once in a while, and it doesn't suggest any change of mindset. Our leaders in all fields do nothing to bring about a genuine change: there is no propagating of a natural lifestyle but even in the summer heat, they press their feet into socks and shoes (!), wear suits and ties (!), and preferably sit in AC offices—the true Brown Sahibs they basically are. A lot could be done to evoke awareness in public on environment cum health issues, as they are inseparably connected. Our leaders have their tunnel view, like the typical *"Yes-butters"* that they are: "Health? Yes, I am concerned with health, but with my health. It not my department." Or: "Environment? Groundwater? Oh yes, I am concerned, but sorry, it is not my department." Or: "Cows die miserably from street rubbish they eat? Sorry for that, but it is not my responsibility, not my department." Or: "Yes, I am working on cleaning up our City and yes, I am responsible for regular collecting of rubbish. But what can I do? The people are just not sensible, they throw away everything."—Question:

"What do you do to enlighten them?"—Incredulous answer: "I?"

e) Fashionable institutions for higher education where business is the motive and not education: as with everything in India, there is an administrative overkill in the educational field, too, leading invariably to hundreds of loopholes to circumvent all the rules and regulations. If you go through the usual curricula, you find the same *kichdi* of subjects in all educational institutions, and, at the same time, the same theoretical approach leading to a high degree of unemployability among youth. The whole set-up is going against sound competition globally, and against creative, innovative minds. On the one hand, we have the 'leaders' in the ministries and administration for educational institutions in India who are deadly against change, and who mainly see their tasks in an overkill of control mechanisms, making convenient exceptions if the monetary incentives are brought forward, and, on the other hand, we have the founders of educational institutions who know very well that such an institutions can be a money-minting enterprise, provided the glamorous façade is appropriately marketed. What really happens inside the institutions, and if they are up to the expectations, is another consideration altogether. Cosmetics won't help in changing the educational system, and here, too, our decision-making leaders are strictly compartmentalised in their approach: no basic changes, but business as usual.

This is the 'development' our so-called leaders provide: cities choking from increasing traffic without prior planning for appropriate infrastructure, environments suffocated by decreasing groundwater, rubbish heaps without facilities for recycling, education businesses called 'schools' to the disadvantage of the students, and so forth. These examples show clearly the poor leadership in our country, and their decision making against the interests of the people and, what is even worse, against a liveable future.

'Development' has to be seen from a holistic angle: in this context we resort to use the term 'positive development' as different from a development perception where there is nothing positive, but only disastrous change to expect.

Learning from the past—not *living* in the past:

> In Nature, the holistic concept is perfectly realised: everything is interrelated. Nature is destroyed because men developed ways and means to interrupt the natural chains of development, the natural interdependence, and because they exploited nature instead of using carefully what it offers—it could be a win-win-relationship, but we have a one-sided exploitative system leading to destruction of natural resources. One of the most hazardous examples is the speedily progressing decline of our water resources.
>
> Nature provides everything.

References

1. Mentioned by many good leaders, quote attributed to Drucker, but also others.
2. See Appendix: "Open Letter to Planning Commission."

3

Leadership, Inferiority Complex and the Brown-Sahibdom

> The British Raj did not encourage settlers (i.e. British). Settlers might set a bad example and 'go native', destroying the carefully nurtured image of the difference, and hence the superiority of the British race. The Raj, it was thought, depended on that image of superiority to enable it to rule so many with so few.[1]

During the British Raj, there was a good percentage of Indians in comparatively powerful positions, albeit not in the supreme decision-making echelons. They were faithful and loyal collaborators, and many of them were not really happy to see the colonial power driven out of the country.

Somehow, when discussing certain issues of efficiency, punctuality, quality consciousness and the like, there is, more than 60 years later, an atmosphere of awe and admiration remembering the "good old days" when the Britishers saw to it that things kept going smoothly. We suspect that part of this nostalgic feeling might come from an inherent wish not to be forced to take decisions, but to have someone to tell you what to do.

Strangely, this behaviour you find especially in the higher echelons of power positions, namely, in the administration. While analysing the misery of leadership in this country, we have to analyse the phenomena from all angles to understand the reasons, and to find solutions. For example, we have to put the following questions:

What Makes the Fascination of our "Colonial Heritage"?

a) From an Authentic Interview:

During the British Raj, the law-and-order situation was much better. Everyone knew his place, and our Babus could not do what they want.

Q: *You wish the Britishers back?*

A: No, no, not that. But sometimes I think it would be better. There is no accountability anymore.

Q: *You mean to say that there was accountability during British Raj?*

A: Oh yes, yes! All were accountable!

Q: *What about the accountability of the Britishers?*

A: ...?

b) From another interview

Q: *Why do people think that under British Raj the situation was better?*

A: The law-and-order situation was better. People felt safe. Now, we don't feel safe. And hard work was appreciated. Now, it is not. Corruption was kept in check, or there was hardly any corruption.

Q: *But the country was exploited from its resources. The people had no civil rights. The caste system was prevailing unchecked.*

A: Yes, there were some flaws. But the caste system is kept alive much stronger through the reservation system. The Britishers appreciated good work and hard work. Now, you don't get anywhere if you have no connections, or if you don't bribe the Babus. The Judiciary was neutral, and it was not so corrupt. The Britishers were not so bad as people say. I would prefer a neutral rule to our Indian rulers. They only think of themselves.

Q: *You would give up your democratic rights?*

A: What democratic rights? We vote, but contesting elections is a different thing altogether. If you have no money to spend, you cannot contest. Those who contest do it for themselves, it is all selfishness. They cheat on the people. This is no democracy, it is a mockery.

Q: *What is your suggestion?*

A: (*chuckles*) Call back the Britishers, ask them to unite the country, and to rule as neutral caretakers. We Indians cannot rule ourselves. We have to be ruled.

Why do we still have the feeling that British habits, "values", etc., are still valid and ought to be kept up?

a) From an Authentic Interview

Q: *You are member of several Clubs in your city. Why?*

A: If you want to be successful in business, you have to be a club member. You meet your business friends there, and you make new friends. Many deals are fixed in the club.

Q: *But: the "Club of Flower Lovers" doesn't seem to be serving business purposes.*

A: There are clubs you have to be member for social reasons. It helps your children in school, and you can take your family there.

Q: *Club nights deprive your family of your company?*

A: Oh yes. I hardly meet my children during the week. But anyway, we always have arguments. An absent father is better than a grumbling one, as my daughter says. But, the club life is very important in many ways. You come to belong to certain influential people in society. Without the club, you cannot do a thing.

Q: *Why have the clubs the same rules and regulations as during the British times, when most of the clubs were off limits for Indian? Why don't you have 'Indian' rules? And why cannot women be normal members in most of the clubs?*

A: These rules are time-tested, that's why we keep them up. And women can be members as wives of members. Why should they want to become members on their own? Single women have different places to socialise. They would not feel at home here.

Q: *Did you ever discuss the matter in the board of the club?*

A: Matter of fact, no. There was no need. As I said, our statutes are time-tested. Why should we invent the wheel anew?

Q: *Just to take up one of the more irrational rites: do you still have (lots of) alcohol before dinner?*

A: Of course, there is usually a lot of drinking before dinner.

Q: *Is that not quite irrational? In continental Europe, for example, people have an aperitif at the most as they don't want to be alcoholised before relishing the food. There is a well-known joke about this strange habit, saying that, knowing the English type of food, one has to be drunk before bringing oneself to swallow it.[2] But this cannot be said about the Indian cuisine.*

A: There might be some irrational rites, but on the whole, our clubs are quite Indian, not English. We are all Indians, and that makes a club wholly Indian.

Why do we Still Show the "Brown Sahib Syndrome"?

a) From an Authentic Interview

Q: Did you ever hear the term 'Brown Sahib'?

A: Yes, I think it is ridiculous. There is no such thing in India. There are no brown sahibs. What do you mean?

Q: *By definition, the so-called 'Brown Sahibs' are those who imitated the colonial masters till they literally merged their personality with theirs and inculcated all behavioural patterns and mindset. This total imitation process is actually a psychotic one. The phenomenon in India applies not only to the generation who worked with the colonial masters and imitated them directly, but the following generations seem to have imbibed the same things. Clearly a very strong influence. That's why I am asking you.*

A: Of course, we have taken over the administrations, the political system, the educational system an many other things, but I never thought about that in the context you put it: the brown sahibs. Yes, we behave very much like them, at least we try to. And it is necessary for discipline.

Indians don't like discipline. That is why leadership in India is so difficult. People don't like discipline, and discipline is of the highest value for good work. Our leaders have to fight hard to establish and continue discipline. I think it is the most important leadership task. Not many leaders know this, and that is why we have not enough good leaders.

Q: *You mean to say that it is sufficient for a leader to keep up discipline?*

A: Yes, yes. The Germans show that.

Q: *The Germans? How? Is it not their creativity and their motivation to do hard work which makes them successful?*

A: Yes, yes, true. But Hitler saw to discipline, and we should have leaders like him.

Q: *Are you serious in putting up a heinous butcher like Hitler as a leadership model to emulate?*

A: You see, you have to break the egg to make an omelette, and some flaws we have to take in the stride.

Why on earth should Indian lawyers be forced to wear black jackets all the time, even if common sense clearly says that in this climate the work efficiency of a lawyer, or of a judge, for that matter, could be very much enhanced by a more convenient dress code? It could easily be done. And it would surely not minimise authority, reputation, status which seems to be so immensely important for the judicial tribe.[3]

Why on earth should a civil servant enjoy the type of submissiveness which is displayed around him/her? And why on earth should this submissiveness be displayed towards his/her family members, too?

When we assume that the Civil Servant is not physically handicapped, why should he not be able to carry his briefcase himself? Why this show sometimes of several people trying to snatch the 'Lord's' briefcase and carrying it all the way like a cherished trophy?

An why should the wife of a civil servant show the same haughtiness and the same arrogance towards servants and other 'inferior' people? Why should she complain that a certain shopkeeper has behaved towards her "as if I was not the wife of an IAS officer"—what should we make out of that? It reveals a mindset that, naturally, the 'wife of an IAS officer' is to be treated differently, i.e. given more attention, subservience, etc., than other people. How can an egalitarian society evolve in such an atmosphere of arrogance and contempt towards others?

Why was the chance to abolish all these old-fashioned, colonially-imposed paraphernalia of power and useless rituals, not taken after Independence?

In preparation for Independence, there were so many battlefields between the collaborative Indian officers of British Raj, and those who were the aspirants of power. We do not comment on the specifics of ego-battles which finally led to the unavoidable partition of India, but we refer to the bitterly fought wars within all levels administration. Everyone wanted to grab a slice of the cake, and many of the former true Gandhians very quickly shed their convictions in favour of wealth and power. India thus resembled a slain animal, a prey to a multitude of creatures out to eviscerate it, and as is usual in such a process, only the leftovers are thrown before the masses. In the name of 'development' India has been exploited and raped almost the same way as the colonialists did, and it is no consolation that this time, it was the Indians themselves doing the dirty job. Leadership in this context could not evolve in 'good leadership' for the following reasons: the British hierarchical system in government, administration and in all other fields was extremely authoritarian as it had to be to deter the "natives" from rebelling. At Independence, the chances for changing the system were not even seriously discussed: it went without saying that a 'functioning' administration had to be kept up, and thus, the whole infrastructure was blindly adapted by the only-too-willing Babus who learnt their job in collaborating with the colonialists. Mora than 60 years after Independence, we still suffer from this major mistake, and we have become a 'complainant society': noticing the evils, but making others responsible for it. It is not the Britishers who should be blamed for our dismal state of condition in education and other important areas, it is *we* who are to be blamed as we are not willing to change a thing. Too much is at stake for our so-called leaders. Good leadership would lead to change, and, where necessary, to drastic change.

Why should a person in his senses wear suit and tie in 35 degrees Celsius or more?

Together with the over-bureaucratised infrastructure, our babus and, in the meantime, all representatives of the middle classes, have adopted a Western style of dress: sometimes it looks quite pathetic, but of course, it is an Indian adaptation. We cannot understand that in spite of climatic adversities, majority of employees still hold on to a dress style which is hazardous to health: closed shoes and socks, suits, shirts and ties, to name the uniform which causes so much inconveniences. No wonder, our babus prefer to stay within their air-conditioned rooms instead of doing their duty and go out to see how majority of Indians have to live. Good Leaders would give good examples to emulate, but we are still in search for them. Now, coming back to the health hazards: is there no awareness of the damage done to the feet (sweating, fungus-prone), skin (over-heated, prickly, allergy-prone, rashes through synthetic fibres), the mostly too-tight belts causing overall physical harm and suffering. Good leaders would know that good work, good performance can only be done by people who have a minimum of feeling good, both, physically and mentally. Clearly, work efficiency must be very much reduced under the circumstances, and all the energy-wasting air conditioning is not really relieving the hazards; the abrupt changes in temperature outside and inside an office lead to even more health problems. With the exceptions of some Southern States, this feature of dress code is to be observed all over the country. India has very conducive traditional dresses which should be 'allowed', very well adapted to the climate, and also handsome from the aesthetic point of view. Why is all this considered inferior? Are we not bold enough to wear our own dresses as long as it fits into modern workplaces?

Case Study (Interview with a Senior Clerk in a Government Department):

Q: *Today, we have nearly 45 centigrade temperature. Why do you go to work with closed shoes, socks, tie and all? Isn't it very inconvenient?*

A: This is the dress code. We all have to wear this. What else should I wear?

Q: *Dress code? Is it written somewhere? Who decides about the dress code?*

A: No, not that I know of. But everyone dresses like this. But yes, it is almost unbearable in this heat. Fortunately, my office is air-conditioned.

Q: *You could wear pyjama-kurtha, chappals, and you would not have to suffer. Besides, the air-conditioning is very harmful in view of health, and also, from the environmental standpoint.*

A: Pyjama-kurtha? You must be joking! Only lower people are wearing it.

Q: *But outside you office, you wear it sometimes, even to functions, weddings, etc.*

A: Oh, that is different. And then, the dress is made of very precious material, like brocade, silk and all, beautiful synthetic cloth...

Q: *What would happen if you would wear cotton pyjama-kurtha in your office?*

A: I would be the laughing stock! People would ridicule me, they would talk behind my back, they would not take me seriously.

Q: *Are you afraid of that? Why don't you talk to them about the health hazards, both, of the 'uniform' and the sudden change of temperature?*

A: They would not listen, everyone wants an air-condition.

Q: As a matter of prestige? Even if it endangers your health?

A: Yes, I think nobody wants to hear that.

Q: You are in a leadership position, and a leader has to be exemplary. Why don't you put off air-conditioning? Why don't you change your dress according to the natural climate? Why are you not proud to wear 'Indian' dresses?

A: I cannot imagine, and I don't think I want that.

Q: You could start wearing chappals, a loose shirt without tie from tomorrow onwards.

A: How could I do that? What would people say? And my wife would be terribly upset.

Q: What has you dress to do with you wife? Why should she be upset?

A: She would be mad because she thinks Indian dress is inferior, our social status doesn't allow this.

Q: But she wears a sari?

A: Oh yes. Only once, when we travelled to US, she tried the Punjabi dress for convenience.

Q: Then, why is she forcing you into Western dresses?

A: Because of prestige. What would people say? Am I a lowly clerk? Am I a lowly peasant?

Q: So, you prefer risking your health in favour of some amorphous social status?

A: What can I do? Everyone follows the dress code. How can I do otherwise?

It goes without saying that there cannot be a single answer to this syndrome of colonial heritage, social status, the urge of showing a distinction between upper and lower echelons, but a few basic explanations might enlighten those who also do not comprehend what is going on, and why, for that matter, even after 60 years of Independence, and in generations who cannot remember colonial India at all, such outdated, irrational, class-dependent, burdensome colonial heritage should still have this oppressive power!

The younger generations are obviously just perpetuating habits and rituals essentially alien to Indian traditions, and also adverse to mental and health conditions in the climate, without questioning the reasons and the usefulness in our modern world. There is not enough self-confidence among the bureaucrats at all levels, among the representatives of the judiciary, and most of the Indian private companies[4] to do away with old-fashioned rituals, whereas in the country of the colonial masters the updating of it has been implemented long back.

The perfection with which British haughtiness, contemptuousness, ritualistic rules and regulations, and the perfidy of power-play mechanisms are imitated and displayed is awesome, indeed! Good leaders cannot evolve out of such a moat of adversities.

The Unadmitted "Inferiority Complex" —On Prestige and Status Consciousness

We have to deal with a vicious circle in the behavioural patterns of our society: a personality who is insecure, feels the urge to compensate and also, to establish an outward façade of sovereignty. His perception of self-confidence is dependent on feeling important and superior to others, which consequently, means showing off, especially in the form of high-handedness, haughtiness, authoritarian gestures and the like towards others. Authentic examples are:

a) An officer calls a clerk from a different room (in some distance) just to pick up a paper that has fallen from the officer's desk. The officer could have picked it up himself in the fraction of a second.

b) An officer calls back his chaprassi from quite a distance only to order him to put sugar into his teacup, whereas he could have done it in no time himself as the teacup stood directly under his nose.

c) demanding special treatment for himself, his wife, son, daughter, father, mother..., as this is 'due to a civil servant'.

Unfortunately, our society delivers the 'goods', like behaving submissive, rendering privileges, advantages, etc., without questioning. How can we expect good leaders could come out in these circumstances? It is obvious that only those who know how to play the game will succeed, and these are exactly not those who have the necessary key potential for good leadership.

It is a really vicious circle: our society allows, accepts, and even encourages these behavioural patterns, which leads to increasing snobbery, contemptuousness, haughtiness. The future generation will be infected by this contagious disease, as their children imbibe it, take it for granted that they should be something special and should be treated specially, and consequently, they would not be able to adjust to 'normalcy', they cannot bear to be treated like any other citizen, and they very often fail to succeed in 'normal' conditions. But, as we all know, their families want them into the power positions and, unfortunately, in much too many cases they succeed at least in this. This way, from where should good leadership come?

On Submissiveness

It takes two to tango!

Look out for people in power positions, but don't look so much at the leaders but observe the people surrounding them, how they behave, how they communicate. This tells you almost everything about the leadership quality. It tells you more than any other observation, that too, about both the players.

If we find the leader enjoying others to bow to him, then all is said and done: he is the leader type we don't want, we don't need. He is the one who has to compensate his insecurities, and he is the one who would not stand up for his people.

But, on the other hand, we have to state that there are too many who allow others to suppress him/her in the first place! Too many people prefer to be mute and cowardly instead of showing dignity, courage and self-esteem.

Of course, the latter behavioural patterns would have disastrous consequences in the case of the usual leader: he has to punish, to harass, to show that he does not allow 'insubordination', and thus, fear prevails, and submissiveness is the answer.

For very selfish reasons, the majority are prepared to submit their real feelings under a (so perceived) 'power' or else, people want to get some of the 'glory' of someone they think is superior, or someone who could elevate them.

There is the well-known 'weaseling around', nodding all the time, conceding everything, trying to please the person through showing their servitude or else, out of an habitually acquired fear complex.

The latter proves to be justified, in many cases.

The "hanging at master's lips", like hypnotised, repeating whatever the master says while exaggerating everything, always ready to dance to the master's tune. A group of them invariably tries to outdo one another, teeth and claws.

"Happy slaves are the most acrimonious enemies of freedom. ... A slave does not want to be free. He wants to be warden of slaves."[5]

How Our 'Leaders' Show Off

The *power of denial*—the most frequent misuse of power, especially drawn out sadistically by personally weak-structured bureaucrats. A leadership position is perceived as a convenient tool of power, and especially weak personalities have to compensate with behavioural patterns of "showing off". Suppression, over-controlling, punishments, humiliation—all these are tools for compensation of weaknesses of 'leaders'.

Some of the most significant behavioural patterns are displayed at all levels of our outdated hierarchies in governments, administration, and in other institutions and agencies, the public-private enterprises included. Interestingly, in most of our purely private enterprises, especially in those which are exposed to the global markets, we observe drastic shifts from hierarchical structures towards a 'lean management' culture, away from the superficialities of titles and other obsolete paraphernalia of power. That makes all the difference for enhancing efficiency in production and decision making!

It has become a matter of prestige to sport some state-of-the-art computer equipment but, when you ask what is practically done with it, you hardly get a convincing answer. Be it that the suitable software has not been installed/developed yet, the internal office network is not yet installed, rules and regulations have not yet been worked out, staff is not yet trained properly—all these excuses for non-performing leaders.

But the new computer looks good, na? (Sometimes, we feel tempted to ask the leader if he knows the 'on' button...)

Compensatory behaviour is supposed to heal or hide deficiencies, and, after a short while, it grows into so-called acquired habits, not to be questioned, just the normal behaviour.

Compensatory leaders, i.e. many persons in power positions have ample opportunities for showing off:

a) He makes it a point that he always arrives late for an appointed meeting so that all others not only have to wait, but he assumes that they will also think he is enormously busy. All this goes together with making lots of noise about how difficult it was to drag himself away from most important tasks, preferably from a talk with the Minister (!) which he had to cut short to come to the meeting. (just observe the faces of the others, or listen in to their mumbled comments: nobody believes it, and all are highly amused.)

b) He usually lets people wait for some time, even when there is a fixed time for the appointment (reasons and behavioural patterns: see above). To make others wait is not only a display of very bad manners, it is, in a certain sense, a criminal offence: you deliberately steal other people's time! A German proverb says that, 'Keeping time is the politeness of kings', and in this context, it refers to 'noble' behaviour as compared with contemptuous wilfulness of those who do not know how to respect others.

c) His office is decorated with all sorts of wall-hangers: certificates (sometimes of a nature you feel urged to ask from what institution, or what it all means), photos which show the leader in the company of the occasional VIP, letters—laminated and/or framed—from VIPs, and all sorts of kitsch from travels abroad.

d) A leader on a lower or middle level likes to display heaps of paperwork, whereas the upper level leaders see to it that files and papers have no place in his office—the paperwork is to be done at the lower levels, and he is here to preside over his kingdom. A computer set on his desk, yes! But e-mails he receives from his PS in printed form, and he dictates his answer conventionally to the steno. What a waste of time, energy and material!

e) Now, the arrival of computers has put the lower and middle level leaders in a very difficult situation: how to show off the workload when there is no paper to shuffle? No heaps of files to be displayed? It might be one of the explanations why there is so much enmity towards modern technology at these levels. It is not so much fear of being unable to grasp the handling of a computer (after all, the mobile phone is not much different!), but it is impossible to show the ceremony of overworked leaders without papers. How many trees could be saved if the already available technical support would be really used? How many work hours would be saved if we would not have two work systems to be dealt with simultaneously? We saw it with our own eyes: work was done conventionally first, afterwards the same procedure repeated with the computer. Logically, it means almost doubling the work, and we need not wonder that so many leaders (and staff, for that matter) are complaining that modern technology has not brought relief but more work.

f) Following procedures in most of our courts of justice, we feel somehow thrown back into medieval times, even when there is a computer, it is not used. How much time would be saved by simultaneously typing statements in the machine which would make repeating of the same sentences by the judges obsolete. A good steno acquires the necessary skills in a very short time, and it saves time for him, too, besides enhancing accuracy and precision of statements given.

g) The display of several mobile phones is another showing off method. Someone with more than one mobile phone must be an important person, indeed! And it goes without saying that the newest, most sophisticated model must be among them. We all know that hardly 20 to 30 per cent of the gimmicks a present-day mobile provides are practically used—why should one use the mobile for things which are more conveniently done on a laptop considering the difficulties of handling the tiny keys?

Thus, compensatory leader has ample opportunities to compensate, whereas all those non-leaders have to resort to other compensatory measures, like kicking stones and doors, shouting at everyone they dare to, delay work (they dare to) and causing suffering for people—even beating wife and children at home. Not that leaders in power positions don't do these things, only they have lots of other possibilities which give them great advantages.

The misery of compensatory leaders is not the misery of the leaders, but the misery of everyone else.

References

1. Quote from: Marc Tully, *The Heart of India*, Penguin India, New Delhi, 1995, p vii.
2. Continental Europeans are very particular with their cuisine, and they look down on the 'uncultured' English food.
3. Also see chapter V., Leadership ... Judiciary.
4. Most of the international companies are much more easy-going, and they prefer a climate-adjusted dress code. Some European businessmen told me that they could not convince their Indian staff to ease their code dress while they themselves did it.
5. Marie von Ebner-Eschenbach, German (Austrian) author, 19th century, quote translated by the authors.

4

Leadership and Civil Society

To define Indian society as a *Civil Society* seems to go without saying, but, there are some doubts we have to express, and here, we try to get a clearer picture by putting our fingers into the wounds of society.

Civil society should have some essential features which we have to determine in this chapter. The terms derives from the West, it has its roots from the era of Enlightenment in Europe, in the French Revolution and, later on, in the coming up of democratic structures in Western countries. As it is broadly understood, it means the non-governmental strata of a society, comprising almost all spheres of life which is not directly determined by governmental rules and regulations.[1]

We can imagine that it is impossible to draw a line between the two; they are inseparably interlinked and interdependent, so that here, without going into the philosophical roots and discussions, we can safely state that the expectations of people in a given country, irrespective of culture, political system and the like, towards civil society is that of a "good" society from which "Good Governance" and "Good Leadership" should evolve. Modern civil societies should have a sound economic backbone, egalitarian values and norms, and there should be, in the more idealistic outlook, egalitarian infrastructure which is a pre-requisite for a functioning democracy. In a functioning civil society, the citizens feel responsible for their society; they have a genuine interest in the welfare of the whole society, and they do not distinguish between "them" (as in other communities, religions, other strata of society) and "we", a phenomenon which is extremely developed in India, and which consists one of the big obstacles for humane development in the country. In this context, we have to point out that the existing Reservation System is one of greatest stumbling blocks towards developing into a civil society that deserves the name.[2]

Now, considering the societal set-up and all the constraints, dichotomies, failures in delivering good leadership, failures in delivering good governance, highly corrupted civil infrastructure, and severe failures in rendering dignified, human living conditions to a vast part of our society, we can state that we might have something like a civil society, but the attributes of a "Good Society", meaning benefiting all citizens equally, cannot be given.

This set-up makes it very easy for exploiters to do their work, and it makes it very easy for the powers in this country, mainly governments, politicians, administration, media and even judiciary, to take advantage according to their own vested interests.

What we observe is the following:

a) We have a majority of mute people who somehow adjust while desperately trying to grab the most for themselves.
b) We have a Reservation system which is tearing the society apart.
c) We have citizens who know all about the all-pervading corruption but don't fight against it.
d) We have an outdated perception of leadership which is acclaimed by those who lead and mutely accepted by those who are 'led'.

A civil society deserving the name cannot be built up, and kept sustainable and lively by authoritarian infrastructure, by meaningless hierarchies, by untransparent rules, regulations and procedures, by unaccountability of institutions and their leaders, by an outdated judiciary system [3]where justice is either delayed or else, the vast majority of people have no access and also have not much trust in, by politicians, governments and administration. These are worlds apart from the ground realities of life of the majority of population, by an overall atmosphere of greediness, ruthlessness and shameless corruption.

A civil society deserving the name needs leaders who are exemplary in their mindset and attitudes to hold up principles of democracy, freedom and justice.

A civil society deserving the name needs a population that shows self-confidence, and questions and punishes bad leadership. Why on earth are bad leaders in this country awarded with parliament seats, power positions and all what comes in their stride? Why are bad leaders re-elected? Why are known corrupt leaders put and kept in power positions?

Not that India lacks able potential to perform better; the potential is there aplenty. But the overall submissiveness stands in the way of change for the better, the overall attitude of having resigned to the present state of condition of leadership, and to put up with it. "Yes, it is bad, but what can we do?" is the most repeated answer when we questioned complaining citizens. Most of the time, the only outlet for frustration, disappointment, anger, rage, is to complain.

Yes, we are living in a complainant society, and the majority of our fellow citizens compensate through complaining, but shy away from subsequent steps. They literally 'turn inside'; they concentrate on their very own interests, thus mirroring precisely the behaviour of their leaders.

> "Social responsibility? Oh no, I have enough at hand to cater for my own needs!"
>
> "Taking steps against a corrupt official? Oh no, he is much too influential, I would only suffer!"
>
> "Yes, I am absolutely against corruption, but what can I do? If I don't bribe, I don't get my things done. At least, not timely, and this is what counts for me."

Thus, the vicious circle repeats itself indefinitely; cynically, we can say that, in this context, our society is divided into two parts: one part which expects and accepts bribes, and the other part which delivers. Our citizens allow corruption to happen because they pay!

A civil society deserving the name cannot, in its majority, allow and support blackmailing structures to strive; the citizens have to show that they don't yield. We cannot blame corrupt leaders only as there are always two sides to a coin: those who demand and those who give. Those who give are as responsible for the conditions as those who take, it is a fifty-fifty game. All those who complain about having to bribe, we ask: why do you think you have to? Have you ever tried to refuse? We have no right to criticise anything as long as we ourselves indulge in the same thing. If we bribe, just to get things done quickly, or done at all, or whatever 'reasons' there might be brought forward, we support a corruptive system, we are culprits ourselves. Complaining about corruption, but corrupting if it is to our advantage, shows the deep-rooted hypocrisy in our society.

We should start to say "No" when we are about to be blackmailed into bribery by our own urge to get things done, or done faster, or better, there is always an excuse, and thus, the all-pervading corruption can further spread like the cancerous societal disease that it is.

But, there is a dream to dream:

> Suppose the majority of our citizens would one day say NO to bribery—what would the corrupt people do? Go to court? Punish? Kill? Yes, that can happen, and it happens, indeed. But it happens very rarely. Even our deficient judiciary system would hardly find ways and means to help them.

It is possible to say NO, and there are people who have the guts to do so. It might not be the easy way in a country where wealth is obviously more admired than honesty, and where the callous display of wealth is considered something very prestigious, even if it goes against the law of the land.[4]

Where are the positive leaders who could be emulated in this context? What we observe in all ways of life are persons who call themselves leaders, but who miserably fail in performing their duties as good, efficient leaders.

We collected a series of authentic case studies when upright citizens were determined not to yield to bribery, and they got their things done successfully, albeit with lots of efforts, and after having to bear with deliberate delays, unnecessary obstacles, harassment, and the like and, of course, all took much more time than 'usually'. We want to show that bribery and corruption is not a 'necessary evil' as some might say, but it is an evil which has to be actively fought against. There are many cases—our own, too—to prove that you can get your things done without greasing the outstretched palms.

Only the citizens themselves can create an enabling environment where bribery is seen as the criminal act it is, and not admired as something shrewd, cunning and intelligent by someone who is luckier than others.

A civil society deserving the name has to build up a perception of good leadership oriented on principles of social responsibility, and not those of mere authority.

The perception of leadership in our society is widely guided by one of the modern mantras: Give us a leader! Give us leaders! Give us leadership! Then, it is assumed, everything will be fine. Send us a leader to follow, and all is well.

Kenneth Galbraith and others, not only economists, have coined the term "convenient wisdom", which broadly means that we all tend to accept as true what is most convenient to us. Thus, having a leader to show us where to go, and what to do, relieving us from feeling guilty for not acting ourselves, and finally, from all responsibility, just suits us fine: it is most convenient, and immediately, it becomes common truth, the above-mentioned "convenient wisdom" determining the overall opinions in a society. What we coined as 'overall submissiveness' allowing bad leadership to strive, is a convincing example for the convenient wisdom in the above-mentioned sense.

What we clearly have here is again the tendency to shove responsibility to some superior power, to someone who might do 'something', but basically, it is the capitulation before taking up tasks one should take over oneself. But expecting the same from others, here: 'leaders', is okay We often come across average citizens who openly admired leaders like Hitler, Stalin, and other more than doubtful personalities, having suppressed their own people ruthlessly, and also brought misery and bloodshed over mankind. Human history, unfortunately, is full of those examples. Since the era of enlightenment, one should think, the perception of leadership has undergone drastic changes. Democratic principles became stronger and stronger, and of course, innumerable human beings lost their life in fighting for them.

The civil society in the twenty-first century should consist of people who are conscious of their own value as citizens in a democratic country; they should accept leaders only in this context: individual freedom that has its limit only where the freedom of another is endangered. Sounds easy? Just let us try!

The fact that India is, by and large, a "complainant society"—this is how we coined it—makes it difficult to motivate individuals for taking initiatives, especially when it come to the leadership issues they are constantly complaining about.

Being asked why they allow bad leaders treating them badly, bad leaders exploiting them, bad leaders depriving them of their democratic rights, bad leaders being corrupt and ruthless, they answer invariably: "What can I do?" or, as variant: "There is nothing I can do", depicting an abysmal lack of hope. A German proverb says:

> If you really want to do something, you'll find a way; If you don't, you'll find an excuse.

This art has evolved into perfection!

The excuses crop up everywhere: it is the mantra for citizens who are not prepared to behave as citizens in a democratic country, the mantra as free-for-all for the self-styled leaders to do whatever they want. It is a convenient excuse for doing nothing, for not standing up against injustice, for perpetually electing 'leaders' who do not deserve the attribute of a good leader.

As long as the individual citizens are not aware that they are powerful if united against injustice and exploitation, there will be no improvement. As long as the individual citizens are not willing to take initiative, to say "No" to suppression and corruption, there will be no improvement. It is the citizens themselves who are responsible for the present deplorable situation where the 'leaders' trample upon them, where open corruption is rarely punished—in fact, those who are amassing wealth are admired for their guts, and a rich person seems to be a good person in the public opinion.

We would like to see Indian citizens waking up from their slumber of convenience and absence of civil courage, and stand up and give their overall thumbs-down for the scoundrels who have built up an evil network of perverse leadership.

Will that day come soon? It will come soon, provided there is a change of mindset and attitudes at all levels, in all sections of society, starting in our educational system which, unfortunately, does not educate in civil courage but in submissiveness.

What can we expect from teachers who punish students for questioning? What can we expect from teachers who are submissive themselves? Don't we expect students to emulate the teachers? What can we expect from an educational system where blunt capitalist business principles are ruling? When money supersedes educational demands, when quantity supersedes quality, and when destructive business principles are leading to deterioration of quality teaching and de-motivation of teachers, then no mature citizens worth an egalitarian civil society can evolve.

But, against all odds and present facts, we do think that there is all reason for hope and a big scope for improvement as we observe globalisation impacts not only in economic spheres but also in overall lifestyle and attitude patterns. The younger generation is exposed to worldwide media influences, advertisements, internet connectivity and contacts, leading to a change in overall behavioural patterns. More and more information about how things can be done differently and more efficiently comes into the fray, and the younger generation imbibes all this with great interest.

Now, viewing this change from the angle of holistic change, we see at present more of the superficial and manipulative influences leading to more and more consumerist attitudes, like it is prevalent in the Western world, but this process has been going on since the last more than three decades with the powerful upcoming of well-to-do middle classes, Western-oriented, and extremely self-oriented concerning responsibilities towards the society as a whole.

From an unknown source:

> I do not want my house to be walled in on all sides and my windows to be stuffed. I want the cultures of all the lands to be blown about my house as freely as possible. But I refuse to be blown off my feet by any.

Showing self-confidence, and feeling comfortable and proud in being part of a nation which provides reason enough to be proud of, and which has all scope for becoming an exemplary society for other nations to emulate would be the very natural attitude for Indian society but, alas, all tendencies go in a different direction. As long as the leaders in our country are not able nor willing to identify themselves in a convincing manner with India as a country with unique features of highly valuable diversities, an ancient culture, a traditional openness for change, and immense richness of material and immaterial resources, we cannot hope that change towards a self-confident civil society will be established.

One of the big stumbling blocks is that we have to mention it again and again, the overall submissiveness in our leaders and their dichotomies: on the one hand, they are callous and use all their influence and power to achieve their individual goals, showing the sort of 'courage' which goes with bulldosing over other's rights and needs; on the other hand, they are permanently all eyes and ears for what is fashionable and gives prestige, and these attributes are distinctly 'foreign'.

What we observe in this context are:

a) widely confused perception of "national" and "nationalistic", i.e. used by politicians and their coterie to whip up emotions with the aim of garnering voters.

b) nationalistic slogans for creating a make-believe atmosphere of "Indian-ness" which has nothing to do with a genuine identification of individuals and communities as "Indian".

c) intolerance towards 'others', as convenient tool for gaining political clout.

d) poor performance of leaders in striving for societal harmony.[5]

e) meekly compromising in political matters concerning vital interests of the country while defiantly insisting on petty matters (blown up to become issues of 'vital interest' for the nation.

f) stubbornly holding on at an outdated educational system which produces the same subaltern, submissive citizens as is the mainstream citizen of present-day India.

g) valuing and admire citizens who go abroad and invest their talents elsewhere.

(to name only some of the burning problems)

A healthy and self-confident civil society appreciates the creative spirits. It does not award those who merely obey and, it has to support future-oriented efforts to make its citizens proud to be part of it. All these cannot be achieved through mainstream pleasantries, through imitating values which might be fit for other cultures, and through superficially holding up misinterpretations of ancient traditions, if and when it fits the vested interests of political leaders.

References

1. From Sokrates, Plato, Aristotle and others, to Cicero ('societas civilis') to myriads of other philosophers through the ages, the term can be traced, but this doesn't make it more distinct. We cannot go into the philosophical discussions here.
2. The issue of *Reservation System* is elaborated in the respective chapter.
3. Dealing with the Indian Judiciary means sometimes running against rubber walls: the bureaucrats and judges behave as if they are feudal lords doing with the people whatever their whims and wishes, dictate and they don't feel the necessity to explain anything.

There is no accountability whatsoever: a judge fixes dates while complainants, defendants, witnesses, lawyers (costing a fortune in India!) are present, but the high and mighty judge suddenly decides not to deal with the matter that day. In one of our case studies, one of the people involved in the case is working with international organisations, and therefore has fixed dates abroad, but repeatedly, the judge deliberately determines court hearing exactly in these timespans. Is it a pathetic vengeance of a simple district court judge in a very provincial town? A provincial judge who cannot hope ever to go abroad or else, who is aware that nobody would want him there? Matter-of-factly, he has his satisfaction—so much so for good leadership!

4. We refer to the many sumptuous marriages, and cases of showing off wealth which is in no proportion of any known income. Besides, lavish marriages are banned by law—but who cares? Who would enforce the law of the land?
5. After the well-known principle of Julius Cesar: *Divide et impera!(= Divide and Conquer!)*

5

The Misery of Leadership in Politics, Civil Services, Public and Private Sector Enterprises and Judiciary

> Sumitra did not try to argue with Harry. Like Too before him, he would never understand. He had no conception of the shifts and makeshifts necessary to hold on to a position of power, and that what appeared to him as bribery and corruption was nothing but a judicious balancing of funds to keep the machinery of government oiled and functioning.[1]

The "Pleasing Syndrome"

We contemplated for some time which chapter in this book would be best suited for including our thoughts about what we call the 'pleasing syndrome', and finally decided to put it here, as this syndrome is closely connected with the all-pervading phenomenon of 'Chamchagiri', and it is observable everywhere: be it in public life, or be it in schools and all academic institutions, or be it in neighbourhoods and families. Also, the patterns of behaviour observable in the 'pleasing syndrome' are the main enablers for continuation of bad leadership.

We have to view the pleasing syndrome from its roots, before we come to the impacts, and from there to the extent it is influencing our daily life and the prospects of sustainable change in society.

Let us first look at an authentic case study (which we came across frequently, always in a similar way!):

> We are travelling in a town, and we need to get help for direction where to reach the street we want to go. We ask someone, and the person is very friendly, seemingly competent, and he shows us the direction where to go, not without giving explicit description of landmarks we should observe. Happily we follow his directions.
>
> But alas, soon we are completely lost, and we approach another pedestrian for help. Again, the person is very glad to help us out, even talking to himself while considering the best and fastest way for us. Finally, he explicitly names the streets to pass and the junctions to cross, accompanied by lots of gestures.
>
> We follow, but soon we are lost again.
>
> We approach a rickshaw man who seems to be quite bored, just waving his arm to indicate that the street we are searching is just round the corner. It was, in fact, and we could have reached there much earlier, had we not listened to the friendly people showing us a way which they obviously had had no idea about!
>
> They just could not admit that they did not know, they wanted to be helpful, to please, and out of this attitude, they caused lots of problems.

Is it so difficult to admit that one doesn't now the answer to a question? Is it so difficult to say 'I don't know'? Is it so difficult to have the common sense to not sending people into all sorts of road adventures, wasting their time and energies, and getting nowhere? How would they feel if they would experience the same?

We would have liked to meet again some of these friendly people, asking them why they behaved like they did—just to understand!

Clearly, such behavioural patterns evolve from authoritarian upbringing, and from being exposed to authoritarian leadership, where there is always the fear to admit to what might be seen as "weakness". In this case, the internal role conflict of a person results in blunt lies, but the person is not aware of lying at all—the all-pervading urge to 'please' gains the upper hand, and suppresses all other considerations about what the strangers might suffer.

Another case study:

> We are observing participants in a leadership seminar. Most of the goings-on were the usual deliberations of "good leadership" in the conventional way, lots of 'control', 'hierarchy', 'discipline', 'communication', and bits and pieces of fashionable pseudo-psychology like 'I am o.k.—you are o.k.', 'I am a winner', 'I am a leader', - only one should believe in it. The trainer finally asked the participants in his jolly manner, "Understood everything? You agree with me?", and they answered in chorus a happy "Yes!" Seminar over, all are happy.

We interview some of the participants:

Q: *Do you think the seminar was successful for you?*

A: Oh yes. It was very successful. I know now how to be a good leader.

Q: *What do you change from now onwards? What will change in your leadership style?*

A: Not much. You see, in my office, I cannot change things. The work is organised from higher up.

Q: *Then, what good has it brought about?*

A: Well, perhaps no direct success. But, for me, I now know that I can be a good leader.

Q: *How?*

A: The trainer told me so. I will participate in his next course, too, even if I have to pay for it myself.

Q: *Then, the seminar helped you in enhancing your self-esteem?*

A: Yes, very much!

Q: *And how was the individual leadership ability assessed? What are your individual strengths and weaknesses to work on?*

A: What do you mean? We are all leaders. We are all able to be good leaders.

Q: *So the trainer told you? Without assessing things like individual personality structure, or assessing strengths and weaknesses?*

A: He is very experienced. He knows.

We do not comment on this in detail. But, what is displayed here, we find almost everywhere:

a) Trainers who please the customers—both, the business partners, and the participants—to ensure further business.

b) Trainers who display lack of competency, but try everything to please the participants.

c) Trainers who display utter lack of ability for self-critique, overestimating their talents and competencies, but are successful because they know how to please.

d) Leaders who are so submissive (to the trainer) that they don't question his competence: the 'pleasing syndrome' at its best!

The fear of possibly being 'disliked' by someone if you express a different opinion is very much obvious, especially in the professional field, but also in other social contacts.[2] Some people are already happy if a certain person is not cross with them, the Indian leaders seem to prepare a very fertile ground for this.

An Indian leader loves to believe in people who admire his/her authority; it is not enough to be respected, but one has to show the required submissiveness, and part of this behavioural pattern is never to contradict a superior. (By the way, our Indian leaders still talk about their staff or co-workers as "inferiors" that says it all.) It is basically all about being afraid, about fear:

a) Fear from risking the career.

b) Fear from being ousted from the benevolent halo of the boss.

c) Fear from losing prestige and/or social status and all the misery autocratic leadership creates.

On the other hand, the all-pervading submissiveness seduces the 'leader' into believing that he is really the greatest, the best, the embodiment of good leadership and, what counts even more, the most superior and accomplished personality. We call this 'personality cult', and we deal with it in the chapter on 'leadership and competency'.

Summing up of the roots for the Pleasing Syndrome:

a) Individual insecurity leading to the inability to admit 'I don't know'.
b) Trying to come up to pre-perceived expectations (What is it that my boss wants me to say, to do? How can I please him? What will catapult me into his good books?).
c) Pressure from autocratic, 'bad' leaders.
d) Constantly focusing and worrying on what the leader's expectations might be.
e) Opportunism as personality structure and/or acquired habit.
f) The irrational urge to be 'liked', or 'loved' by others (starting from childhood, continued in school, and furthered by authoritarian leaders).

Some observations:

> The boss calls someone from the staff. The person enters the office room showing his subservience through a clear body language: almost half-bent, anxiously looking on but avoiding direct eye contact, totally focused on the boss but not looking at the visitors (which would have been the normal behaviour!). The boss bellows his order, and subsequently, our man seems to shrink to half his size. Every half-sentence of the boss is acknowledged with an almost breathlessly uttered 'yessir, yessir'. He makes his exit by clumsily going backwards, never taking his eyes from the boss (is he afraid that the boss might throw a dagger at him?), and on the way our man knocks down a flimsy coffee table. The boss howls "Out! Out!", and our man nearly trips over his own feet in his hasty retreat.

We all feel extremely awkward, but the boss is quite happy and comments, "Idiot! Idiot! All Idiots!" before he continues our discussion as the most charming and jovial man he wants us to see him.

We are guests in a typical middle class home, gorgeously coloured artificial flowers, heavy upholstered furniture, glass-cases with all sorts of kitschy artefacts, even a toy doll (blond!) has found a prominent exhibition place—not to be toyed with! We try to sit comfortably while trying our best not to dislocate the various dollies decorating the armchairs at all the strategic points where you try to rest your arms and back—dollies everywhere, on the table, chairs, sofa, and gorgeously coloured, too, an assault to the eyes.

We inquire about children, and to our astonishment, the youngsters who are just entering the living room are introduced like this: "This is my son Arjun, and this is our daughter, Savita."After this, Savita is serving water, chai, snacks, whereas the boy is just sitting on the sofa, looking bored and obviously anxious to flee the place. The parents immediately start talking about the qualities of the children and of course, both of them are 'toppers' in school—while listening to this, we observe their awkwardness, and feel pity for them[3]. Finally, they are forced to 'perform': the boy has to show his talents as dancer a` la Bollywood, whereas the girl has to recite some poems. Both obey like sheep. The parents seem to bask in the performances, they beam at us as if we just had the greatest enjoyment in life. It is absolutely clear that the children suffered at being paraded like this, and that they did not want to obey, but they did without any protest!

It was a pathetic sight: the children doing their best to please their parents, knowing well that they would incur dire consequences if not, and, somehow, we had the impression that these children are already conditioned to obey, to please.

What can be expected from them when they grow up? Just the same subservient behavioural patterns they were

> forced into from early childhood. Is this the material which would develop into good leaders? Definitely not: they are forcibly deprived from developing into mature individuals because they imbibed the 'virus of pleasing', thus never learnt to question, to protest, to stand up to their own feelings and wishes. They will emulate the all-pervading societal hypocrisy shown by their parents ("Our children are toppers", even when they are far from it), and they will—consciously or unconsciously—take revenge later on as leaders who should never be.
>
> Here, we see one of the manifold root causes why India has such a deficiency in good leadership: how can good leadership evolve from forced submissiveness?

Analysing leadership qualities in the above-mentioned groups—civil servants, politicians, judiciary, leaders in public-private, and still in some private (Indian) enterprises - we certainly have vast potential of 'intelligence' at hand: civil servants have to have at least a comparatively high level of cognitive intelligence[4], whereas these features cannot generally be said about other groups of leaders, like politicians, or entrepreneurs, for that matter. In fact, the narrowed-down perception of 'intelligence' as a cognitive ability, is only one of the many variants which makes a person intelligent or not, which makes a person suited for a certain task or not, but certainly, it has nothing to do with key abilities for making a good leader.

We can observe entrepreneurs having not much of cognitive intelligence or formal education, but they might have full potential of key leadership abilities which makes them extremely successful as leaders and that, too, as good leaders.

The same applies to politicians who sometimes show a great potential for leadership and, if the respective politician is genuinely committed to serve the people, he would become very successful[5].

Alas, the prevalent system of all political parties benefits mostly those who are the 'toppers' in adapting the qualities required: no individual opinion, but subservient to the respective party's high command, all in view of the ultimate goal: power (and the wealth which comes with it).

Similarly, the conditioning of our civil servants (including IPS and IFS) shows the same features, and we cannot hope for the better as long as the 'pleasing syndrome' is determining career prospects and the overall expectations of middle class people's aims and objectives in life.

There is the overall confusion and misperception between 'being polite', respecting others', showing 'manners', i.e. good behaviour, and the urge to *please*. Calling a spade a spade is somewhat tabooised, lest someone could find fault with it, lest it might have adverse consequences.

Unsuitable Measures

There is a lot of misunderstanding concerning trainings for leadership as various trainers and/or consultants try to convince people that everyone could acquire the skills for good leadership, and that everyone could be 'groomed' as leader. It goes without saying that these postulations are utterly wrong: if a person lacks the key abilities for good leadership which can only be assessed by suitable tools and competent psychological evaluation and analysis, there is no trainer in the world who could transform him/her into a good leader. As the German proverb says: "You cannot transform an ox into a race horse."

Lack of good leadership is especially observable in the average personnel of our judiciary: you get the impression that the mindset of judges usually is one of self-righteousness and pompousness which would prevent anyone from having a natural, intelligent, and emphatic relation to one's own personality and also, to those of others.

In the case of the judiciary, this fact is of utmost importance as it perfectly mirrors the abysmal conditions within our third estate; in reality, the third estate is not independent at all but prone to influences of the influential, and prone to bribery as almost all other institutions of power in India.

At no instance in the making of a judge or a lawyer, the issues of 'leadership' are even touched; if we add the fact that 'management', 'organisation', 'cost efficiency' and some other important topics are completely alien to the curricula and the—few—internships, so that we need not wonder about the inefficiency of both the professions. On the one hand, the judges have no idea about work efficiency, or cost consciousness; on the other hand, the lawyers do not demand it as they are very much interested in delaying cases for the benefit of their own coffers. This way, the system is very well developed: hands in gloves against the interests of the clients! Where else in the world do we experience that simple cases need more than 25 and even 30 years even to be taken up and, finally, decided?

Most of the complainants might be dead and gone by the time the judiciary generously decides to deal with a file. Meanwhile, the lawyers have earned their cut albeit they have not deserved it.

We collected various case studies in connection with absolutely negligence on the side of the judiciary[6]

We sincerely ask why official India thinks it could go on as if everything would be well functioning? The Indian judiciary system allows a certain section of judges and lawyers not to render or bring about justice but granting benevolent or malevolent judgments, depending on favourable or not-so-favourable conditions in the interests of the judges and/or the lawyers. The clients who seek justice are literally lost in space.

Let us only look at decisions concerning high positions in our higher judiciary courts: the (few) judges who stand up against lack of transparency, corruption, delaying justice, inefficiency, haughtiness and pompousness, and the all-pervading self-righteousness of their colleagues are punished by delayed promotion, by being transferred to 'unimportant' courts and, finally, they won't be promoted to positions in the Supreme Court.

Recently, all media were harping on 'corruption in the SC', but what consequences were taken? None at all. Everything is just going the usual path, certain judges were not promoted, others were, and, to top it all, we have a vigilance officer who himself is suspected of criminal activities (as of now, he is still holding the position).

After all, the last Chief Justice of the Supreme Court of India had the callousness of objecting to the demand for transparency of assets of judges, and this stand gained him the position of Human Rights Commissioner after his recent retirement. To our opinion, this is a blatant violation of what one could expect from a representative of the highest protecting institution in a democratic country, the judiciary, who is expected to protect human rights in a country where there is a lot to improve in this field. There are quite a number of upright judges who would deserve this position, and would come up to the expectations, but, alas, they are merely tolerated as one cannot remove them during their tenure, but they never get a prominent or profitable position after retirement[7].

We have to ask: who takes these decisions, and what are the reasons behind?

Why do those judges who stand up for unbiased judgments and transparency not get the appreciation they deserve?

We all know the answer: they are thorns in the flesh of the well-oiled corrupt machinery, and, as they cannot be eliminated altogether, they have to be made mute. They don't please the machinery, thus manifesting a threat. That's it.

Good leadership is a term unbeknownst, and it has hardly any relevance at all in our courts of justice.

Case study:

> A case is to be heard in a provincial District Court. The complainant, his lawyer, some witnesses, the defendants plus lawyer, everyone is present, everyone is patiently waiting for His Highness, the judge. With a delay of more than 15 minutes, the judge enters the courtroom, he does not look at anyone, he does not apologise, he takes his seat and starts reading the newspaper.
>
> Nobody says a thing! No one objects! Long faces all around, shuffling of paper, of feet, and the longest face in the room,

> that of the judge, is still looking down on his newspaper—otherwise, looking literally down on the people.
>
> After some time, he looks up with a bored facial expression, and finally says that today he has no time to hear the case as he is expecting some important visitor from the High Court. One of the witnesses tries to explain to him that he came thousands of kms to testify, but this judge just refuses to listen to anyone and anything. He rises and leaves the courtroom. But before, that he fixes the next date, more than two months later, and in spite of the fact that the complainant informed him earlier that he would be abroad. Also, he refuses to listen to anything a person in the courtroom tries to convey to him.
>
> He displays a pompous, arrogant, contemptuous behaviour which discredits all expectations of sovereign, balanced, confident personality, but shows a mousy underdog who happens to have grasped a piece of power and needs to exploit it to full capacity to compensate for all the shortcomings he instinctively knows he has, and that he desperately tries to hide.

One thing is sure: as long as the Indian judiciary suppresses its real potential and allows the mice to kill the lions, nothing will improve. Good leadership would be the answer, but: who is really interested? Can we expect decision makers who are bad leaders themselves to become advocates of good leadership? Hardly![8]

We have all the right to demand good leadership in all fields, and the judiciary is challenged to come up to the expectations every citizen should demand.

The Misery of Non-Performers in Leadership Positions

Non-performers are worse than those who perform poorly, or else, perform disadvantageous to the task which should be fulfilled. Poor performers evoke critique, they can be identified by their mistakes, and there is very often scope for mitigation, be it through transfer or through removing him or her altogether. With poor performers, there is always a scope for putting a finger into the wound, for identifying what went wrong, for showing the mistakes.

In the case of non-performers, we have to deal with a much more complicated situation:

> The non-performers know very well that they don't come up to any expectations, and consequently, they have to do whatever they can to hide this fact. They have to put in a lot of hard work and cunningness, and a lot of war-like efforts to ward off dangers from probable rivals; so, there won't be energy and time to concentrate on the work for which all the non-performers are paid, the same way as the performers.

The Art of Non-performing for Solid Money

It is very easy to define: by taking up a job, a person goes into a contract, promising to do work against a salary. If he does not perform, he commits a crime: cheating, accepting money for nothing. We never came across a case where a non-performing leader was taken to task for this very reason. It seems that non-performing does not exist in the vocabulary of Indian leadership.

One of the greatest worries of a non-performer is to suppress any talent in the vicinity who could evolve into someone showing that work at hand can be done properly and efficiently. The staff of a non-performing leader is a poor lot: this leader will see to it that emerging talents will be turned away, if need be through evil methods, like harassing them and/or make them do inferior work (giving no work at all and accusing them of non-performance is a further method of frustrating and demoralising otherwise able staff), and that only under-performers will do work. Thus, a *negative selection* of staff is built up, the prospective danger for a non-performing leader is avoided.

In this context, the non-performer is afraid of creativity and new ideas in his surroundings, like people are afraid of snakes or like the devil fears the holy water.

Such leaders, or, more precisely, persons in leadership positions, cannot allow to have real performers around lest their own performance might be compared with it.

This leads to the well-known *vicious circle,* shown step-by-step:

1. Someone gets into a leadership position but has no key leadership qualities/skills. This happens quite often as the usual selection procedures do not assess these, and also, the more or less automatic promotion system—after seniority—does not contain assessment of performance and hardly competency.
2. The 'leader' gets rid of all persons around who have these qualities or seem to have them; he removes or suppresses the good performers.

Results:

3. Overall performance becomes worse and worse.
4. Second line leadership grooming is not executed, is not possible.
5. Performance evaluation is not executed, is not possible.
6. Overall performance goes down the hill.
7. Non-performance, waste of resources, circling around instead of going forward.

It is comparatively easy to identify *pseudo-leaders* if we apply the following defining categories by observing and evaluating their presences or absences. The four categories serve as tools for assessing key potential for leadership qualities:

1. decision making
2. setting aims and objectives
3. motivation (self- and others)
4. controlling (in the sense of assessing performance)

Concerning point 1, it is obvious, that a weak leader tries to *avoid taking decisions*. We can observe a high degree of creativity in inventing multitudes of excuses, and unfortunately, due to lack of accountability, those leaders can get away with almost everything.

Case study (the situation):

> The head of a department in a State Government Ministry for Forestry. His responsibilities comprise decisions about

afforestation measurements in connection with earlier loss of forests, mainly due to mining activities and road construction. We are informed that vast areas of land which were declared for re-forestation lay barren since many years, and in the process of desertification. Also, these and surrounding areas of agricultural land already showed a dramatic and progressing decline of groundwater level.

Excerpt from an interview:

Q: *Why is no afforestation taking place?*

A: Oh, that. There are lots of difficulties, yes, difficulties.

Q: *What difficulties?*

A: Not enough funds, and the people there don't want forest. They want agricultural land. They are against afforestation. They protest. What can we do?

Q: *According to our information, huge funds have been allotted, and it seems that these funds are already spent. For what?*

A: We had to build up the right infrastructure for plantations, but there is lack of water. Big, big water problem.

Q: *You spent the funds for water conservation? For replenishing the groundwater?*

A: Not exactly. It is a difficult situation. We had to request experts to research the problems. Lots of studies have been done, some of them are still under way. We are studying the reports to find out the best way. Our funding is just covering the expert consultancy.

Q: *You cooperated with the Ministry for Water Resources and the Central Ground Water Board?*

A: Hm, no, not exactly. Afforestation is not their business.

Q: *So, you spent the funds for private expert consultancy? Why not using the expertise of our water authorities?*

A: Well, you see, there are lots of difficulties. They have their own work to do. They won't have the time to work for us. This would need too much time.

Q: *But too much time is already gone. The rapid decrease of groundwater level is almost irreparable.*

A: What can we do? We need the experts. We have to follow their advice. And they need their time, they do thorough research.

Q: *Suppose your officers go through the reports: how can they evaluate them without their own expertise?*

A: They evaluate the suggestions after feasibility. That is money and some other considerations. Difficult, very, very difficult.

Q: *These areas are deteriorating rapidly, and the surrounding agricultural land is already suffering a lot. How will you solve these problems, and when?*

A: The problems of surrounding areas are not our responsibility. The Ministry of Agriculture has to deal with that. We cannot do everything.

Q: *Do you have an action plan?*

A: How? We still have to evaluate all the reports and studies, after that, we have to see for funding. The action plan will follow. We cannot give other information at present. Good decisions have to ripen, they cannot be taken in haste.

Q: *But the original funding is already spent, and nothing has been done.*

A: Expertise is necessary, and you have to spend money. With further funding, steps will be taken, problems will be solved.

(We terminate the interview, as things are going in circles)

Concerning point 2, a weak leader specifically avoids setting clear aims and objectives. The two main reasons are that it could lead to make him accountable for failures and, at the same time, he is not able to define them: except, perhaps, for his own career and greed, he has no clear plan or vision which would enable him to develop aims and objectives as a precise plan of action.

He re-acts instead of acting in this context, and the processes of re-acting are slowed down as much as possible, for reasons given above.

Point 3, the ability to motivate oneself and motivate others, appears as almost absent in a weak leader. The prerequisites of personalities for motivational achievements are mentioned in the chapter on Leadership and Motivation, but here, describing the deficiencies of weak leaders, it is obvious that someone who cannot motivate himself is unable to motivate others.

Someone full of fear in view of decision making, someone who meanders around everything which could make him responsible or accountable, cannot muster the strength and courage for committing himself to anything.

Motivation as a driving force for action and change is considered very dangerous by a weak leader. Change is the utmost threat: wherever there is something unknown, unpredictable, or something which could reveal this constant feeling of insecurity and fear, he has to re-act.

He focuses permanently on these issues, and this is the reason why he is obsessed with suspicions: he feels surrounded by adverse forces, he cannot trust anyone lest his deficiencies might come into the open, and this leads to truly paranoid behavioural patterns. He feels permanently observed, scrutinised, even persecuted, and thus, he leads a truly miserable existence.

Now, we cannot blame the deficient leader only: we have to question a system which allows deficient leaders to wield power, and we have to blame those who put those persons in leadership positions without assessing competency and ability, and also not assessing the performance regularly. But, as it is, these superiors mostly come from the same ranks, and they just feel better as if they are surrounded by people like themselves.

Going into very simple facts of human psychology, a deficient leader has to compensate for his lack of self-esteem, lack of self-confidence and the resulting insecurity by showing off his leadership qualities or else, what he considers leadership qualities. These are the leaders who have to show authoritarian behavioural patterns, they are the ones who think and behave after the rule: a leader has to show others what to do, a leader has to have everything 'under control', the latter leading to what we coined the 'controlling overkill', stifling good performance, and highly de-motivating.

Not trusting anyone means, logically, that he cannot truly appreciate achievements or performances of others. Thus, he cannot execute the most important task of a leader: appreciation!

Leaders with personality deficiencies, shortly called 'weak leaders', suffer from the urge to compensate their insecurities, and they desperately try to hide these through various behavioural measures. We already mentioned the authoritarian methods, but we can observe a wide range of additional behavioural patterns, like

a) The well-known 'Yes-butting': Yes, it is quite well done, but... The message is clear: it is not good enough! The motivational impact: devastating!

b) Suggestions are not accepted, and worse, some time later, the same suggestions are brought forward as own ideas of the leader.

c) He is not easily accessible: like all authoritarian leaders, he has to show power the way that others are always put into place, and their place is inferior!

d) He is not able to accept critique, and he cannot admit mistakes; at the same time, he blows up errors and mistakes of others. Such is his mindset:

> the more others are tainted, the more he is shining. Thus he tries to build up and keep the façade of superiority.

e) What he fears most is being ridiculed, moreover, he is constantly suspicious that someone might ridicule him, and this can develop in real paranoia. But ridiculing others is very satisfying—another way of compensating. In this context, we observe a lack of genuine humour, and a simple joke can be very dangerous on the background of his generally suspicious outlook.

f) People who do not respect and accept themselves in all their strength and weaknesses cannot respect others.

If a 'leader' lacks basic key potential for leadership, he cannot learn or train to be leader. Basic deficiencies in a personality structure cannot be changed. This fact is well established, and we have to be very careful not to fall into the traps of manipulative so-called trainers/consultants who promise to be able to produce genius leaders out of everyone. Lack of key potential cannot be substituted or levelled through leadership trainings and the like, and we have to blame all those consultants and training institutions who promise to heavens of leadership wherever people are stupid enough to pay for hollow promises. Only most irresponsible trainers would make such promises, and their manipulative marketing skills yield success: people believe what they want to believe, in these cases to become super leaders, even when they secretly realise that they are not made out of the right stuff.

Instead, good trainers should asses the real potential of individuals, give them leads and make their findings transparent; this 'personal SWOT analysis' would help to find the way towards a fulfilled and happy life.

We have to question basic competencies of the above-mentioned trainers or consultants[9] as they seem to suffer from one or both of two major 'diseases': greed and ignorance, and, being trainers, they also spread the disease!

In any case, it is a betrayal of people who are not careful or cautious enough to scrutinise the offers from consulting institutions which should be done diligently before enrolling in leadership courses.

In the same way, our leaders in decision making seemingly do not care a straw to assess the quality of courses; most of the time it is sufficient for all frauds to hand out glossy prints of seminar programmes, bragging about their achievements. They know that there will be no quality control, and that they can promise whatever they think will bring the assignment. And some good bribes always help, and it will also help in getting further assignments.

How much money is wasted in dubious leadership trainings leading to nothing?

How much money is wasted in 'seminar tourism'[10] camouflaged as leadership trainings? It could be invested in developing a good integrated system of career planning comprising assessment of leadership potential in the first place, custom-tailored workshops and seminars, and subsequently monitored after principles of success and failure[11]. Recently, we came to know about a highly expensive seminar held in our capital for senior leaders. It was titled "Management and Motivation through Clapping", and its programme showed clearly all the nonsensical bogus training. Anyway, the participants had good time while clapping, they had a good day free from work, and perhaps, they are still happily clapping away in their offices.

Thinking Ahead and Thinking Beyond—Alien Land for Deficient Leaders

Leaders without visions cannot evoke the necessary hope for change or hope for improvement, nor can they motivate others to do the same. This is the point where we essentially define 'good' and 'bad' leadership, and all the nuances in between.

How can anyone 'lead' the way when he is not conscious nor clear in his mind about his own direction, about where to go himself?

How can anyone 'lead' the way when there is a virtual blockade concerning the future, no visions nor future-oriented mindset and attitudes?

As the well-known proverb goes: "Those who do not have a goal, don't go anywhere."

We made the experience that many deficient leaders did not even comprehend what we were talking about when we raised the issues of 'visionary' leadership.

Why should they have or develop visions when there is so much to do at present? Is it not good as it is? Why bring about change when everything seems to go smoothly? (a few snags here and there—what the hell!)

Why should there be change when things were 'always done like this'? Visions are things for people with no work at hand, dreamers and those living on clouds high above. The connection between good leadership and the ability to think ahead and beyond seems to be almost absent or else, a frightening thing.

The confusions with the perception of 'visionary thinking', besides a blunt inability to understand, lies in the personality of a deficient leader himself: he cannot allow himself, or others for that matter, to go beyond what is practice up to now, he feels insecure by the very idea of change, he cannot think in terms of taking risks. Also, he perceives visions as something that has nothing to do with what he sees as 'reality', and (t)his reality is the only way to help him through the day.

> We vividly remember a discussion when such a leader elaborated on 'realities of life' and 'people who are living in the future, and they don't see the realities, and they refuse to recognise the constraints and problems of leadership'...'they don't see that there are impossibilities', and so forth. Our question on how a country can survive and compete internationally without thinking forward, and thinking impossibilities, he brushed away: "Visionaries are dreamers, they live on cloud nine. We have to deal with the harsh realities, and we'll deal with future realities the same way we always did. We deal with the facts, and we are the ones that keep the country alive and running." We tried to make it clear that good leadership includes both, dealing with the day-to-day realities, and also, evolving visions for preparing the future. But he would not have it: "Where is the time for that?"

The convenient excuse 'time' as a free-for-all for doing nothing.

For most of us, the excuse "Where is the time?" does not come as a surprise; it is the most used term in connection with inefficiencies of all sorts when, matter-of-factly it is either admitting subconsciously that he cannot organise his work or else, just the usual excuse on which there is hardly anything to say.

To express it unmistakeably: the excuse 'no time' is very convenient, and it conveys some other messages, too, which come in handy for enhancing one's prestige and/or reputation:

a) a person is terribly busy, has an awful lot of work,
b) a person is very much in demand (by superiors, or by people who seemingly count),
c) a person has immense responsibilities,
d) a person has to undertake lots of travels (also abroad, preferably),

whereas, in reality, this person is just not able to organise the work efficiently so that things can be done systematically, and after setting priorities, as it should be.

In this context, the all-pervading leadership problem shows its especially ugly face because time efficiency is a synonym of work efficiency, and our leaders do not exemplify attitudes to learn form and to emulate.

Our leaders show the path, oh yes, but it is the most bumpy, man-hole ridden paths that they make the people walk on, drive, get along. At the same time, the leader's paths are quite smooth, soft to the sensitive feet, and most convenient for all the needs of a leader. The time factor is obviously the most important is that it serves as *vade mecum* for almost all shortcomings because nobody questions the way in which the leaders are squandering away the precious good of 'time'.[12]

It has become a fashionable thing to talk about the 'burn-out syndrome', as is the general perception that only very important people, the real big leaders, suffer from this disease having come upon us from the heavens of shark-capitalist economies. Only, this perception is far from true: 'burn-out' can grip everyone who is doing work under constant pressure, and here, we have to differentiate between people, 'leaders' who create the pressure themselves and suffer accordingly, and those who are in working conditions where they have to bear permanent pressure.

Creativity at its Most Productive—For All the Wrong Reasons

Another salient feature of an incompetent leader is the fact that he/she is extremely inventive in finding excuses and also always puts the blame onto others. When things go wrong and/ or are not running well, the 'leader' has nothing to do with it.

All through history of mankind we find good and bad leaders while historians define the 'good' and 'bad' after their own values or vested interests, depending on what was achieved for their own kith and kin. When there was killing and bloodshed in the millions, it is always the 'others' who are to blame. Especially interesting is the fact that religion has always served as an excuse for the most horrible mass killings, and the religious leaders did not hesitate to sanction it.[13]

'Good' and 'Bad' cannot be defined as absolute values at all: we all have our individual perceptions, and in different cultures, we find very different values for what is good or bad. The terms have to be seen as depending on socially accepted norms in a given time and situation.

> Let us look at a family of pickpockets: the most admired person will be the best pickpocket, he is considered 'good', whereas someone in the same family who cannot master the required skills, is considered 'bad'. It does not make any difference that the family is happily embedded in a society where the social norms are against pickpocketing, and where the laws of the land are punishing their profession. Professional success is what counts, and if you are wealthy, people admire you—even if they suspect your wealth might be ill-gotten[14], as wealth is the ultimate goal, and power and money are the modern mantras.

Terms like these, 'truth' is also among them, cannot be defined absolutely, but we can establish criteria which can help to find a reliable description or definition after certain parameters. If we decide to understand the terms in view of a humane society, we have made a big step forward: 'good' in this context would bring about everything positive, bring about hope and happiness, whereas 'bad' would be the opposite. We can judge 'good' and 'bad' after criteria of happiness for all mankind, and our forefathers, irrespective of culture and specific creed knew this very well, knowing that the fundament for happiness is hope:

Hope is the Pillar
That holds up the World,
Hope is the dream
Of a waking man.[15]
(*Pliny the Elder*)

Where there is a will, there is a way.

Earlier in this book, we elaborated the facts and reasons of the missing *will* for bringing about sustainable change, and of course, this is closely connected with the ability and will to evolve visions, to encourage others to evolve visions, and find ways and means to put them into practice. This is one of the most important and also, most challenging leadership tasks, and now, let us get a good picture of our average leaders in this connection.

Again, we hardly find visionaries. What we mainly find are the 'Yes-butters', eager to please everyone, especially their superiors, but, at the same time, there is always a 'but' to rely upon as excuse for doing nothing. The bureaucratic wolf thus hides himself in the 'creative' sheepskin for disguising perfectly the fact that he is under no circumstances willing to oblige.

We never met more people thinking of themselves as highly visionary and creative than in our government offices, and the density of occurrence of self-styled 'high performers' is nowhere higher than there. We can safely take recourse to results of various socio-psychological studies establishing the phenomenon that people overstress the importance of personal attributes in exactly the reverse proportion they have themselves. That means, for example, a basically insecure personality is disproportionally authoritarian as this provides the perfect mask for him: he has to show that he has power, he likes to be a 'doer' (shoving people around), he makes people admire him and keeps them dependent from his bene- or malevolence. Whereas, a strong personality doesn't need to show off, he convinces through natural authority as against artificial one, and people listen to him without being asked to do so.

If you ask the self-styled super-performers for practical examples of their extraordinary achievements, you invariably draw a blank. The usual answer, given with a shrug and an appropriate sad mimic is: "If only I would find support", or "If only I had the funds", or "If only I had enough staff", or "If only I had the time" (*sic!*), and endless litany, and, in itself, admittedly creative. But creativity is never better than in people who want to find excuses for their own shortcomings.

Thus, we have to add the "If Onlys" to the already mentioned tribe of "Yes Butters".

Authentic case study:

> We discussed our 'Models for Replication' which would bring about drastic change in abysmal living conditions for unemployed youths in villages with a high government official in an Indian state. Our models are quite unconventional, and implementing them would lead to enhancing entrepreneurial spirit while, simultaneously, it would do away with dependencies from governmental grants and subsidies, leading to self-entrepreneurship and enhanced employability, thus reducing interferences of bureaucratic authorities and powers.

As expected, we met with polite interest but utter lack of commitment.

Q: *How could you support our efforts in the village?*

A: You see, I am always interested in supporting development. Actually, development is our daily work...(*laughs heartily*). Your concept is very, very interesting. We should have more people like you.

Q: *Hm. Can you give us your ideas about support at grassroots level from your department?*

A: Well, we have to discuss it. Let us discuss it. We have to be careful, the people might not be interested.

Q: *Why?*

A: We had some development projects there, but they were not successful. The people there are not interested. They demand everything from the government.

Q: *What type of projects?*

A: I think agriculture, yes agriculture. New plants and some road construction, I think.

Q: *What was the problem?*

A: Well, I don't know, really. You know, I was not in this position at that time. But I think the people didn't cooperate. They want the government to do everything for them.

Q: *Have you been there? Did you talk to the people? What are the problems?*

A: Well, no, I could not go there. You know, where is the time? Nobody has time these days. What can you do? But I get all information I need.

Q: *Let's go back to our concept. How do you think you could give support from your department?*

A: Well, it is not so easy. We have to observe the official channels, and everything has to be done officially. It needs time, but where's the time (*laughs*)?

Q: *We are not talking about funds and grants, but about making contacts with local officers, for example, opening doors with the village authorities.*

A: Well, difficult, very difficult. The people expect everything from the government, they don't want to work. They want money, money, money. What can you do? There is not enough money.

Q: *What do you think are the advantages of our concept?*

A: Well, well, highly interesting. Very interesting concept. I am impressed. We should work together.

Q: *Yes, this is why we are here. What type of cooperation would you suggest?*

A: Give me some time. I'll come back to you. It is difficult to decide, but sure, we'll cooperate. I support your efforts whole-heartedly.

Q: *Would you like us to give you some more details, some more information?*

A: I'll let you know, I'll contact you. Yes, yes, I'll contact you. I have such a workload, I cannot say yet. But I wish you all success. Please keep me informed, keep me informed...

(Needless to say that there was no further reaction from him.)

A few months later, on our request, we had another meeting with this officer. Jovially, he inquires about the progress of our activities, but is obviously not really interested. He continues to talk about people he met, especially VIPs, quite the name-dropper.

As soon as we mention that we had met his Minister who is personally interested in our concept, he suddenly calls his PS and asks for the file. Hectic activity spreads around as the file is not to be found, and, after some time, we decide to terminate the meeting. The gentleman is desperately trying to remember what we talked about earlier, but it is clear to us that he has not paid any attention to our concept, he has not the faintest idea why we met him last time, and what we were discussing.

Thus, a worthwhile venture in the interest of improving grassroots conditions through re-structuring and taking unorthodox steps has ended before it began.

Another victim of leadership without vision and commitment.

This case study also shows clearly that weak leaders would never commit themselves to something they consider unpredictable, new, unexpected, even when they are able to understand that there would be all scope for success. They would not understand a dynamic mindset like:

"Let us be realistic—let us try the impossible!"[16]

Globalisation as Excuse for Non-Performance

You ask government officials, civil servants, and even entrepreneurs of a certain kind why they complain about the influences of globalisation, and you will invariably be answered:

Global players, China, World Bank, IMF, etc., are out to bad-handle India.

Needless to say that all those are in fact non-performers, obsessed with their self-created paranoia, but the issue is a very burning one: no doubt, globalisation influences economies and societies everywhere (as the name says), but it also opens wide vistas for performance and success. Why should India stare at it like a rabbit shortly before it is devoured by the snake? Sure, India's economy and politics are heavily influenced by external powers, but the essential question is: How do we play the game? Do we continue to complain, or do we take up the challenge positively? Do we assess the various chances and opportunities?

It seems at present that only a few of our Indian global players have successfully taken up the challenges, but alas, our politicians just lack the vision and the will to follow them, not to mention our civil servants who sit comfortably in their cosy offices, spiralling around themselves, inventing and re-inventing themselves continuously, as if there is no outside world to be concerned with.

India has to take up the already established influences of globalisation as a unique challenge to make the best out of it. To complain about globalisation means to shut the eyes before things which cannot be reversed and, at the same time, to forgo the chances that lie in it.

In this context, too, we have to mention the all-pervading cancerous disease of corruption which makes us suspicious as sincere political and business partners. Good leadership at all levels could mitigate this negative image, albeit it may take a long time. Re-establishing trust is much more difficult than establishing trust in the first place and holding on to it.

Good leadership has to continuously monitor and question the outcomes of all efforts, be it from Government's side or else, from other agencies and businesses. It is a fact that Indian businesses do not strive as would be possible because of inherent obvious flaws concerning reliability and quality consciousness.

One of the most inefficient sectors in our economy (and bureaucracy, for that matter) are the GRS (Grant-Rebate-Subsidies) which are most corrupt and rampant, and spoil all sincere efforts to create self-reliance and overall trust at all levels. To make a positive impact in this respect in a short time would be very easy: the key words are convergence and coordination.

Evaluating/Grading/Judging/Consequences

These key words have to be linked up with each other efficiently by:

a) Inclusive approaches bottom-up (also involving youth as future of the country).
b) Holistic planning for sustainability.
c) Accountability.
d) Making use of un-used or under-used facilities.

All the narrow-mindedness of our average leaders.

In view of the opportunities, chances and necessities in our globalised economies, international contacts are mainly restricted to cooperation with global players in the private sector, and, what is worse, to pseudo-cooperation with international agencies in the fields of "Development Aid", deepening and widening dependencies and submissiveness. The IWF and UN agencies, but also the very big "Development Aid" organisations, are most prominent in this context.[17]

Communication with international grassroots agencies in administration and local elected bodies are almost absent, and it is deplorable that our administrators and politicians have no idea how valuable it could be to learn from each other: be it in view of efficiency, citizen-oriented policies, inclusive decision making, creating awareness on burning issues like environmental threats, population policies, and establishing peaceful relations.

We found the average leaders deplorably disinterested, and they would only respond interested when there were trips abroad or substantial funding in the offing.

The Bureaucratic Overkill

Weak leaders develop great skills in creating and re-creating bureaucratic procedures, and the reasons are very obvious. Bureaucratic procedures, rules and regulations provide the most untransparent infrastructure which serves as almost impenetrable screen for hiding what one wants to hide: mainly the fact that efficient performance and delivering the goods are absent.

Furthermore, this impenetrable infrastructure, through its official character, provides a fertile soil for corruption; this and other to-be-hid factors in the daily life of the average bureaucrats are already dealt with in previous chapters.

We have to ask why this highly inefficient, in terms of benefiting the country and its people, could develop, and why it is allowed to spread further like a cancerous disease. There is a bundle of answers to this and, here, we mention the most pertinent factors.

After Independence, India has blindly adopted the already highly bureaucratised infrastructure from our colonial masters and, since then, is very busy in creating and re-creating more and more obstacles in the way of smooth functioning, citizen-oriented procedures, and cost consciousness, the latter almost absent in the mindset of the average officer and staff.

Accountability would be the key term, at least for mitigating the most harmful consequences, but who would take up this Herculean task? Those who are benefiting from the existing state of condition surely not, and here we are confronted with the biggest obstacle: those who are benefiting would be in the (power) positions to bring about change, and there is no way to make them do so.

Then, the governments could set up a committee for streamlining and setting up 'accountability agencies' which would end up in the usual stalemate: committees in India have an enormously long shelf-life, they go on and on, they move in circles, and after ages they come up with almost nothing. After all, committee members benefit from their being committee members only as long as a committee exists (we refrain from using the term 'works'), why should they put unnecessary haste into the task? In the case of 'accountability agencies', who should man them? Obviously, in the present set-up of the civil servant system, the same people who should be monitored. Old Cato in ancient Rome had asked the question: "Who censors the censors?", and that is exactly the crux of the whole problem.

Only self-confident and mature citizens, independent and committed thinkers could do the job, but, in the overall attitude of submissiveness, there would be a very long way to go, even if we were lucky to find people who possess the above-mentioned attributes, who fulfil these parameters.

We can safely state that we have a veritable bureaucratic hydrocephalus growing by the day, thus contributing to the ever spiralling waste of public money. This fact cannot be played down by the mere formality of establishing some committees for reducing costs in administration, as these committees are bearers of the bureaucratic disease themselves, as already mentioned above. As yet, there was no effect or impact whatsoever resulting from these committees. On the one hand, the members of the commissions are officers or similar position-holders themselves, thus having no interest at all in bringing about change; also, they are not exposed to any accountability—they get their additional salaries for their committee work without having to deliver.

Our average bureaucrats are mainly busy with re-inventing themselves permanently by creating more and more obstacles, like unnecessary paperwork, making people run from one place to another to collect their requisite documents and meaningless papers, stamps, signatures, thus leading to the ever-growing bureaucratic hydrocephalus and finally, to the present bureaucratic overkill.

We could easily learn from other countries where, through methods of Organisation Development and well-trained, competent staff, bureaucracy has been streamlined. But who should want to bring about this change when all involved are profiting from the present condition? The mindset of wasting and siphoning away public money without accountability is the biggest stumbling block to prevent improvement.

We call the whole set-up a bureaucratic overkill, corresponding with the obsession for 'controlling overkill', the disease from which all weak leaders are suffering.[18]

The maniacal obsession to control has landed us in completely unmanageable tangles of hierarchies that cannot be explained in reasoned terms. It has mutated into an automatism, continuously self-inventing, and spiralling into more and more mechanisms, thus throttling creativity, transparency and flexibility. It induces fear in all who are subjected to it, exactly what is intended, as fear is the ultimate tool for those who want to suppress, be it in administration, all bureaucratic setups, or be it in religion and community-centred spheres of life.

True, if one feels insecure, one also feels constantly suspicious that something might happen that could be dangerous. So, something must be done to fortify the so-feared crumbling bastion. And, if one happens to sit on a leadership position, one has all the freedom to substitute fruitful monitoring mechanisms with senseless controlling mechanisms, and exactly here we have the biggest obstacles to make administration efficient:

Fear and confusion!

We estimate that in Indian administration, government department, judiciary, public and public-private enterprises, educational institutions and all connected set-ups around 40 per cent to 50 per cent of personnel could be cut down to economise expenses and bring about efficiency. This could be done by applying the not-so-difficult instruments of *Organisation Development* if only there would be competent leaders to push it through. Such steps can only be taken when there would be a viable action plan for a certain period, revamping organisational structures, qualifying all those whose jobs have become redundant for other employment. A step-by-step plan can easily be worked out by competent experts in organisation development issues, preferably in close cooperation with experts from countries that have successfully revamped their civil services. In view of the plight of millions of Indians who do not have even the minimum resources to live a dignified live, such a drastic effort should be highest on the agenda of our politicians. But: do they sincerely want it? We doubt that very much.

Only when the average citizens wake up, when they realise that they are cheated and neglected by those who should do their level best to improve living conditions, only when they put pressure on all decision makers at all levels can change can be achieved. What we observe at present is the constant rise of greediness by the wealthy middle classes which cannot grab enough, and leaders who come from the same strata of society and, logically, by following the same patterns, are not interested in any change.

> You can't reform politics if you can't reform politicians, and even Mahatma Gandhi had not been able to do that.[19]

The same applies to all strata of our administration and the above mentioned agencies, foremost the judiciary, where we observe an unbelievable self-righteousness, clinging desperately at outdated, almost medieval infrastructure and behavioural patterns.

In contrast to Marc Tully, we are convinced that things could well improve, if only the—hitherto frustrated and suffering—competent leaders would unite and thus become strong enough to make an impact. [20]

'Monitoring' is widely perceived as mere 'control' which means that it is not seen as a motivational instrument. Also, 'monitoring' is usually reserved to 'leaders', and all monitoring concepts are, due to vested interests and accompanying wrong perception, adverse to inclusive approach, another vicious circle.

Thus, the whole perception of leadership, especially good leadership, is in a very perverted stage: valuable instruments of good leadership are twisted and half-baked, and essentially, all 'leaders' just want to remain 'leaders', without accountability, without even having a defined perception of 'good leadership', and what is expected from them in particular. All behavioural patterns in this context are *evasive*, the best method to ensure that they won't to be taken to task.

It is always others who are 'bad leaders', leadership qualities are always lacking in others, and, if one's own leadership comes into question, it is always the inabilities of the 'inferiors' which might give such an impression.

In reality, when we analyse the average situation, a person in a leadership position in India has a sort of wild card which enables him to just do or not do whatever is at stake. We have to see clearly that when co-workers and staff don't come up to expectations, it always comes down to lack of good leadership. To understand, we have to put the following questions:

a) What are the parameters of selection of staff/co-workers?
b) What are the parameters for proper training/ qualification?
c) Is there transparent, inclusive planning of how to monitor performance?
d) Is there proper appreciation?
e) Is there transparent, constructive critique including follow-up measures?
f) Is there regular personal contact/rapport between staff/ co-workers and leader(ship)?
g) Is there an atmosphere of "same eye-level" and mutual respect?

We found a negative to most of the questions, and precisely here is one of the various root causes for the lack of good leadership in this country.

The Misunderstandings about "Charismatic Leaders"

In India, the term 'charismatic leader' is widely misunderstood: the mantra of power and money makes even the most nondescript persons into accepted leaders, and the magic of the same blinds the people.

Usually, we perceive the term 'charismatic' as a specific quality or attribute of a person different from the average individual, showing exceptional abilities, mainly the impact on people making them voluntarily into followers. Distinct communication abilities are the means of transport for 'charisma', establishing instant rapport with individuals or masses of people. Unfortunately, the display of attributes which are not related to individual abilities, namely, *money and power,* are utilized as substitutes for genuine leadership, and the Indian masses seem to be easy prey for those superficialities and make-believes.

The attitude of easy appreciation, acceptance and submission leads to a pseudo-legalisation of so-called charismatic leaders, and this is one of the root causes for many evils in our society.

In the same way, the majority of people in India are all too ready not only to accept, but to admire and revere charlatans of all kind, be it the self-styled 'spiritual leaders', influential politicians, or holders of powerful positions in administration or judiciary.

The multitude of 'holy' men and women with huge followings, the undisputed obedience towards people whose reputation—seen from a rational perspective - otherwise is more than doubtful, speaks for itself, and it is a shame that we are only too eager to submit to and support all types of personality cult, making weak leaders into those who strongly believe in their 'right' to lead, and believe that they are able and good leaders.

We have to open our eyes for the evils in our country which are deterrents for sustainable development and change, and we have to fight with determination if we want our country to mature into an egalitarian society and are able to compete in the globalised world. Let us hope that it is not too late!

Observations off the shelf:

> The highly ritualised style of living in India, having its base in religious tradition, but has become camouflage for

social suppression, is mirrored in the 'ritualised' social norms in the organisational patterns of society and, as religion (and with it, the fear-induced submissiveness) demands it, makes everyone prey to submit to them. Tradition is well and good as long as it not a deterrent for a society which is wedded to democracy and secularism, and which should not submit to outdated concepts. Learning from tradition is very important for a given society, but living in the past is a catastrophy!

For example, the 'Guru', the mostly self-styled person is an unquestioned authority, and this explains the existence of hordes of self-styled, very business-minded 'Gurus' overflowing the country and also, the masses of foreigners venerating them like Messiahs, as this helps them in their escapist tendencies from their own societies under the banner of an amorphous 'spiritualism'.

To exemplify: Two of these propagators of 'spiritualism' are the well-known Sri Sri Ravi Shankar and the unavoidable, media-savvy Ramdev[21] who even talk about 'scientific spiritualism' with hair-raising postulates. None the less, business is soaring, and all the money "goes directly into the lap of heaven", the latter maybe the name of their Swiss Bank Accounts" (to quote someone unknown). Really, one has to admit: world champions of public relations, charismatic leaders, economic sharks in the disguise of lovable dolphins!

Summing up we can say that there is not much incentive for good, able leaders with genuine key abilities for leadership to come up and take over leadership tasks in this country; they have to fight a majority of peoples, colleagues, who don't come up to the expectations of good leaders, who enjoy much more privileges and appreciation from their superiors whereas the committed leaders have to fight against suspicions, intrigues, and all sorts of obstacles. On top of all this, their superiors very often punish them for their 'being different' by delaying promotions and/or transfer them to presumed 'bad' postings. It goes without saying that this damaging machinery could de-stabilise even very strong personalities, and we know about various cases where able, committed officers change their attitudes and style of work towards the more convenient, opportunistic way of functioning. Pressure from family, friends and relatives increase the change of behavioural patterns towards a complete change of mindset and attitudes towards less and less commitment. Furthermore, the colleagues ridicule him, even ostracise him socially and professionally. Only the strongest survive in these conditions, and they have to go their way alone. It is not much consolation that he can hold his head upright and stand tall to his convictions, there is a high price to pay.

We do think India cannot afford to go on and on following these patterns: awarding unwanted behaviour, while punishing the ones who could bring the country forward.

References

1. From: Ruth Prawer Jhabvala: *East into Upper East*, Counterpoint (Perseus), Washington, 1998, p. 65.
2. We do not go into the fact that sometimes, due to certain psychological defects, people tend to contradict everything, just to try to make themselves more 'interesting' in the eyes of others. This phenomenon is not rare, and it applies mostly to disgruntled human species who compensate for a perceived lack of appreciation by snubbing others.
3. Indian middle classes seem to produce only 'toppers', there cannot be anything below for them. The problem is that the children develop a sense of loss: parents love them as long as they contribute to the 'prestige' of the family, and if they fail in the obviously most important field of performance in school, they develop utter insecurity. In many cases, children just fall into despair. No wonder that India is 'topping' the world statistics in suicides among children and youth: what a shame!
4. The term 'intelligence' in this book is defined not by its usual lopsided cognitive dimension, but encompasses all variants of 'intelligence', like emotional, etc. It is the holistic approach which points to the fact that the cognitive factor alone might make the worst type of leader, and that is why the selection of leaders in administration is so abysmally deficient.
5. Unfortunately, in the power structure of the established political parties, those natural leadership talents are very rarely allowed to come up within a party: they are considered to be very dangerous for the existing 'leadership', and they might endanger the whole exploitative set-up.

6. See Appendix: The Speed of Justice, an authentic case study.
7. The same applies to courageous civil servants in this country.
8. See Appendix: "The Speed of Justice", after an authentic court case, not yet completed as the case still drags on, and the article "The Indian Judiciary System, An Overview".
9. Unfortunately, the tendency of "grooming leaders out of everyone" comes from certain exclusively business-minded 'US-schools' that state: 'Everyone can become a leader.' This type of training/ consultancy developed from trainings for insurance and other field agents who had to be brainwashed into thinking that their self-motivation depends on thinking they are 'the greatest', and that they can achieve everything if only they want to. Self-criticism is out. Honest psychologists, consultants and trainers know better, and they don't subscribe to these false and individually dangerous theses.
10. 'Seminar Tourism': meant as perks, special benefits for 'special' staff, in the disguise of seminars or other educative ventures. These events usually take place in favourite tourist spots (for example: Kovalam, Goa, places in the Himalayas), and whole families are also taken there—paid for by the employer, namely, Government departments, using taxpayer's money.
11. See Appendix: "System of Leadership Training Modules".
12. Logic requires the following explanation: 'time' is a given dimension which cannot be influenced by humanly possible ways and means; it passes whatever we do or make during the passing of time, that means, we can neither 'save' it nor 'waste' it. The only thing possible is to make the best use of the given time, and the best way to do so is after simple organisational rules of priorities and other efficiency-enhancing measures which would give enough room for recreational purposes, too.
13. For example: during the many wars between Germany and France in the timespan of several hundred years, the priests on both the sides blessed the respective soldiers and the weapons, and they requested the same god to make them victorious; till recently, Catholics and Protestants in Northern Ireland killed each other in the name of their religion; the crusaders killed thousands for land and money in the name of a 'peaceful' religion; presently, the whole world has to suffer from religious fundamentalists who kill in the name of the 'peaceful' Islam, and last, but not least, Hindu fundamentalists kill in the name of an otherwise decidedly peaceful philosophy.
14. Clearly to be observed in the way the 'aam aadmi' elect and re-elect the openly corrupt politicians, and there is hardly any protest against corrupt administrators or people serving in our judiciary system.

15. From: Dean Koontz: *Twilight Eyes*, Headline Publishing Group, 2007.
16. Most probably by Che Guevara.
17. The specific evils in the practised so-called development aid are their fundamentally exploitative aims and objectives: 'helping' in case of emergencies, like natural disasters, rendering aid to mitigate the actual sufferings, but not helping in establishing holistic sustainable development which would prevent the need for help in the future. Recent examples are the ever-recurring floods in various parts of India, the disastrous receding groundwater levels leading to desertification, etc., where technologies are available to prevent these, but they are not implemented. Thus, "development aid" is a shortsighted eye-wash, whipping up emotions in the international donors, but the ultimate aim is keeping the victims dependent, so that "development aid" will continue as big business for the so-called developed economies.
18. See previous chapter.
19. Marc Tully: *The Heart of India*, Penguin India, New Delhi, 1995, p. 130.
20. See Appendix: 'Forum for IAS Performers', a platform where dedicated performers will meet, exchange their experience, co-ordinate their activities, and collect and publish 'Series of Performers Presentations' to practically show the way to sustainable change.
21. An example of his dubious messages: he offers to 'heal' homosexuality through his 'spiritual methods', thus inducing the unfortunately rampant opinion that homosexuality is something unnatural, a sort of disease which can be 'healed'. Fact is that homosexuality is just an variant of nature's gifts, and homosexual people are as 'normal' as anyone else. His vast influence will deceive people into further persecution of homosexuals. See Appendix: Article on Homosexuality by the co-author of this book, Dr. Kamal Taori.

6

Leadership and Reservation Policies[1]

The fact that our present-day reservation policies are enshrined in the Indian Constitution makes it very difficult to attack it and solve all the problems evolving from it.

Quota policies is always the tool for those who want to hush up realities, who want to do some repair work in obvious damaged circumstances, but, at the same time, it is clearly a method of evading realities.

The majority of our 'leaders' strongly support reservation policies as they have to keep to their own vested interests and to those of their supporters. With reservation, we have some justification for social discrepancies and unfortunately, a tool for misuse, hindering the process towards an equal society instead of furthering it as is loudly propagated by those who have to lose a lot if reservation would be abolished.

Reservation has developed into the Holy Grail for greedy individuals and communities, thus cementing the disharmonies in our society. It is most cynical to pretend that reservation would harmonise society, would support integration of communities, or else, would help levelling the social and economic gaps.

In reality, reservation policies are tearing our society apart, in full view of everyone who has the will and the capacity to analyse and to understand, but political correctness and other vested interests prevent them from fighting this system.

From the economic point of view, reservation and quotas lead to supporting incompetency, while suppressing potential and abilities which could contribute to our economy successfully competing in the era of globalisation. In our environment where merit is not suitably awarded, but irrational considerations keep up a system of suppressing talents, we cannot expect economy to become sustainably strong.

Off the Shelf

In Western countries, we have some elements of 'reservation', too: political parties have introduced quotas for women in good faith to promote female politicians coming up as good leaders; the same way, legislation provided better opportunities for women to find employment both, in the civil service and also, in the private sector enterprises. The laws of the land prescribes that in case of selecting from a group of applicants for certain jobs, and under the condition that suitability and qualifications are the same, the female applicant has to be given the job. In the same way, advertisements for jobs have to be phrased so that there is no gender preference to be interpreted, lest the respective advertiser will be punished under the law.

The reality is quite simple: as ever before, employers have full freedom to choose the best qualified person for a job, and it would be very difficult to prove that gender discrimination was applied. On the contrary, employers usually put the main emphasis on qualification and other requirements (communication skills, etc.) than on gender, and this non-gender-biased attitude has led to very successful results. Of course, there is the fact that schooling and higher education are completely free from gender biases, the fact that—especially in Germany—education is free (including school books), and meantime, most of the universities charge a nominal fee for enrolment, the accessibility to highly qualified jobs is very easy.

Germany has quite a lot of jokes on the "quota" issue, like the following:

> A staunch enemy of quotas says that he has no objections whatsoever concerning quotas for women in political parties. Asked why, he says: "If an incompetent male politician is substituted by an equally incompetent female, what difference does it make?"

This joke says a lot about the confidence in the abilities of politicians, but, at the same time, it reveals an important fact: in all other areas where competence is required, like in public and private businesses, quotas necessarily lead to enhancing incompetence, and these are fields where it matters! From all over the world where access to good and also, higher education is easily available, gender biases are diminished and almost non-existent.

But in India, where education at all levels has become a big business to the disadvantage of quality education, we cannot expect gender biases to disappear. Parents in India still give more importance (and money, for that matter!) to their male children than to their female ones, and education for girls is very often considered a way to enhance the chances for marrying them off into a higher strata of society—the 'market value' of a girl increases in the still dominant flesh market.

Thus, gender equality in leadership is still confined to a very small minority of women, most of whom are propelled into the limelight of political leadership through their family traditions, and the same applies to most of the few women entrepreneurs. We do not provide enabling environments where women are encouraged to develop their abilities, their talents, and realise their dreams. Our—male—leaders are not interested in having to compete with able women, and the few exceptions do not change the overall abysmal picture.

A civil society cannot afford to substitute privileges of certain groups with privileges for others; our reservation system is a conglomerate of positive and negative discrimination, but basically, it is utter discrimination.

A civil society has to have the strength and the will to remove all stumbling blocks in the way of an egalitarian society, if it cannot muster the strength and courage, it doesn't deserve the name 'civil' or 'democratic'.

Reservation is the most unfit tool in view of overcoming the caste system and other evils, as it strengthens it further. Isolating groups and communities from certain privileges by giving these to others is just eyewash. It perpetuates the evils in society, and it deepens the rifts between social groups.

> ... the policy of positive discrimination enshrined in the Indian Constitution has led to a further crystallisation of caste identities even if the goal of that policy was to eliminate inequality arising out of the marginalisation of certain castes.[2]

We have to deal with the problem of discrimination as such, and discrimination always leads to positive and negative consequences, for one or the other. The middle classes seem to have softened the sharp edges, but only on the surface. They, too, are benefiting or else, suffering from the system. Good leadership would mean using all existing potential of a society, and not being afraid of female competition. Male fiefdoms as per gender have no place in a modern society in the twenty-first century.

In a democratic set-up, reservation has no place whatsoever as it only functions through discriminatory mechanisms. The same applies to 'minority rights' which has become another of the many political mantras, used as excuses for all sorts of injustices.

A democratic country should have one constitution and the subsequent legislation for all citizens, irrespective of gender, creed, or community. There should be no place for separate laws and privileges as this only brings about further discriminatory facets in the patchwork of Indian society.

It is so obvious: those who are benefiting try to hold on and further expand the benefits while those who are not benefiting are trying to gain the same advantages. Needless to mention that any benefit which is given to one group has to be taken away from others.

In this way, reservation and minority legislation enhance disunity in society. At the same time, such conditions are providing a hotbed for suspicions, greed, jealousy, tensions and hatred.

In this context, we have to mention the highly corruptive practises of dealing with reservation. There are ample examples of blatant misuse, like changing caste (and tribal) names in order to gain the privileges of BCs, OBCs, and MOBCs, these made easily possible in conspiring with government officials. We could sarcastically foresee that, if this process goes on long enough, the whole of India would consist only of the above-mentioned groups, and, logically, reservation would then be obsolete.

In present times, we are confronted with some of the results of the abysmal failure of policies which try to achieve a peaceful and prosperous society with precisely the wrong means: it is like trying to douse a fire with the help of petroleum or, as a German proverb says, 'Employing a goat as a gardener'.

What India needs is leaders who are able to commit themselves to sustainable development in the interest of every citizen, and to achieve this, they have to be authentic, dedicated to this task, courageous and uncompromisingly honest, and they have to stand up against injustice and all evils in society.

Where do we find them?

Hardly in the upper strata of society where corruption is rampant, and the non-corrupt are constantly risking their professional career and social standing. We have to radically propagate a drastic change of mindset and attitudes if India should 'shine', not as a hollow political slogan but as a challenge for everyone.

Our severe problems with Maoists, with Islamic fundamentalists and terrorism from different corners cannot be solved with the conventional methods of tit-for-tat, but only through a broad social consensus by abolishing injustices, prejudices, exploitative mindsets and very deficient infrastructure, and working for equal chances for everyone.

Good leaders would work for awakening society, lead to maturity in decision-making, to social responsibility and would work for abolishing conditions which perpetuate injustices. They would be courageous enough to point out the evils, they would not shy away from calling a spade a spade instead of hiding behind the smokescreen of 'political correctness'.

> The poor steal for the sake of hunger. If they had enough to eat would they steal? Black-marketeers become leaders, whereas those who are driven to steal by hunger are considered criminals.[3]

It seems that India is prone to repeat all mistakes over and over again:

a) It was a mistake to introduce Reservation in our Constitution, albeit meant only for a limited period. Even 6 decades back, it was known from reliable researches that it is an instrument of discrimination which is detrimental to social harmony. Instead of learning from facts in other countries, and against all experiences in our own country, it was not terminated but continuously extended. It has grown into a gigantic beast which in fact swallows up all hopes for sound and sustainable development.

b) It was a mistake to allow Reservation issues becoming an instrument for undercutting and diluting democratic values by misusing it for vested—mostly political—interests and gains.

c) It is 'politically incorrect' to criticise the reservation system lest someone's feelings cold be hurt. Yes, it hurts to put the finger into the wounds of society, and ours is a very, very wounded one. To heal the wounds, we have to uncompromisingly fight for an egalitarian society: the Constitution applies to all citizens, irrespective of their creed, community, and other factors which are labelled as 'minority rights'. All citizens should have the same rights, they should be under the same laws of the land,

and there should not be any exemption. Those who feel they should have 'special' rights and laws are free to leave the country.

d) In the name of 'protecting religion' and 'traditional social values' (who defines these, and who decides?) the reservation system is blatantly misused for either gaining advantages on the cost of others, or blackmailing people into submission.

e) The reservation system is extremely harmful in view of efficiency in all institutions—governmental and others -, and also for our economy. It puts shackles on and restricts sound development, and it negates the necessity of merit and good performance.

f) Its purpose to overcome the caste system and rendering chances for the hitherto suppressed and exploited has been perverted into the contrary: it is cementing the caste system further, and it is tearing our society more and more apart.

g) thanks to the reservation system, we have the most astonishing feature that big chunks of our society are desperately trying to become acknowledged as somehow 'inferior' groups or communities, only to take advantage of the privileges the so-called backward castes (and the various other terms) enjoy.

Where are the leaders who are courageous enough to fight against reservation? We have found some, but there are not enough as yet to make a difference. The problem is that the topic "Reservation" is widely tabooised. The cancerous disease of political correctness prevents people from speaking out what they really think. In private, we found many like-minded people from all strata of society, but most of them are not prepared and willing to stand up for their opinions, lest they have to suffer professional and social ejection.

The fact that the Mandal Commission has further cemented the machinery of reservation and made it almost impossible to find a way out, further deepens the divide within our society.

But, hope is a great initiator of social change, and we do think that there will be a drastic change towards an egalitarian society—if not through our leaders, then through enlightened and courageous citizens!

References

1. See Appendix: Article by the authors on reservation policies.
2. Quote from: Sharankumar Limbale: *The Outcaste (Akkarmashi)*, Oxford University Press, New Delhi, 2003, p. XV.

7

Killers of Good Leadership: Dependencies of Leaders

Our main intention in this book is to describe the type of leader India needs in contrast to the average leadership we have at hand: the type bathing in superficialities like mass appeal, social prestige, undeserved appreciation and the like, and we point out the necessary qualities of leaders India deserves on the background of our misery of leadership.

India doesn't deserve to be exploited by individual and group-led vested interests. It deserves leaders who understand the needs of our people and, at the same time, have sufficient abilities to develop visions which would lead us into a bright future.

In view of the abundant natural resources and manpower, India has all potential to become an A-League global player.

Alas, the image of India shows hardly that: our politicians and our decision makers in public and private fields—with very few exceptions—do not enjoy a very good reputation globally.

We requested various people in Europe, businessmen and representatives from NGOs and governmental development aid agencies, to spontaneously describe their Indian counterparts in characteristic attributes after their own experiences. These are the significant characteristics (in range):

a) Not very reliable, inscrutable, making false promises.

b) Over-smart, tries to exploit, as business partner not very trustworthy.

c) Opportunistic, always trying to please verbally.
d) Superficially friendly, but lacks real humour.
e) Exaggerating, bragging, boasting, always "the best", the "fastest", the "biggest", *etc.*
f) Very adaptive, but suspiciously so: not genuine, not quality-conscious.
g) Easily to be influenced, often changes opinion after (business) partners, but only on the surface.
h) Defiant when criticised, tends to sulk, always justifying instead of explaining.

These qualifications agree with an article by Shri Mohan Murti[1]; the following are quotes from the original article, titled:

> Is the nation in a coma? Europeans believe that Indian leaders are too blinded by new wealth and deceit to comprehend that the day will come when the have-nots will hit the streets.

Shri Murti is describing his experiences being exposed to various questions in a panel discussion in Frankfurt, Germany, consisting of some of the most prestigious economy-oriented newspapers, and representatives of some of the biggest car-makers and insurance companies in Germany, all of them multinationals operating in India. The auditorium consisted of mainly CEOs of well-known European business houses.

Shri Murti was the only Indian present. Shri Murti especially describes the situation:

> After the panel discussion, the floor was open for questions. That was when my "moment of truth" turned into an hour of shame, embarrassment — when the participants fired questions and made remarks on their experiences with the evil of corruption in India.
>
> The awkwardness and humiliation I went through reminded of The Moment of Truth, the popular Anglo-

American game. The more questions I answered truthfully, the more the questions get tougher. Tougher here means more embarrassing.

Questions ranged from "Is your nation in a coma?", the corruption in judiciary, the possible impeachment of a judge, the 2G scam and to the money parked illegally in tax havens.

It is a fact that the problem of corruption in India has assumed enormous and embarrassing proportions in recent years, although it has been with us for decades. The questions and the debate that followed in the panel discussion was indicative of the European disquiet. At the end of the Q&A session, I surmised Europeans perceive India to be at one of those junctures where tripping over the precipice cannot be ruled out.

Let me substantiate this further with what the European media has to say in recent days.

In a popular prime-time television discussion in Germany, the panellist, a member of the German Parliament quoting a blog said: "If all the scams of the last five years are added up, they are likely to rival and exceed the British colonial loot of India of about a trillion dollars.

.....

One German business daily which wrote an editorial on India said: "India is becoming a Banana Republic instead of being an economic superpower. To get the cut motion designated out, assurances are made to political allays. Special treatment is promised at the expense of the people. So, Ms Mayawati who is Chief Minister of the most densely inhabited state, is calmed when an intelligence agency probe is scrapped. The multi-million dollars fodder scam by another former chief minister wielding enormous power is put in cold storage. Prime Minister Manmohan Singh chairs over this kind of unparalleled loot."

An article in a French newspaper titled "Playing the Game, Indian Style" wrote: "Investigations into the shadowy financial deals of the Indian cricket league have revealed a web of transactions across tax havens like Switzerland, the Virgin Islands, Mauritius and Cyprus." In the same article, the name of one Hassan Ali of Pune is mentioned as operating with his wife a one-billion-dollar illegal Swiss account with "sanction of the Indian regime".

A third story narrated in the damaging article is that of the former chief minister of Jharkhand, Madhu Koda, who was reported to have funds in various tax havens that were partly used to buy mines in Liberia. "Unfortunately, the Indian public do not know the status of that enquiry," the article concluded.

"In the nastiest business scam in Indian records (Satyam) the government adroitly covered up the political aspects of the swindle — predominantly involving real estate," wrote an Austrian newspaper. "If the Indian Prime Minister knows nothing about these scandals, he is ignorant of ground realities and does not deserve to be Prime Minister. If he does, is he a collaborator in crime?"

The Telegraph of the UK reported the 2G scam saying: "Naturally, India's elephantine legal system will ensure culpability, is delayed."

.....

This seems true. In the European mind, caricature of a typical Indian encompasses qualities of falsification, telling lies, being fraudulent, dishonest, corrupt, arrogant, boastful, speaking loudly and bothering others in public places or, while travelling, swindling when the slightest of opportunity arises and spreading rumours about others. The list is truly incessant.

My father, who is 81 years old, is utterly frustrated, shocked and disgruntled with whatever is happening, and said in a recent discussion that our country's motto should truly be *Asatyameva Jayete*.

Europeans believe that Indian leaders in politics and business are so blissfully blinded by the new, sometimes

> ill-gotten, wealth and deceit that they are living in defiance, insolence and denial to comprehend that the day will come, sooner than later, when the have-nots would hit the streets.
>
> In a way, it seems to have already started with the monstrous and grotesque acts of the Maoists. And, when that rot occurs, not one political turncoat will escape being lynched.
>
> The drumbeats for these rebellions are going to get louder and louder as our leaders refuse to listen to the voices of the people. Eventually, it will lead to a revolution that will spill to streets across the whole of India, I fear.
>
> Perhaps we are the architects of our own misfortune. It is our *sab chalta hai* (everything goes) attitude that has allowed people to mislead us with impunity. No wonder Aesop said. 'We hang the petty thieves and appoint the great ones to high office.'

Indian leaders consider themselves undoubtedly brilliant, and they are not aware that it is mainly due to their deficiencies that India's image is severely tainted.

The All-important Ego Clashes

In a circle of top level civil servants who usually meet before dinner (they normally dine at home if they are not invited by someone) in their club for chatting, conspiring, gossiping and drinks, you can observe the most interesting and intriguing communication patterns and, best of all, the hardly disguised ego clashes.

If one of them cracks a joke, thus drawing overall attention and, mostly, appreciation, there is invariably someone else who tries to crack an even better one and, also invariably, the best-applauded jokes are those on the cost of presently absent colleagues! No matter that the person(s) at whose cost everyone is highly amused might be present the next evening, and no matter that invariably one of those present will gleefully tell about it, the game is too tempting not to be played.

After all, ridiculing someone who moves on the same societal and professional level means that all the others feel automatically superior. But, these are the indirect ego clashes. There are lots of very direct ego clashes which are played in a more sophisticated manner, comprising all information available, and also, the invented ones. In the club, you find the small in-groups, whispering in a corner somewhat away from the main circle, let us name them as A and B. Their distinct separation, and the fact that they must have 'secrets', not to be openly discussed, gives these in-groups a lot of importance. Someone who has a secret is superior to those who have none. During a long evening, you might observe several of these in-groups meandering here and there, always in sight of the others, but never in earshot.

We don't speculate about the contents of the visibly conspirational set-up, but it is quite possible that they just exchange information about where to buy the best pair of socks, the same way housewives may exchange their cooking recipes. The basic intention is to show that there is something not meant for everyone's ears, and this alone makes the whole display of secrecy worthwhile.

Now, speculations start racing in the brains among the left-outs: why those two? They are normally not on friendship terms. What do they talk about? Is there a transfer in the offing? A promotion? In this case, I should be promoted after seniority! I have to take aside C immediately, he must know. Or is there something else to do with my department? Do they have a plan to harm my career? Or, is A questioning B about meeting his wife several times? Do they have an affair? (The latter speculation gains momentum when it is furthered, like an innocent question at home: "Is it possible that B is having an affair with A's wife?", as this will be spread as "B is having an affair with A's wife" in the form of grapevine, rapidly growing into a 'truth'. The same applies to all other speculations, providing material for gossip, and for tainting others.)

Concerning professional matters, the egoclashes come in a more brutal form, albeit mostly very polite, and very deadly: The head of a ministerial department, C, is asked by the minister to give his opinion about a colleague D, whom he knows well, if he should be made head of a new commission. Our man knows that his colleague has ample competence to head the new commission, but his immediate concern is of the additional importance such an assignment would render to D. Would it make the man more important? Would he come more in the limelight? Would he be more frequently present in the media?

Now, our department head has to decide after only two considerations:

a) Is the outcome of the work of the new commission likely to make positive headlines? Would it be a feather in the cap of the colleague?

b) Or else, is this commission doomed to fail due to the issues which it has to tackle?

Thus, the decision is easily made: in case of yes to (a), the answer is a definite NO, decorated with all details so that the assignment would not be given. In case of yes to (b), there would be no other person on earth to be better suited for the task. In any case, it would be disadvantageous for the colleague D.

Later on, when both meet in the club, there will be another secret meeting in the corner where our man discloses what is going on and, where he assures the colleague of his unwavering positive support. In case the candidate is very keen to get this assignment, he might even offer material award for his active support which, of course, is gratefully accepted. When the ministerial decision is out, and not in favour of the candidate, but to colleague E, our man will again have a 'secret' get-together, assuring him that he went out of his way in supporting him, but that—most probably—colleague E worked against it, seemingly having crept into the Minister's ear. In case he got the assignment, C will describe in all detail how fatal a blow it would mean to D, and that he, C, tried his utmost to prevent it in the last minute so that no harm would come to D's career. Our C would feel triumphant all the way, his ego is boosted, and he is happy for the time being: the game is won!

The egos have clashed, and the more mischievous egos are always on the winning side.

Reference

1. Co-founder of a consultancy company "Indus Consulting Group LLC", working also in Europe. He is former Europe Director, CII, and lives in Cologne, Germany.

8

Leadership and Media

The Indian media sometimes play a very dangerous game; in short, it is the art of making leaders out of literally nothing, accompanied by the art of preventing genuine leaders to rise, subject to certain conditions.

Like in some election campaigns in Western countries, especially in the US[1], the Indian media have learned the art of building and destroying at will, i.e. according to the will of those who pay them enough. This state of condition makes the postulate of "Fourth Estate" as a proud, independent, and self-confident power in a democratic country a mockery.

How else is it possible that influential people get away with open corruption and other criminal activities without a scratch?

How else is it possible that the same people retain influential, power offices?

How else is it possible that these same people just continue misusing their power and influence, violating the laws of the land with impunity, and callously damaging and destroying those who try to stand up against them?

As long as the media are hands in glove with them, they are protected, and, unfortunately, the majority of our citizens stay mute, gazing at the spectacle spread before them, and feeling utterly helpless.

Similar to the phenomenon of submissiveness as a salient feature of behavioural patterns of the average Indian employee at all levels, even in the highest echelons of power, we observe the spectre of media as mainly subservient to the highly efficient duo of power and money.

The media are considered to be the fourth pillar in a democratic set-up (as independent from governments, industries, and all lobbyists and pressure groups), but the reality shows a quite different picture.

Here, we talk about all media, print-, audio- and visual, as all of them show the same features: majority is subservient to the above-mentioned influences, journalists are bought in the millions all over the country by vested interests, and the TV is another source of sometimes severely negative impact. TV has massively changed the landscape for those who want to shape the country and the public opinion after their own interests, and we cannot repeat it often enough: these interests have nothing to do with the real interests of the country and its people.

When politicians, or their kith and kin, own large media imperia, as it is the case in some States, we cannot expect unbiased reporting.

But, as we all know, but only few admit to it, the public opinion is the published opinion, and TV has become an extremely powerful source for influences creeping into the minds, eroding what is left of common sense and rational thinking, and this applies to both, rural and urban areas alike.

Talking with representatives of publishers, especially those of dailies, they will complain about the number of readers going down, about high salaries for journalists (in spite of the fact that a majority of Indian journalists are freelancers which makes us sometimes feel sympathy for them even when they are corrupt), but, in the meantime, most of them are involved in TV productions and are doing quite well in the vicinity of the all-pervading inventing, suppressing, misinterpreting news as against sincerely investigating, reporting and seriously informing.

From a discussion with a senior journalist[2] from a nationwide daily, also working for TV from time to time, he answered to our question about scandal-mongering, especially in TV:

A: "It's what the people want. They want to see soaps as it distracts them from their own dissatisfaction, they want to see

VIPs involved in scandals as it supports their tendencies for self-righteousness, and they relish it gleefully when a top gets toppled. Just look at the public reactions to the scandal around the marriage of Sania Mirza, or the ongoing tussle of IPL and Mr. Modi. Almost everyone is of the opinion that he deserves what he got. And an MP involved with a hitherto unknown girlfriend while still married adds a lot of spice to the whole affair. The public loves that, and so, the media deliver. The competition is brutal, and we are all dependent on selling. Don't blame the media but blame the public."

We ask about the fact that media are very powerful in creating public opinion after the motto "The public opinion is the published opinion", but he brushes this away:

A: "No, that is nonsense. The media only take up what is already there. They might exaggerate sometimes, but basically, they only take up issues the people already have in their mind."

Q: We insist: What about the responsibility for factual information? What about journalists who are biased because they are paid mouthpieces of politicians and industrialists?

A: This is mostly fiction. Media want to sell, to earn money, and they inform accordingly. Journalists are seldom paid for being biased, perhaps they express their personal opinion which might be biased. They might be affiliated to a certain political party. Can you expect them to report adversely?

Q: But, the fourth power is supposed to be as neutral as possible in order to function as a corrective force towards Government and industrial power wielders?

A: Yes, yes, they express this, too. They mirror the public opinion, as I said.

Q: Then, about half the population is not mirrored in our media?

A: Might be.

Q: Perhaps, those have nothing to say?

(at this point, we decided to call it a day)

The above interview shows clearly that money is the driving force, and, as competition became very tough with the private channels, with the floods of magazines intended to cater to the fast growing middle classes, ways and means have to be found to be successful in this battlefield.

We are much more interested in finding out what, other than money, propels the leaders in the media, the editors and owners of publishing houses, to do what they do, and to neglect, to distort, exaggerate, or omit completely what one should think they ought to present. At best, they allow their staff to act like this, at worst, they force them to. As there are indeed a few more positive exceptions from the above pictured rule that are quite successful in the market, we are not convinced that the argument of 'competition compels us' is the answer to the disputable statements above; we try to dig deeper. We try to compare 'subservient' media to 'courageous' ones, and we have to concentrate on the print media. The reason is that in the TV market, we could not find a single channel we would consider 'courageous'[3] in the sense of delivering unbiased information and holding against the mainstream, including the educational channels.

Entertainment has to be superficial, we agree with that, but soapy series about (mostly) family conflicts that would not exist if the authors would not invent them, lead to a dangerous public mindset, like 'We are lucky not to have these problems, conflicts", etc., or else, one can identify him/herself with the story, but is unable to solve the problem in real-life conditions. Furthermore, we have all these freak shows where mostly quite ordinary people display their most personal issues just to enjoy a few hours of 'name and fame'.

In the same way as people tend to accept as 'truth' what they see in print, they tend to even more accept what they see and hear.

Where can we trace responsibilities of the decision-makers? We are not able to do so.

Some decades ago, we could observe owners of print media like Shri Goenka of the former *Indian Express* acting courageously, and even risking persecution and arrest, together with lots of the journalists of this paper. He definitely showed good leadership, and the journalists felt encouraged by him.

Now, look at the development: the proud paper has become the *New Indian Express*, and we cannot see any difference from other newspapers anymore. Clearly, it is a question of leadership in the highest echelons, and we just ask if being successful in competition should not result in doing things differently? What sense does it make if, in a highly competitive market, different products are not different at all? We are unable to answer this.

In the context of our book, we try to evolve some suggestions for good leadership in the media:

a) Wipe out dependency from lobbyists and Government circles (don't try to please the high and mighty, don't accept benefits, be it in 'kind' or otherwise).
b) Encourage journalists to investigate more, and better, for that matter (let them find issues of burning importance).
c) Show the younger journalists the joy of their work; show them how much confidence they build up in performing sincerely, honestly, and with determination.
d) Stand by the journalists if they get into trouble (like in conflict areas, where police and Government don't like to be investigated, or when they are subject to harassment by the high and mighty who might be disappointed by some truthful reporting).
e) Appreciate thorough investigative work (release time pressure in those cases).
f) Clamp down on corrupt journalists (point the way by either re-organise the payment scales to fight incentives for being corrupt and, most important of all, be a good example yourself).
g) Create a consciousness of social responsibility (show that you are not only catering to the influential strata of society).
h) Be a good paragon for journalists to emulate, at least to learn from.

i) Put influence on improving the quality of colleges and universities that teach journalism (like building up round tables with these institutions where the matter of improving quality is discussed, demand improvement by giving suggestions, send good journalists as lecturers).

j) Expose corruptive practises and show the young journalists how rewarding it is to be courageous and straightforward.

We also should learn from sincere friends in foreign media, albeit there are not many. Marc Tully is one of them:

> I had to become involved; I had to become part of India—at least that was the way I saw it. Some have argued that I became too involved, that my reporting was prejudiced by my affection for India. For my part I have never been able to understand why British journalists who are open Francophiles, overt admirers of America or enthusiasts of some Western country which they report are not likely to be accused of being partisan, but correspondents who identify themselves with countries whose cultures are not European or American are regarded with the gravest suspicion.[4]

In this context, we have to go into the works and influences of the so-called lobbyists. Lobbying in India—as mostly elsewhere in the world—means essentially bribing parliamentarians to put pressure on the legislation towards the respective vested interests. Needless to say that lobbyism is at its most successful for those who can pay the most, thus, logically, serving the interests of big entrepreneurs or big black-marketers, or both in amiable combination. Small and medium-sized enterprises cannot afford to lobby, albeit some are quite successful in using blackmail and other threats. Leadership in this context means the ability to cunningly develop the best ways and means to get the influential person(s) into their own fold.

The European Union has ventured into a model of voluntary transparent "Registration of Lobbyists" (in the European Parliament in Strasbourg, and the affiliated agencies in Bruxelles). Of course, the problem of corrupt politicians cannot be completely averted by this model, but it is a big step forward to more transparency.

Charismatic Leaders?

Another field where the media play an exorbitant role is the way they create leaders. We have to explain what is happening:

In a country where too many people are obsessed with the idea that if only the right leaders would be provided, everything would be well, it is easy for the media to build up persons of their liking as "Charismatic Leaders". The full force of influencing people's minds and consequently, their opinions, is shown in pre-election times: the media can build up or destroy leaders, that much is sure. And they really do!

We all know that it is done, we all know hundreds of examples, but we cannot exactly describe what is really going on, and why. We can describe the decisive role of the media in artificially creating a charismatic leader out of the blue, meaning: out of nothing which would justify the attribute 'Leader'. The game is well-known, and it is called "How to make a Leader", and our media are happily playing it.

An authentic case study:

> Take a nondescript would-be politician, perhaps from a family of a well-known politician, who decides, or better, his family decides so, to become a national political figure. The party affiliation is pre-determined as per family/father/grandfather, and now, ways and means have to be found to get him into the right circles, to make a political product out of him.

It is easy to convince the party colleagues that he is the right man, provided the above-mentioned troika family/father/grandfather is influential enough or else, there is an influential 'Godfather' in the party who wants to propel him into the limelight.

Said and done, he has to be made 'known' and, it goes without saying, depicted as a dedicated, visionary, gifted young politician who knows all the answers to the country's problems. No matter that he has almost no political experience, no matter that he only hesitantly gave in to the troika's wishes, no matter that he has not much of formal education, no matter that up till now, his life circled mainly around spending family's money, and no matter that he has no idea about politics as yet. He need not, he will be told and taught as we see later on.

The next step by the wily strategists (the troika and other party bigwigs) will be to introduce him step by step to the public, and what is a better opportunity than a big event like a national party convention where he will be hailed by all and sundry as the next big leader. The big game starts here.

Unavoidably, the genuine abilities of our future leader is thoroughly examined, by experienced campaigners, by consultants, and the like. Finally, it is decided that he has to undergo a rigorous personality change. Our man is only the typical 'mommy's boy', not eloquent or brash like some of his contemporaries. "We have to 'develop' him", is the motto of the hour, and this process has to be fast. He should learn:

a) How to speak properly
b) How to use body language
c) What to say at all
d) When to say nothing

and similar things, chalked out by the the appointed consultants.

Meanwhile, our man is convinced that he is made for leadership, albeit still lacking orientation, and somewhat doggedly, he submits to all the efforts.

Finally, one of the consultants states: "I cannot make a racehorse out of an ox", and quits his service, knowing that he won't ever be consulted by this party.

What to do now?

One of the consultants for 'personality development' has the most brilliant idea, that is changing the earlier parameters: "We style him as the 'man of the people', the humble, down-to-earth person who is only interested in uplifting the downtrodden masses. Thus, he need not be eloquent, he just has to show some humbleness, even clumsiness, which the masses will love.

He only has to repeat phrases we'll stuff into him, and he has to act as if his special charisma lies in his utter humbleness." Applause from the party.

The media are informed well in advance, and they are provided with lots of information about the leader-in-the-making, only that they are not informed that he is no leader at all, at least not as yet. The party convention in full swing, our man stands his ground: he had learned his phrases, he touches all the available important feet when media coverage is around, and he shows the right expressions while mentioning the plight of the poor masses which he will mitigate and, possibly, remove. His body language is in tune with what he says, and he is easily accessible by the media.

Thus, a new star is born, the charismatic leader out of the blue!

The background story reveals that lots of money went into the coffers of almost all people who matter in the media, and local journalists, too, received their share.

From one day to the other, our man is boosted up as a national hero, anointed by the media to be the saviour of the poor, the man who will rid the country from all evils.

But the burning question is: did the people really buy it? And if so, why?

They obviously bought it: our charismatic superman is at present representing a constituency in the Lok Sabha, albeit in the opposition. And nobody ever heard about him from then onwards (and perhaps never ever after).

If our media are prepared to indulge in these types of gimmicks, so convincingly that the local voters and large parts of society believe it, then we have to state that enormous danger is imminent. Will we have more artificially created leaders in the future? Do we already have this type of parliamentarians, 'servants of the people' who have no idea what they are doing, and even less what they are supposed to do? What if this becomes the favourite game of hands-in-glove politician and media persons? Will it lead to parliaments of robots, remote-controlled by the party bosses and their affiliations? Of course, they are leaders, but of the kind we don't need and don't want.

In our chapter on "What is to be done" we come back to the constructive role the media could play—if only there would be the will!

References

1. Where less than one third of the population with voting right goes to the polls at all - can we call this democracy?
2. He also guides interns, young journalists, and he delivers lectures in several renowned colleges and universities. This means, he is a leader—but where is he leading?
3. If our readers know some such channel, we would be grateful to be informed!
4. Tully, ibid., p viii.

9

On Planning—The "Something–Someday-Somehow-Someone" Syndrome[1]

While analysing planning and planning processes, especially the official planning institutions in India, we could not but remember one of the most famous songs of the unforgettable Beatles (selected quotation):

> He's a real Nowhere Man,
> Sitting in his Nowhere Land,
> Making all his Nowhere plans for nobody.
> Doesn't have a point of view,
> Knows not where he's going to,
> Isn't he a bit like you and me?
> Nowhere man, please listen,
> You don't know what you're missing,
> Nowhere Man, the world is at your command.
> He's as blind as he can be,
> Just sees what he wants to see,
> Nowhere Man, can you see me at all?
> Nowhere Man, don't worry,
> Take your time, don't hurry,
> Leave it all till somebody else,
> Lends you a hand. ...
>
> He's a real Nowhere Man,
> Sitting in his Nowhere Land,
> Making all his Nowhere plans for nobody. ...

Stunningly realistic: we feel it applies to all our leaders in the fields of planning, it describes realistically what is matter-of-factly going on in the name of 'planning'.

It seems to be a gigantic waste of time, resources and energies, securing lots and lots of jobs for our 'nowhere men' so that they are free to make all their plans for nobody.

In the context of our book we have to ask sincerely: where is good leadership in planning to be found? Do our 'Planners' have any idea of the expectations one should have for results and implementation? Do they have any idea of the parameters of competence they should come up to? Do they have a sense of the ground realities? Do they have connectivity with the 'masses' they are supposed to work for?

Where are the necessary elements of sustainability, convergence, and cost-consciousness to be seen? Or, does it matter to them at all?

'Sitting in their Nowhere Land'—how can they focus on realistic needs or impact of their planning efforts, having no connectivity with the real India?

We feel it necessary to mention at least two main deficiencies[2] and mistakes which are salient features in our planning processes, i.e. validity and reliability of data used for planning, and the practicality/implementability of schemes.

Concerning validity and reliability of data, we encountered the following interesting case which would be amusing if it would not be deadly serious in its final impact:

Situation: We talk to a clerk in a District Collector's office somewhere in India, and we ask him about his work and about his job satisfaction.

Q: *How many years have you been working here?*

A: Around 23 years. I was promoted eight years back last.

Q: *What is the main type of work?*

A: I am responsible for collecting and sending statistic data to the State authorities and to the Centre. Very responsible work. And timely, timely. Time is always pressure. Sometimes it is too much. The District is too big.

Q: *Do you hail from this area?*

A: No, I come from the neighbouring District. I have lived in this town since I got the job here. Also, my wife was born here. Her family is here.

Q: *What do you like in your work?*

A: It is not dirty work, it is good work. We have good salary, and we have lots of freedom.

Q: *Freedom? In what sense?*

A: You see, the DCs come and go. Normally, they need one year till they understand what is going on here, till they know the important people and all. Then, they do some work, and very soon they are transferred somewhere else. The same procedure starts with the new DC, and so on. They don't really become acquainted with the District, and they need our help. In fact, they are dependent on us. And we tell them what to do (*chuckles*).

Q: *How do you make use of this dependency?*

A: (*Smiles*) You see, one need to tell all. One need not tell certain things. Or, sometimes, one makes small things very important to distract from really important things, if so necessary.

Q: *You mean to say that you manipulate issues for the DC for your own gains?*

A: (*Smiles broadly*) Oh yes, I have colleagues who do that. Of course, I don't!

Q: *Coming back to your specific work. What are the main data you have to collect? Is it difficult to collect?*

A: All numbers, of people, their livelihood, if they are in agriculture or other professions, the unemployed, the number of families, the BPL, the children, the schools, so many things!

Q: *How do you collect the data? Do you have a time schedule for recurring data?*

A: I note down the changes, but normally, I collect the numbers when I am asked to do. The Department of

Statistics sends request, they send forms to be filled. I have to go to places and collect the numbers.

Q: *There is time pressure?*

A: Oh yes, lots of pressure. But (*smiling*), sometimes I already know, and I don't have to go and see.

Q: *Then, how do you make sure that your data are up to date?*

A: Oh, there is never much difference. Usually, I can do the work just here in my office. Where is the time to go to places?

Q: *Your boss, the DC, is he checking your work?*

A: Normally not. He knows that I do my work smoothly. He trusts me. And he has so much other work to do.

Q: *You mean to say that you are the master of the 'numbers' in this District?*

A: Oh yes! Nobody doubts my numbers. I have lots of experience, and I deliver everything they need. I know what they need.

Q: *Your numbers are taken without cross-checking?*

A: What do you mean? Cross-checking? For what?

(End of interview)

We got similar results while talking to other clerks in other Districts, and in other States, and we are deeply worried about the quality of data the Government authorities are working with. From the above interview, it is clear that the bulk of data are highly doubtful from the angle of validity and reliability, and that means, logically, that evaluation and interpretation lack the same, and another aspect closely connected with this is the time factor: judging from the quite open answers we got from our local 'experts' in the fields of collecting data for the official statistics, the data are mostly delivered with big time gaps. That means, between the actual data collected (if at all they are valid and reliable at all), the delivery and the subsequent evaluation, there are time gaps of sometimes more than one year, or even more. This shows clearly that the data material cannot mirror the actual situation at the ground, and thus cannot be considered valid material for evolving proper plans.

Now, referring to the subsequent Governmental schemes and projects on the basis of the evaluation and interpretation processes done by the respective Departments of Statistics of States and Centre, and again evaluated and interpreted by the respective Planning Commissions, we cannot but despair.

The lack of good leadership which, in this field, should yield valid and reliable data for positive change from grassroots level upwards, is the root cause for all the failures we observe in the highly lauded Governmental development schemes and projects.

Good leaders would be committed to deliver solid, valid material from which we could draw information needed for sustainable development. Good leaders would know about the importance of clear facts, and they would see to it that their clerks would realise the importance themselves, that they would be motivated to contribute to their level best to support sincere efforts of mitigating sufferings, and alleviate poverty, to name only the most pressing tasks of our time.

Q: At present, we have the impression that it does not matter at all as there is no accountability, nor is there any attempt to develop sustainable positive development. The top planners know the deficiencies very well, then, why do they not see to it that these deficiencies will be tackled? A very experienced officer in the Planning Commission expressed his view on this very clearly when we asked about the quality of the data material.

A: We have to use the material we are getting, and surely, sometimes we doubt the figures. But what can we do? We have no time to check and re-check as this would mean more delays in the whole planning processes. We don't have the staff to go and check, this is not our responsibility. Also, in the average, the doubtful data will be levelled by the data which are correct because of the gigantic figures we are provided with. So, we have a quite good base for our planning.

Q: Then, why is it that most of the schemes and projects are failures considering the money which flows into them, and the factual outcome, especially in view of sustainable improvement?

A: You cannot say that. There are very good schemes which serve the poor, and they are functioning perfectly.

Q: You agree with us that most of the schemes are merely mitigating some urgent problems, like food security, unemployment, health issues, but these are not what we understand by sustainable development.

A: We have to set priorities. When people are hungry, we have to feed them. When they are unemployed, we have to create employment. When there are health problems, we have to mitigate that. These are the present-day challenges we have to tackle. If urgency is there, how can we concentrate on sustainability? The people would not understand that, they want help immediately. They don't understand sustainability.

Q: But helping in emergency situation does not necessarily exclude sustainability. Why are these activities for timely help not connected with future-oriented planning for sustainable change?

A: Oh, but we do plan for the future!

Q: How? Please give an example.

A: Like the NREGA, the National Rural Employment Guarantee Act, now re-christened "MGNREGA.

Q: But MGNREGA is quite blatantly violating Gandhiji's philosophy, as we see it, especially considering the fact that this scheme does not create real employment, but is just another form of dole.

A: Oh, you are wrong in that. People get employed through this scheme, they earn their livelihood!

Q: But it is artificial employment. It is not suitable for enhancing a sustainable employment infrastructure as it is not encouraging rural entrepreneurship; in fact, it is a continuation of giving alms to people whereas they would need rural enterprises, sustainable job creation and efficient steps to qualify them.

A: At least it is a good step forward. Rural enterprises are difficult to create, people don't have the mindset for it.

Q: You mean to say that people in rural areas are less talented for entrepreneurship?

A: Quite so. We have our figures and our experiences. We know what people can do and what they cannot do. Enterprising people go to the cities.

Q: There are no business opportunities in rural areas?

A: I would not say that. But it is difficult. There is no proper infrastructure.

Q: What about the idea of creating conducive infrastructure? Would tat not be a better step forward?

A: The enemy of development is too much hurry, too much haste. We have to proceed step by step.

Q: Are more than 60 years of Independent India not more than enough time to build up rural infrastructure conducive for entrepreneurship?

A: It is all a matter of priorities, you see; our GDP is rising and rising. Our economy is developing like anything!

Q: You will agree with me that the GDP does not reflect the living conditions in rural India but shows the middle and upper classes benefiting, whereas the rural population is almost excluded from the economic progress.

A: You cannot put it like this. If the economy is striving, the society as a whole benefits.

Q: How?

A: As I said, a progressing economy leads to benefits for all.

(End of interview[3])

Logically, we have another vicious circle at hand: without good leaders in planning, there cannot be good planning, there cannot evolve sustainable positive development for the masses. Planners who are detached from the ground realities, who work on obsolete data which are not only outdated till they reach the planning offices, but are also obtained through quite doubtful methods are in no position to do the needful.

We could not find proper cross-checking on the reliability and viability of planning data, but we found an overall negligence concerning the quality of planning, and also, the same negligence concerning future impact of schemes and projects from a holistic viewpoint, but mainly the phenomenon of 'tunnel views', uncoordinated and more or less reacting to policies of showing that something is done, money is spent, if only 'the people would understand'. Our leaders in planning processes are very quick in pointing the finger towards the ignorant masses who are not responsive to the good they are receiving, and who are basically an ungrateful lot.

Thus, planning processes are not adjusted to realities, and they cannot be made useful for the vast majority of our citizens. Any social scientist who would publish 'results' on the basis of such dubious sources would be shunted out of the academic and expert's community with derision and sneering.

Our planners are seemingly unaffected, unmoved by any self-questioning, and the fact that nobody else questions them, makes them all the more self-righteous. The absence of accountability creates a type of leadership who cultivates a mindset of arrogance, and this is all the more deplorable as the same people could immensely contribute to the welfare of the nation as a whole, and not only to the welfare of roughly one-third of our population, city-dwellers, mainly.

We have to question all those who are responsible for the officially sanctioned *natak*:

> Why do we spend so much money on planning processes and decisions which do not result in the aims and objectives of sustainable development?

Why are the rural areas still neglected, and why are projects implemented which only serve the aim to further establish more and more dependency[4] instead of instigating self-reliance and sustainable development?

The term 'sustainable development' is widely used to describe the efforts of the planners, but it is a hollow phrase as long as the prerequisites for sustainability are completely ignored. It seems like erecting big buildings on shallow, sandy ground, and the unavoidable collapse of these buildings leads to more and more futile planning.

As long as planning processes are executed as ways and means for keeping lots of people comfortably busy while rational and practise-oriented parameters of success are not put in place nor applied, we cannot expect any improvement. In case someone questions the outcome, there are lots of excuses which come faster than a mouse finds a hole. The overall deplorable picture of Leaders in Planning is executed as an end for itself, like a wheel constantly turning but not getting anywhere, and we describe it as follows:

> There is the planning of planning of planning...,
> and what we hear from the Leaders in Planning is what
> we coin as the 'Something-Some day-Somehow-Someone
> Syndrome':
> Something should be done.
> Something will be done.
> Some day it will happen.
> Somehow it will function.
> Someone will see to it.
> Someone will coordinate.
> Some day it will start.
> Some linkages will be established.
> Something will come out.

And, who will be responsible? No one, Nobody, everything is left to the omnipresent Nowhere Man!

References

1. See Appendix: 'Open Letter to Planning Commission'.
2. Other deficiencies we find are in the lack of inclusiveness of schemes or projects, in the lack of accountability of planners and implementers at all levels, in the lack of cost consciousness of the

planners and implementers, and also, in the lack of counter-action concerning corruption and other widespread misuse of public money.

3. Sometimes, one has to end a conversation before utter despair sets in—this was such a moment.
4. For example, the much lauded introduction of the (MG)NRES is the enemy of self-initiative and entrepreneurship as it keeps people in dependency instead of enabling them for self-reliance. We also know that big chunks of the funds for the scheme are grossly misappropriated, and no consequences are to be seen for those who violate the rules and regulations. To top it all, it goes now under the name of Mahatma Gandhi who would have definitely fought tooth and nails against it! The fact is that through MGNREGA not a single sustainable job creation has been achieved, thus, the same mistakes are repeated over and over, totally neglecting the reasoned principles of holistic sustainable development.

10

Holistic Concept of Good Leadership

There is a very confused perception of efficiency to be observed in India.

Widely, people think in terms of "speedy delivery", leaving aside the most important factors that consist of quality and reliability.

In concordance with the overall submissiveness, it seems to be more important to deliver "somehow" than to do a job properly. Also, the one who requests delivery hardly reacts to the many deficiencies which are obvious. We describe here the main factors which make efficiency to very difficult to attain:

a) Unsystematic approach, planning and working.
b) Confusing haste with speed—both, in decision making and actions/work).
c) Wavering of decision making (for fear to do the wrong thing), no steadfastness.
d) Leniency towards influences (from cronies, superiors, trade unions, other pressure groups).
e) Lack of focusing on the tasks on hand (thinking and doing several things at one time).
f) Lack of clear fixing aims and objectives.
g) Lack of applying holistic approach including future-orientation in the form of visions and anticipation of holistic development.

Concerning our leaders, we are sorry to say that they hardly give a good example that people could emulate. Usually, somebody who attains power enjoys to wield it, to show that he/she now has to tell others what to do. In a certain sense, we would not mind if that would be really done, but in reality, they need to perpetuate an appallingly authoritarian style of functioning, thus depriving themselves from creating enabling conditions where creativity and new ideas could continuously improve the overall performance.

Grooming self-responsible, efficient workers means that the leader has to be initiative in encouraging the people to come up and to develop their potential.

The best way for our average leaders to sail happily and unscathed through all disturbances which might crop up is the motto:

Mistakes and failures can only be avoided through doing nothing.[1]

Learning from Competent Critique

An Indian "leader" hardly admits to mistakes or failures—it is always *others* who are to blame! He confuses quick decision making with hasty ones, is not able to act or react with flexibility (for fear it could undermine his authority); he doesn't allow himself to show quick grasping of new ideas from others, especially not from his 'inferiors' (for fear that it would not be a feather on his cap but someone else's); he avoids any risk-taking and any taking over of responsibilities which are not closely defined as his own, where he cannot easily wriggle out, and he displays a pathetic inability of strategic and tactical thinking, a pre-condition for proper planning.

On Bureaucrats

Oh, how happily they dwell on their so-called procedural necessities, rules and regulations: they deliberately invent things to prolong a process which could be done nicely in 10 per cent of the time; at the same time, they apologise profoundly, putting the blame on rules and regulations and on their superior who is depicted as a stickler to book; they look you straight in the eyes and invent at the same moment some additional stumbling block. Just see the intensively mischievous glittering in their eyes! And, if something especially nasty has been successfully done, they need at least one week to recover from the over-joy.

Key Potential for Good Leadership

In the field of professional human relations, there are only two basic patterns of behaviour which are closely interlinked, and which makes them efficient:

1. Respecting the dignity of others
2. Keeping up one's own dignity

A German proverb says that *if you don't respect yourself, you cannot respect others*, and that is very true.

The fundamental pre-condition for the above given two points is assessing and accepting one's own personality first, which includes constructive self-criticism as well as accepting constructive criticism from others. Admitting errors and/or mistakes does not diminish the necessary natural authority, but enhances it, provided the errors and mistakes do not come from incompetence, ignorance or arrogance.

Co-workers know very well that nobody is without weaknesses and failures, and they appreciate the integrity of a character who admits to them, but they resent:

a) arrogance, haughtiness
b) incompetence in superiors
c) suspicious attitudes (disguised as "control processes").

All these are the biggest obstacles in the way of sustainable motivation.

Another German proverb says:

> Accept a NO as an opportunity, a chance to find an even better solution. Knowledge conquers resistance and obstacles.

There are some important basic principles which have to be carefully explored:

a) Do not behave towards others in a way you do not want others to behave towards you.

b) Do not ask people to do things you would not be prepared to do (yourself).

c) Do not view your staff as "inferiors" but consider them as "co-workers"

Building up (Youth) Leadership in Villages

In view of so much neglect of business opportunities in rural India, we have to go into the problem of how to build up sound self-esteem which would enable the rural population to take their fate into their own hands. Practical perspectives and awareness of the resources which lay unused would be the first step towards self-reliance, and it would encourage people with leadership potential to take the initiative.

In our earlier chapters we elaborated on the fact that our top level leaders have lost the connectivity to grassroots level people and issues, moreover, they persistently avoid to connect with them. The local leaders, even those who are genuinely interested in improvement and sustainable development, are left in the void and, unfortunately, many of them emulate the behavioural patterns shown by the top level leaders.

It would be of utmost importance, an uncompromising necessity for local leaders—political and in administration—to include the local people in planning and decision making. Thus, farmer's self-esteem would be built up, and planning would be improved by the knowledge and experiences of those who are subject to planning processes. The same way, the term 'marketing' should be properly used: not as mere 'selling and buying', but as a valuable tool for customer-orientated production and profitable distribution. Here, too, many fatal mistakes are made: we transport goods from thousands of kilometres away into States where the same goods could be easily produced locally, thus making the goods more expensive, and depriving the local producers from doing good business. Opening up the local markets for local products would require a change of mindset, and also, it would require a massive change of policies. Good leadership would recognise the opportunities of local markets and marketing.

In this context, the introduction of *suitable IT* is of utmost importance. The well-known slogan "Bringing IT to the villages" has been used mainly as a vehicle for vote-catching but not for measures which would make sense in view of sustainable development. In almost all States there had been activities in distributing IT equipment in rural areas, but these have not yielded the promised effects of positive development. The reasons are very obvious:

a) Before elections, funds are allocated for distributing personal computers and internet connections, but there was no concept for bringing them to good use in view of improving business opportunities or living conditions.
b) In areas where there had been some planning for practical use, the training was either not sufficient or there was no time-wise coordination, so that training efforts came out to be just waste of time and money.
c) There was no preparation for suitable software which would support business and marketing efforts at grassroots level, or support administration procedures for the local people ('E-Government is a far cry from being of good use for the people!).
d) The equipment could not be brought to good use because of frequent power failures and the lack of power-back-up infrastructure.

The latter point brings us directly to another most important field of action where able leaders could achieve immense improvement, namely, the areas of non-conventional, renewable energies combined with issues of environment protection, i.e. water conservation and organic farming.

In view of the ever increasing flight of young people from rural areas to the cities and towns, we have to find ways and means to encourage and enable youth to stay and bring about change in their villages through identifying and supporting business opportunies in the villages. To achieve this, good leadership is of utmost importance, giving perspectives and showing the way—there is all the necessary potential available, it only has to be brought out.

We developed practice-oriented business models which could bring about self-employment and also improve employability of the younger population. One of them is the "SECE" model, "Self Employed Change Entrepreneur."[2]

Leadership and Competency

Sometimes you get the impression that the people know what they are talking about. But very soon, you discover that they know (almost) nothing about it but they think that they know all about the topic. Or else, they convincingly pretend that they know. And the worst of all, they get immensely applauded for their nothingness.

Thus, after some time, even the intelligent frauds among them believe themselves to be the greatest.

Why else all these useless, hollow speeches? Why these endless hollow speeches? And why is it that the audience seems to be almost unanimously impressed? Did they hand over their intelligence to the doorman? In the latter case, let us hope that under all the magic of nonsensical speeches they do not forget to pick it up again while leaving!

One of the salient features of the misery in Indian leadership is the fact that those who are led are too willing to submit themselves to a "position", and in case they feel dissatisfied, unappreciated, de-motivated, they personalise their grudge towards the person who sits on the leadership position, but hardly ever they question or even discuss the issue of leadership as such.

Maybe, there is a hopelessness evolving from the fact that change is not in the offing, that their leaders are not encouraging change, and that they would feel endangered in their own jobs if they ask for change, but we do think that there is an overall leniency towards devastating types of leaderships: "What can we do? Nothing. We have to bear."

Logically, there cannot be any repercussion or something instigating a re-thinking process in the leaders, like introspection or self-criticism—why should they? The derive their rights from their position, and they don't question that they are always the best choice in case they are in a leadership position.

The issue of how to select the able, competent people into leadership positions is not really 'an issue' in India, as too many influences, having nothing to do with the issue of 'good leadership', are allowed to enter the fray. In politics, it is the utility value of a person which decides a posting or the necessity to yield to pressure groups of certain communities. In administration, it is seniority (not a category which would convincingly provides good leaders), personal bonds created through sycophancy, nepotism and accidental acquaintanceship and, in other fields, the same categories are applied. We did not come across proper assessment for key potential of leadership qualities, nor did we find decision makers who were interested in introducing such methods.

The head of a government department bluntly told us that it would be a waste of time as no consequences would follow on the results. "Promotions and postings are not rationally decided but after personal likes and dislikes," was the most devastating statement.

Logically, such decision making is detrimental to all efforts towards improving leadership situation; it is also detrimental to efforts trying to create enabling environment for good leaders to come up and perform.

Good leaders in this country are viewed with *suspicion*: "What is their advantage? What do they gain? Why should they be determined to bring about change?" and some such thoughts.

Surrounded by *suspicious* minds, an able leader can hardly be successful. People just don't believe that someone can think and act in the interest of the people, of the country, instead of trying to grab as much as possible for oneself. The mainstream mindset is adverse to change and proactive, participatory leadership: people who are leaders have to lead, and those who are not, have to be told what to do. Period. Leaders are not questioned, and thus, leaders are sacrosanct; they are not accountable, and people try to please them instead of demanding performance from them.

We are aware that change of mindset in matters of mainstream conscience is something like a Sisyphean, a never-ending task. But our decision makers could start to improve conditions by introducing a time-tested, flexible method for assessing key potential of leadership qualities *before* a person is assigned a leadership position.

We developed a reliable and valid system of assessing the key abilities which yields all necessary information to select the right person[3]. The salient features for our assessment are the following criteria, combined with complete transparency of results and also, intense feedback and counselling :

a) Assessing key abilities
b) Building up strengths and competencies
c) Becoming aware and dealing with weaknesses
d) Building up self-confidence

The Mantra of 'Leadership' as an Excuse for Doing Nothing

The most appalling feature in Indian society is not so much the cry for an amorphous "Leader" who would set everything right, but the widespread admiration for "Hitler" as a 'good leader' in Indian establishment, especially in the well educated middle classes, and it reveals an abyss of disinformation. We have to ask what is taught in history and ethics in Indian educational institutions, and what could be the driving force for demanding authoritarian societal structures and dictatorship in a democratic country. Hitler was an uneducated, highly neurotic butcher who, unfortunately for the then Germany, found an able and evil ideologue in Goebbels (for the theories and the marketing of the 'product Hitler'[4]).

Speeches for Speeches' Sake

It is so tedious to have to listen to the droning along of the professional speakers who don't know how to structure a speech, and also how and when to end it; Most of them don't want to come to the end: it is too sweet to bathe in the attention of an audience!

Most of them are 'armchair experts', on the push of button they can talk about each and everything, without saying anything. No doubt, we come across well-phrased speeches, even entertaining ones, sometimes sounding visionary also, especially when rendered by political leaders. In the end, it comes down to the fact that nothing is really intended to be implemented. As the proverb goes:

> People talk about tomorrow, but they behave like yesterday.[5]

One of the best examples is listening to interviews by media persons. The interviewer takes a lot of pain asking direct questions concerning a certain issue, whereas the interviewee answers in a stereotyped way: the same answers to various different questions, and, what is most astonishing, the interviewer accepts it as if he would have got the information he wanted! Why do they let them get away with it? Why don't they insist on proper answers to clear questions?

On Selfishness

Selfishness is an integral part of self-confidence and dignified survival. As long as it is not exploitative, it is necessary for any good leadership, and for a dignified individual life, and, most important, for knowing what to aspire, where to aim, what to do. We coined it 'positive' selfishness, and it is a prerequisite for self-confidence, for orientation in life, and for self-assessment. Positive selfishness is widely not understood as a very positive driving force for all those who want to achieve their goals, their dreams, everything they have in mind for themselves to put their energy in. Positive selfishness enables people to be constructively self-critical, learn from their mistakes, be assertive in their activities, and also respect the positive selfishness of others.

On the other hand, there is the 'negative' selfishness, defined by ruthlessly pursuing one's own wishes and plans, unscrupulously exploiting others, invading others' interests for one's own achievements. This negative phenomenon of selfishness has become a salient feature of modern India's leadership picture, showing visionary potential only in the narrowed-down fields of an individual's or a clan's interests.

Usually, "selfishness" is only understood as something negative, in spite of the fact that almost everyone is "selfish" in one way or the other. But, in the end, 'being selfish' is always used as a negative attribute, especially by those who don't accept and respect other's interest, which they feel as 'selfish'.

In this ocean of misunderstanding and misappropriating, we have to point out that the term 'selfish' is one of the many already-mentioned tools for blackmail: if I placate someone as selfish while the person is just standing my—selfish—way, I create a guilt complex. Who wants to be called selfish? And, what would people say? The same old ritual in putting blame on others while I am indulging in exactly the same ways and means as the person I am blaming. And yes, it is the old blame game, it is always the others, or the circumstances (or the gods, or fate, or the stars, or whatever—or all of them combined) who are to blame, never me!

An able leader is positively selfish; he knows where he wants to go, and he knows how best to arrive there. On the way, he applies methods of constructive self-criticism; he learns from mistakes; he corrects himself; he listens to others; he admits weaknesses and mistakes and, most important of all, he respects others in their—positive, non-exploitative—selfishness.

Leadership and Motivation

One of the great misunderstandings or misperceptions we came across our researches in leadership in India is the fact that the term 'motivation' is widely perverted into creating or doling out a kind of essentially material incentives to bring people to do what a leader wants them to do.

Bluntly speaking, this is, in the case of crudely financial and/or promotion-related measures, nothing than another type of bribery. In case of benevolent behaviour on the part of the leader, or perhaps some leniency in the case of general misconduct, frequent leave, misconduct towards citizens who seek their services, misconduct towards colleagues and others, non-performance, etc., it is just another signal for deficient leadership.

The same misunderstanding applies to another term: loyalty. We noticed that 'loyalty' is understood as submissiveness and yielding to everything the leader might demand or decide. Furthermore, there is the opinion that 'loyal staff' has to keep everything under the carpet what might endanger the status quo or, what seems to be even more important, everything which might taint the reputation of a given department or smaller unit.

Clearly, this is a very sick perception; what is shown here is not loyalty out of a free decision of a staff member, but slavish obedience, driven by the usual forces of the 'pleasing syndrome' and fear of losing ones job and/or status.

The same applies for the term 'solidarity', which again is reduced to slavish obedience in the case of the relations with the leader, but it is a different thing altogether if we refer the term to the same level within the staff: here, the leaders feel the danger if staff members show solidarity among themselves.

It is much better to 'divide and rule', the old bad, but still in some way, efficient method of authoritarian leaders.

What we miss altogether is a modern "Loyalty Management", that would be required by mature, good leaders as an efficient tool for creating a sense of belonging within an organisational unit, and that would provide enough free space for staff members to decide for themselves.

The main rule for a good leader in relation to genuine motivation is:

> Create an atmosphere of commitment where everyone does his/her work out of self-motivation as contrary to staff who expects their leader to tell them what to do and how to do it.

You might now argue that this is easier said than done, and we agree to a certain extent.

Staff members who are used to be told what to do cannot develop self-motivation to speak of. There is always the fear that it might not appeal to the leader, the fear that they stick out their heads too far, the fear that colleagues might harass them, and many other real or more amorphous fears. The average employee is not prepared for being self-confident, even when professionally highly qualified; this evil starts early in our educational system where children are not allowed to be self-initiative and creative, and it continues in the normal context of most job conditions.

It is the task of a good leader to give real incentives in this context. In the following we mention some of the very many measures that should be implemented:

> First of all, a good leader has to assess qualification, potential and organisational setup of his unit. The methods are very easy, provided the leader goes about it unbiased and with clear parameters for executing a simple SWOT analysis, and it has to be done in a transparent, inclusive manner so that the results are reliable. Moreover, inclusiveness would bring about or strengthen mutual trust, and, if conducted properly, yield valuable suggestions from the side of the staff.

We came across a case, where a well-meaning leader unfortunately conducted SWOT analyses non-inclusive, and he was perplexed to consequently experience loss of trust, defiant resistance and other disadvantageous reaction from the staff.

Let us examine this authentic case

The situation has become worse than it has ever been; the leader felt that "the staff is not mature for that", a notion that is only partly right. Whereas he intended to improve working conditions and an overall increase of efficiency, 'happier' employees, and better communication, he was utterly disappointed

What went wrong?

That is easy to tell: he went about his endeavour secretly, like a parent prepares for a surprise for the child who knows that there is something in the offing and speculates about, and is only waiting for the gift-wrapped thing to surface—but here the analogy ends. Whereas the child builds up positive expectations, looking forward to finally receiving the gift, the staff members only know that 'something', some change, might be in the offing and, as we know the more negative mindset of average employees, a high production of rumours sets in, the well-oiled machinery of gossiping gets into motion, and it escalates with the day.

When the well-meaning leader finally opens his gift box, nobody wants to accept it, it has become a totally negative image.

What were the basic mistakes?

1. The leader wanted to improve things towards better leadership, motivation, create a more self-confident staff, etc., but he applied exactly the wrong methods. Conducting analyses on, let us say, work efficiency and the like, requires trust and cooperation from both sides; if that is not established beforehand, the whole endeavour is doomed to fail. What is worse, the atmosphere of distrust increases, and thus, further positive development is almost done with.
2. He did not define the aims and objectives beforehand, and subsequently, he could not fix the parameters of success.
3. He did not clearly plan the *modus operandi*, the course of action, nor the procedural method.
4. He did not think in terms of inclusiveness and was not aware of the advantages to tap the experiences and professional insight of the staff.
5. He was not aware of the highly motivating impact an inclusive *modus operandi* would have created.

What should he have been done?

1. Conduct a meeting with all staff present, informing them about the venture, explaining the aims and objectives, and also the advantages that could be achieved for staff, work quality, job satisfaction and work efficiency. He

should also point out the advantages for himself and for the whole unit as he would incur loss of credibility if he would pretend to do all this only in the interest of the staff. Nobody would take that. The meeting should have a precise agenda with the clear expectation of operationable suggestions from the staff, and it should conclude with giving responsibilities to all those who come forward. It should end with fixed dates for rendering suggestions, and for the next meeting.

2. One or two days prior to the first meeting (not too early as this would lead to unwanted gossip-mongering, thus loss of productivity), we advise to send a short paper to everyone working in the unit (including lower clerks, sweeper, etc.) containing the basics of the plan, the aims and objectives and, most important of all, the expectation of constructive suggestions from the staff.
3. We advise to conduct the follow-up meetings as what we call "Reception Meeting", i.e. there should not be a coffee house atmosphere of cosily chatting around, having tea and cookies, only unnecessarily prolonging the meeting. This gives the unmistakable message that business is intended, and that the main aim is to improve the overall efficiency.
4. Depending on what is suggested, and on what is agreed upon to do, a step-by-step plan after precise priorities is to be set up while the monitoring[6] and reporting is fixed.
5. A feasible timeframe is to be fixed and precisely followed.
6. If financial issues are involved, they have to be calculated and the process of procuring funds has to be set in motion.

In the whole venture, the leader should play the role of the moderator. He is just the "first among equals", making it clear that he pays attention to the staff and takes up their suggestions if feasible, but that he has the responsibility for the whole set-up, and finally, he is accountable both for success and failure—the most important step towards good leadership.

Many good planning ended in failures because priorities in the step-by-step plan were not precisely fixed, or else, while not applying the above-mentioned milestone monitoring system, the necessary flexibility of exchanging or including steps was not included, thus leading to severe setbacks.

In the course of action, many single measures will crop up, like trainings for the staff, assessing potential, re-organising procedures, even move staff members from one workplace to another. All these must be part of the step-by-step plan and implemented accordingly.

The Appendix shows a graph[7] on the most important training units for good leadership and for acquiring the skills to encourage the staff for building up sustainable self-motivation. It would include not only a change in behavioural patterns towards 'same eye-level' attitudes, and a transparent system of awarding good performers and appreciation, but also openness in pointing out the facts to bad or non-performers with the aim to support them in improving. If proper measures should fail, a good leader has to decide about consequences, in the worst case scenario remove or transfer the person.

If these measures are not consequently followed, or even diluted, and, what would be worse, only taken up in selected cases, the whole endeavour would be doomed to fail, and the leader, with all his good intentions, would lose all credibility.

a) Training should contain unconventional ways of behaviour.

b) Questioning taboos.

c) Acting after necessities (functional way of leadership).

d) Evolving self-confidence and creativity.

To sum up: Leadership has always to be seen in the context of motivation, and leadership has to function as a catalyst for self-motivation.

References

1. A German proverb, used to describe utter failure in leadership performance.
2. See Appendix, SECE, Model for Replication.

3. See Appendix: "Module for Holistic Leadership Training", part of our system for "Holistic Personality Development" (conducted by the International Institute for Holistic Research and Voluntary Action (India-Germany)).
4. Dr. Goebbels himself could not aspire to become the leader of the Germans as he was physically handicapped, a fact that made him as neurotic as his accomplice Hitler. But he had brains, and a German proverb says that the 'intelligent villain is always more dangerous than the less intelligent'. Both evil cronies brought such bloodshed and misery to millions of people that one feels nauseated at the mentioning of 'Hitler' as an able leader.
5. A German proverb, source unknown.
6. See Appendix: "Milestone Monitoring System", in: Marla/Taori, *Operationalising Holistic Human Development—Food for Thought and Ideas for Action in the Rural Context*, Concept Publishing Company, New Delhi, 2007.
7. See Appendix: Graph on leadership training.

11

What is to be done?[1]

From all our researches and analyses, we developed a simple profile for a good leader. It can be applied in all fields where good leadership is essential for high efficiency, it should be used as valuable parameters for decision making in selection processes for leadership positions. At the same time, the parameters should be used in educational institutions, like the various management schools, for building up the right type of leaders, and they should be used by individuals to test their own abilities and to find out their strengths and weaknesses.

The following describes some of the unavoidable measures for improving the overall leadership situation. We selected the most important ones, and we are also of the firm opinion that without the will for 'stirring and steering', nothing can be achieved which could sustain.

Selected Tools and Methods for Better Leadership

Some key words for changing mindset and attitudes, to influence the present tendency for avoiding decisions, and for punishing those who have visions and try to implement them:

a) Re-group

b) Re-allocate

c) Re-form

d) Re-discover
e) Re-search
f) Re-evaluate
g) Re-gain
h) Re-learn (putting things into different contexts, open up to new vistas in given contexts).

Key Attributes

Self-confidence paired with distinctive ability for continuous constructive self-criticism, and empathy combined with basic respect towards every human being.

Key Skills

A good leader has to master the tools for organisation development in combination with tools for management to bring about the necessary change required for a continuous improvement processes (see below) as one of the most important motivation forces.

We have to come away from the usual pseudo-motivation of the average leaders: the Triple-C Syndrome (Chatting: for *gossiping*—Chai—Chamcha), as it is detrimental for both motivation and self-motivation.

To start with improving leadership and motivation, there has to be an overall sweep-up in approaching hitherto conventional measures:

a) Training should contain unconventional ways of behaviour.
b) Questioning taboos.
c) Acting after necessities (functional way of leadership).
d) Evolving creativity + boldness both, in leaders and people who are to be led.

CIP—Continuous Improvement Process

No doubt that India has abundant potential to perform better, almost in all ways of life, and, for that matter, especially in its economy.

But if the so-called leaders, the self-styled leaders do not have such potential. What can we expect? Leaders should *perform* so that others can emulate them.

The CIP method is very simple to apply, provided the leader understands the method and implements it. It is basically a psychological motivational tool which requires a drastic change of mindset: from the "Just-so" syndrome to striving for excellence. The leader has to start with a thorough inventory of the efficiency of his own workplace, including his abilities in the field of soft skills. He has to be mercilessly self-critical, combined with a positive, constructive outlook. His own change of mindset and attitudes is the very first step into the right direction.

From his 'inventory', he develops a series of behavioural, organisational, and coordinating points which he makes into his personal to-do plan, time-bound, and starting immediately, for, we all know: 'tomorrow' means in reality 'never'.

At a very early stage in the process, he should explain his intention of bringing about an overall improvement in the work environment and job satisfaction to the staff, and he invites ideas from all of them. He should make his expecations clear so that there cannot be the doubt of another 'trick' or 'trap' where the employees are lured in. He should also make it clear that CIP has to be carried on by all, and that it cannot function when only a few would follow the line.

Observing the CIP (Continuous Improvement Processes) for changing mindset and attitudes, would bring about several distinct advantages:

a) A natural, positive approach to the given work.
b) Good leaders would encourage the system by following it themselves.
c) It would create vibrant platforms for continuous positive change.
d) Good performers would be appreciated, whereas non-performers would be brought to task.

In India, there are hardly genuine good performers in the position of power, but, as all wanting personalities, they expect performance from others, up to the extent that they claim other's performances as their own.

A well-known example to illustrate this behaviour and also show the 'public opinion' generated by the 'publicised opinion':

Let us look at the development in the Indian Railways during the past decades. Various Railway Ministers had failed earlier to bring about improvements and mitigate the hardships of the travellers. Now, in the past decade, there was a lot of improvements, like in the overall railway services, the quality of trains, the customer orientation of the staff, the condition of the railways stations, the electronic facilities, etc. Do we believe that it was the titanic brain of the respective Railway Minister of the past years who conceptionalised this change? No, but we have to appreciate that the respective Minister did not hinder these improvements to be implemented as was the case with his predecessors.

Let the Minister be hailed for what was achieved, and let us appreciate him for the fact that he allowed his staff to implement necessary steps, which plans they might have had in their drawers since long. A good leader need not be a great brain, but he must allow competent others to do what is necessary. In this context, this Railway Minister showed good leadership, and we don't mind that he was hailed as the hero of railways!

But, in reality, it must have come about like this: Some able and competent people serving in Indian Railways have conceptualised several measures so that the Railways improve their services and establish more customer-friendly conditions. Then, a new Railway Minister was appointed, and this is always a good opportunity for submitting concepts as the new person wants to show that something is done differently under his or her aegis. Thus, the smart Minister will take up new suggestions, and, if funds can be made available (sometimes even if not), will see to it that they are implemented. Luckily, during Lalu Prasad's aegis, things undoubtedly changed for the better, but they were mostly steps taken which should have been done long ago—outside India, most of the standard facilities which are hailed as almost revolutionary improvement, go without saying since long back.

Now, another Railway Minister introduced improvements mainly in favour of the own election turf, and this comes up to biased and corruptive performance. But all these things are done by our 'Leaders' in full public view, with all impunity, and no steps are taken to prevent it. And what is worse, the public just accepts, even appreciates—that is the way good leadership is punished and bad leadership is awarded!

Coming back to our topic of how to bring about good leadership, we developed seven categories:

1. No additional funds required—rather saving money.
2. Policy changes leading to re-appropriation.
3. Building up people's confidence and self-reliance.
4. Inviting ideas from the people (through websites and replying, using public functions as forum for ideas, and not for hollow speeches and garlanding VIPs, etc.) and implementing good ideas if suitable.
5. Inclusive planning bottom-up instead of top-down.

6. Involving AIS at all levels with clear accountabilities (the IIIII-Model—Innovative Implementable Ideas and Ideas for India—as success model for performers).
7. Consequently following the path of strengthening secularism (Indian Constitution applies to all citizens alike, there cannot be 'special' citizens with their own rights[2]).

Good leadership would do its utmost to coordinate all variants of leaders for efficiency and sustainability, like in the following groups/agencies:

1. Political/Governmental
2. Cultural/spiritual/religious
3. Educational
4. Health - Sports
5. Community-oriented
6. Business (private + semi-private)
7. Military
8. Civil Services including Police Services

All these groups, agencies, organisations, have their own agenda, and, in present-day India, they all isolate themselves from others. This is the main reason why good leadership is lacking power: envy, jealousy, a spirit of 'fiefdom' encompasses almost all spheres where good leadership would be required.

We do hope this book might upset lots of 'leaders', and some of them might start contemplating where in the above chapters they might find themselves. We want our leaders be shaken up from their complacency, we want them to get angry; like our "Stirring and Steering Group"(s)[3] we suggest in all units to be set up for evolving creativity and change for the better.

As an old German proverb says: "A fish starts stinking from the top."

References

1. For details see the next chapter on Holistic Training in Good Leadership
2. See chapter on Reservation Policies.
3. Stirring & Steering Group (SSG) meant to disturb the usual trot of "we always did it like this", thus creating an atmosphere of creativity towards improving efficiency and job satisfaction for all.

12
Holistic Training in Good Leadership

True, our leaders both, in the public and private sectors, are undergoing very fashionable trainings, workshops and the like regularly. Lots of money is spent for these events, and obviously, it has become a matter of prestige to participate. Just observe the ferocious in-fights in the departments for being 'sent' to a seminar, training, workshop, something on those lines.

We call that 'Seminar Tourism'. It has to be understood as another type of perks, and the height of all these is that sometimes, the families of participants also take part. Of course, not in the formal seminar, but in the informal part which constitutes the main part of the whole event, usually.

Just ask participants after they come back from a 'Leadership Seminar' about their experiences, what they have learnt, and what they have put into practice, and you will soon find that not even the contents of the seminar can be told.

Another big problem is the fact that there is no quality control, both of trainers and/or type of seminars. No follow-up activities are taken up; no parameters of success are developed at planning point; sometimes it is triggered off by hints from some officers whose colleagues were sent for a seminar; sometimes a direct colleague refers to his staff as much more satisfied after having been sent to a seminar, and many other reasons. More or less, it goes like this:

a) A leader gets the idea that the leaders in his department should get some appreciation which would boost up their motivation and make them less grumbling.

b) Sending them to a seminar preferably in a beautiful spot and a star hotel (like Kovalam beach in Kerala, places in Uttarakhand, Himachal, etc.)

c) Choosing the event is easy; a leader of this kind will anyway be flooded by offers for seminars, and he will be surrounded by trainers and consultants. Moreover, his entourage will also be flooded by these so that the decision making goes, usually, through the channel of the greased palms.

d) Now, choosing the participants: in our hierarchies, 'seniority' is the magic word, and it decides most of things, note: not 'competency'! We came across authentic cases where leaders were sent to a seminar only a few months before their retirement!

e) It goes without saying that quality assessment, analyses of necessities for a respective seminar and the like are alien words.

What about all those millions of rupees spent for leadership seminars, workshops and the like? How are the trainers and the consultants selected? How is the quality assessed?

One of the great mistakes in this field is that leaders frequently fall into the trap of people, i.e. trainers, consultants, etc., who say that everyone could be trained as a leader. The fashionable message of trainers: "I am okay—you are okay", whereas in reality, neither I am (always) okay, nor is my fellow human being necessarily okay, let us face this!

Sincere psychology tells us that it all depends on certain key abilities an individual is born with, and also, to a certain extent, on enabling surroundings, like a child growing up in an atmosphere of dignity, love and encouragement, has all the pre-requisites to develop as a good leader, provided it is born with the already mentioned key abilities.

If you would force an individual into training behavioural patterns of 'leadership' without assessing these key abilities and be sure about, this person would become a very unhappy, and a very unsuited leader.

Unfortunately, as in several chapters mentioned before, the perception of 'leader' and 'leadership' in India is somewhat confused. A person is attributed leadership qualities as soon as this person sits on a leadership position; hardly anyone questions his abilities, performance and other requirements that a good leader should show. It is like an actor assuming a role, only actors are very often better scrutinised in their performances.

Thus, people make it very easy for non-performers to assume roles they are not made for. And, once in a leadership position, they would not relinquish it, they would never admit that they themselves feel not suited. They prefer acting before showing 'weakness', when, from a psychological point of view, it would show great inner strength to do so.

We have hordes of self-styled consultants in India who, along with many colleagues in the US, state that everyone can be trained as a 'leader', only they have to undergo their respective training!

The following shows tools, training modules, suggestions, appeals—all in view of improving leadership and overall conditions in our country. We appeal to our readers to contact us with comments and constructive critique!

Appendix—
Selected Models for Replication, Training Modules, Selected Open Letters and Documents Connected with Leadership Issues

Dual System of Professional Education

The German Dual System of Professional Education which is worldwide acclaimed to for its high quality standards, cannot be easily transferred into Indian conditions, as there is no proper infrastructure, especially from the "schooling", the more theoretical view. Also, the fact that in India menial labour is looked down upon, stands heavily in the way. Nevertheless, with some modifications, a model system could be established which will:

- — enhance the self-employment and also, employment perspectives considerably, due to its inherent organisational/management skills,
- — enhance the quality of skills considerably due to its standardised high-quality level,
- — bridge the gap between demands from the production side (high quality standards) and the actual training,
- — will be replicable all over India to name only the most important advantages of the system.

The Dual System consists of two vital parts which have to be closely interlinked and coordinated:

- — "Professional" schooling
- — Private Company or Public-Private Enterprise for dual apprenticeship

Precondition for setting up the model is a systematic plan which contains all skills and knowledge required to fulfil all standards of a certain profession; this plan is to be designed by both school/teachers and the respective company, and carefully coordinated. All skills and knowledge is to be phrased operationally so that the overall quality standard control is secured at all stages (like "the apprentice is able to responsibly perform..."). This plan is the so-called "Professional Profile".

To design this profile, experts (masters) in the respective professions have to be consulted and also teachers have to be identified/trained who can cover the schooling. Both sides have to work closely together and agree in all aspects.

The schooling comprises not only the theoretical implications of the respective profession, but also business skills and knowledge like management, organisation, accountancy, banking, environment protection, leadership, cost and tax issues, etc.

The company rendering the apprenticeship has to:

— employ the apprentice by providing work places and render all skills necessary in practice, thus having the advantage of a work force at the same time, albeit slightly reduced,
— pay the apprentice a certain "apprenticeship salary", which is, of course, a nominal sum to ascertain the livelihood of the person—this is an investment in future high quality workforce!

Both, schooling and practice is conducted in alternate phases, like, for example, three months schooling, three to four months practice, and so forth. It can also be conducted in a "parallel" way, where working and schooling alternate, like, four days work, one day school, or twice a week half-a-day school.

In Germany, a dual Professional Education comprises usually three years, ending with an examination in both fields, which is supervised by the Chamber of Commerce/Chamber of Artisans.

For Indian conditions, this time can be reduced considerably, according to the agreements between the three coordinates (Employer—School authorities—

Chamber of Commerce/Chamber of Artisans—for the experimenting phase we suggest our Institute, in close collaboration with the local authorities supervise the scheme), after fixing the goals.

h) Concerning our prospective model, we have all freedom to fix timings and also, examinations cum certificates according to the modifications.

i) The International Institute for Holistic Research will provide samples of "professional profiles" and expertise to transfer the system into Indian/local conditions for evolving a suitable plan of action. Also, the Institute will provide presentations and training for all sides involved.

The main initial problem will be to find enterprises which will join hands in this venture. They have to be convinced that their initial investments (salary + proper training on the job) will pay off in the end, supplying high quality workers in the future with standardised skills.

Overview

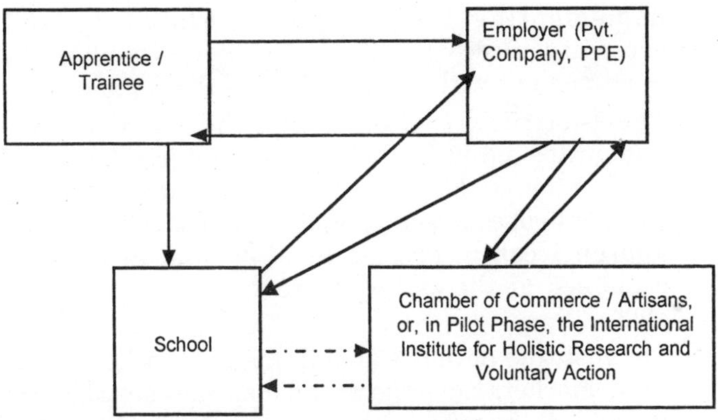

"Dual System" means:

— direct link between Apprentice/Trainee and the employer (2 parties agreeing on an apprenticeship contract)

supported by

— schooling institution (providing theoretical skills, issuing performance certificate)

— Chamber of Commerce/Artisans, or, in pilot phase, the International Institute for Holistic Research and Voluntary Action (supervising the proper proceedings, conducting the examination, issuing the qualified certificates)

Implementation of Pilot Model "Dual System of Professional Education" (DSVE)

a) The Institute will identify and select genuinely interested local persons from:
   i) Private Enterprises and/or Public-Private enterprises
   ii) Local authorities to assist and get trained in continuously supervise the performance
   iii) Educational institutions (polytechnic, and otherwise practice- and future-oriented)

   As Partners in the Dual System of Professional Education, and establish a committee/association with the aim of implementing and guiding the pilot project on the basis of the DSVE developed and submitted by the International Institute for Holistic Research and Voluntary Action (India-Germany)

b) The Institute will take over the practical steps for implementing and monitoring, evaluating and, if necessary, modify the phases timely in consultation and in agreement with the members of the Committee.

c) The Institute, together with the members of the Committee agree on the "professional profile" and also, on all other conditions concerning the pilot project, like work-/school contract, apprenticeship salary, duration of apprenticeship, precise level of qualification to be examined at the end of apprenticeship, examinations, etc.

d) The Institute develops an information brochure on these lines, markets the project, and identifies suitable youths to undergo the pilot apprenticeship. There will not be any gender discrimination in any profession whatsoever.

e) The Institute identifies suitable teachers[1] and rooms for the "schooling" part; renders training for the teachers both, in theory and practice, also in modern teaching methods for youths, and supervises proper proceedings. Entrepreneurial skills and attitudes are integral part of the model. Bureaucratic infrastructure will be reduced to the utmost minimum.

f) The Institute will monitor the implementation processes, the performance of all involved, and render after-implementation monitoring in agreement with the Committee. In a milestone-system, the Institute will regularly check and evaluate the results during the whole process and report to the Committee.

After successful completion of the pilot project, the model would be propagated and replicated all over India.

Irmel V. Marla/Dr. Kamal Taori

SECE-Model[2]

The SECE-Model is a successful concept for self-employment. It is designed in two main fields of activities: inside the village, and outside. Here are the graphs to illustrate the concept:

Approaches outside the village

External Contacts and Cooperation

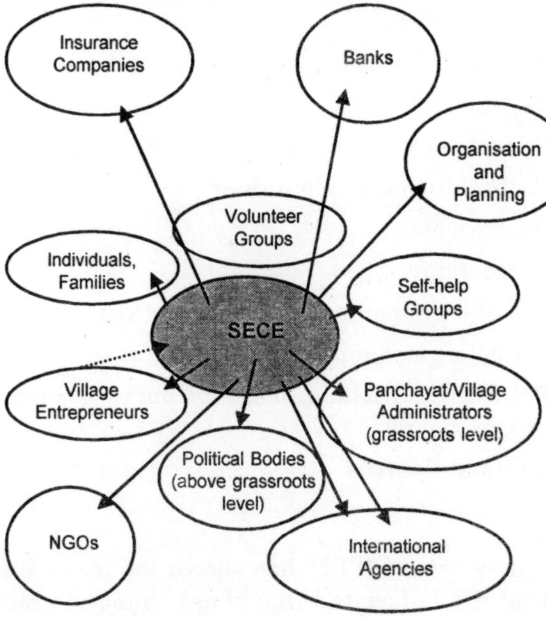

Approaches Inside the Village

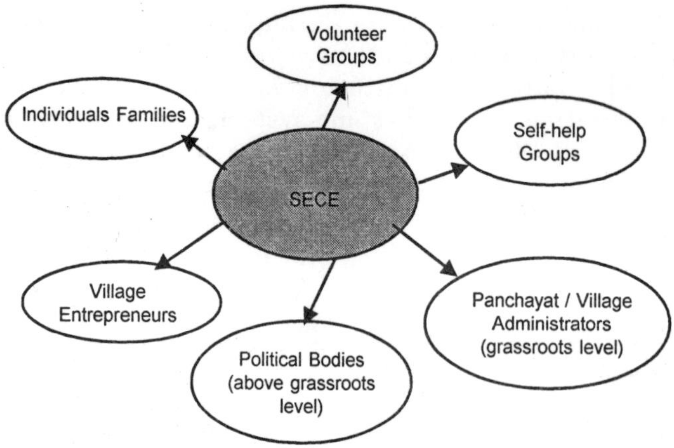

Irmel V. Marla/Dr. Kamal Taori

Holistic System of 6Ps

Our basic approach to viable enterprises contains the following elements for success:

a) **P**ubiic
b) **P**rivate
c) **P**anchayat
d) **P**rofitable (non-exploitative)
e) **P**rogressive
f) **P**artnership

If need be, the system is expandable to "9Ps"

a) **P**ress (all media resources)
b) **P**olitics (politicians, political parties, parliamentary commissions)
c) **P**ublic Resources

Remark

The usual system of "PPP" has shown too many weaknesses, most of all the failure to bring about change in mindset and attitudes and benefits for the village people; also, there is too much temptation and scope for fraud, and not enough scope for monitoring/control and transparency. From what we analysed, the PPP-ventures are all more or less totally corrupted, from both the sides, and are prone to even enhance their squandering away of public money.

SoEZ (Social Economic Zones)

In view of the many problems resulting from and also, of the doubtful results from the much lauded SEZs, we developed the concept of: SoEZ (Social Economic Zones).

The SoEZ is a new concept with thrust on the social element in it, in contrast to the well-known SEZs where the social part plays no role at all. The basically good idea of introducing better possibilities for rural entrepreneurs is distorted by the fact that it only renders privileges to the big players while neglecting the needs of the ruralites, all is done under the banner of boosting employment and entrepreneurship, but this proved to be all futile.

SoEZ is based on our holistic approach to action where it is imperative to involve all concerned at grassroots level and to integrate sustainable development with entrepreneurial spirit in action.

We are of the strong opinion that the already well-established companies seek ways and means of tax exemption for higher profits do not need and also, do not deserve these special advantages as it enables only those who can invest heavily to flourish further whereas the local entrepreneurs cannot compete. The official SEZ would clearly bring further disadvantages to the rural entrepreneurs in all competitive fields where the big players have all power to suppress the smaller ones.

The concept of SoEZ shows a way to combine both: support efforts for sustainable entrepreneurship by catering to the local needs and also, strengthen local entrepreneurs in their ventures.

The legislature and all the elected bodies down to the grassroots representatives should feel and act in the interests of the local people to strengthen their potentials by removing obstacles in the way of sustainable entrepreneurship. These obstacles consist mainly in tax issues, obstacles in acquiring land, bureaucratic hurdles in establishing enterprises and many more of these.

What is to be done?

First of all, the gap between the legislature and the grassroots necessities have to be bridged, they have to work hand in hand, supporting each other.

1. What is the difference between SEZ and SoEZ?
   a) The organised sectors had always the best from the government, banks, taxation policies, market, universities, etc., while the proposal for SoEZ visualises "organising the un-organised", and develop social economic improvement with social thrust.
   b) The SoEZ works on convergence, 6Ps[3], cost-reduction, equity, participatory, holistic and inclusive approach.
   c) The globalisation requires localisation by involving the community and, thus, the people concerned.
   d) The basic difference between SEZ and SoEZ is of approach, attitudes, mindset, learning from past mistakes which show an overall neglect of laws of nature.
2) What is the USP of SoEZ?
   a) It is around marketing-driven, or Marketing-Led Activisation Processes (MLAP).
   b) It is cost-effective, bankable, convergenistic, and propelling the cause of self-employment, viable investment, and policy-corrective mechanism.
   c) As per local conditions, it is flexible, and it has its emphasis on social, cultural, environmental, and even political compulsions.
   d) It builds up good leadership from the bottom.
   e) It revolves around Panchayati Raj institutions and, combined with RBHs, could be the only answer for tomorrow, it could lead to Gram Swaraj.

3) Who will operate, manage, run, coordinate the SoEZ?
   a) Suitable representatives of the local community, PRIs, NGOs, SHGs, ...
   b) Support could be rendered by NRIs, Central and State Governments, elected bodies at the grassroots level, all levels of administration
   c) Networking and exchanging experiences through suitable use of IT.
4) What is the role of Panchayats, PRIs, NGOs, and the local community in the SoEZ?
   a) They have to play the crucial coordinating role as all the facilities which are made available to the SoEZs would naturally be provided through single window service.
   b) They would be forced to develop transparent communication methods, thus creating an atmosphere of mutual trust, accountability and constant information.
5) What could be the role of our IIHRVA/RBHFI? We could take the lead in :
   a) Inclusive initial planning activities
   b) Facilitating business-led contacts
   c) Training and turnkey consultancy
   d) Monitoring and follow-up activities
   e) Further develop efficiency

Irmel V. Marla/Dr. Kamal Taori

Disaster Prevention versus Disaster Management![4]

Our Institute has developed a valid concept cum practical tools for "Disaster Prevention" instead of "Disaster Management, the latter supported by the Standard Operation Procedure Manuals (*SOP*). The "SOPs" are widely useless, as they are designed by Administrators and/or Experts, non-inclusive and, what is worse, collecting dust in offices while, in case of a disaster emergency, nobody would have the time to go through them.

Also, continuous training after the SOPs is not conducted. We observed that after emergency measures, nothing else is prescribed in the SOPs which would sustainably prevent disasters in the future. There is also no provision for change of mindset and attitudes, especially at local level.

Efficient Disaster Management cannot mean the usual handling of catastrophes as and when they suddenly fall from the heavens, at the best following SOPs which usually are out of date or, not at hand, and much too impractical to be helpful in a given disaster situation. They also serve very often as tool for blaming those who react spontaneously, and to put the blame for poor performance onto those who at least do something. The highly hierarchical, compartmentalised infrastructure in administration is a main stumbling block against efficiently tackling the problems and, on the other hands, it is very conveniently used to find and punish scapegoats.

We are of the opinion that it is necessary to widely substitute the SOPs with our concept of "Continuous Operative Procedure" (COP), which focuses on improvement at the grassroots level, on disaster prevention, and on flexible response to acute.

In short, our concept is based on grassroots experiences, awareness, and inclusiveness, and it would prevent many "disasters" (natural or else) to happen in the first place.

The following shows the outlay of our concept:

Central requirement is the setting up of a local Disaster Management Task Force (LDMTF).

We also should not only see the emergency problems but also tackle the continuous disasters which accumulate and increase with time, like social problems of children and youth suicides (especially high incidences in Kerala), ostrasisation of HIV-infected persons, leadership and awareness problems in rural areas concerning holistic environment protection (list is not complete) and, as can be learnt from recent disasters concerning the abysmal state of condition of life-saving equipment due to lack of maintenance, and lack of trained local people in first aid; those conditions are rampant everywhere in the country. Overall change of mindset and attitudes, together with active support from upper levels of decision-making, i.e. rendering responsibilities to local level, would lead to sustainable prevention and/or mitigation of the problems.

To sum up, our Institute conceptualises directly implementable action plans (adjusted to local conditions) and render the necessary training for those who are supposed to take over responsibilities and perform, and this can only be sustainable if a grassroots level TASK FORCE based on voluntarianism and self-responsibility is built up on the following (basic) lines:

For "Task Force" building up:

a) Connecting with SECE[5] (Self-Employed Change Entrepreneur)
b) Thrust on voluntarianism and self-responsibility at grassroot level
c) Monitoring—training (percolating down, and TtT—Train the Trainer so that continuity of efforts is ensured)
d) Assuring sustainability and support by local authorities

We are also of the opinion that the outlook towards "SOPs" should be radically changed towards our concept of "Continuous Operation Procedure Plan" (COPP) for the following reasons:

a) SOPs are mainly used as excuses for doing nothing.
b) "Standard" means usually the restriction of flexible handling which again means, that necessary measures might be hindered by narrow-minded sticklers to the letter.
c) Lots of work time and money is wasted in developing them.
d) In case of emergency, they are not really helpful as nobody has time nor is interested to go through paper.
e) They are usually not updated.
f) Grassroots people are not involved and aware of SOPs.
g) No proper continuous, monitored training and freshing-up measures are conducted.

On the other hand the concept of COPP would provide a continuous process of creating and keeping up the level of awareness in all fields of disaster prevention and also create a new mindset of self-responsibility while giving all successful scope for Disaster Prevention against Disaster Management, wherever possible.

Irmel V. Marla/Dr. Kamal Taori

Example of District Action Plans, or Village Action Plans

This Action Plan was first conceptualised in 2006, and later on developed into detailed specific programmes to enhance its flexibility.

The Plan was sent to the Government of Maharashtra, to District Authorities, and to various elected bodies at grassroots levels. It had been received with interest but was not practically and seriously taken up as yet.

Wardha District Plan for Action—Details for Viable Small Enterprises and Convergence

To enhance self-employment and employability, there have to be distinct perspectives and viable concepts. Most of the concepts would require initial funding, but this should come through loans and/or repayable funding, for example, development funds with the Panchayats could be used as revolving funds to support establishing small enterprises.

Thus, self-motivation would be ensured, and a simple tool for milestone-monitoring would give security in the first phases of implementation.

Quality training in skills and management tools will lead to success.

Our initial findings while visiting some villages in Wardha District show that there is preparedness of younger generation in taking up challenges, at least they are eager to listen und also, verbally, are willing to work with us, and come up with good ideas.

The holistic approach however, has to be explained and understood so that "development" can become a positive driving force in various areas of action. Usually, schemes for self-entrepreneurship fail due to these main reasons:

a) Lack of market-driven approach
b) Lack of self-motivation initial funding
c) Lack of support from elected bodies and administration
d) Lack of skills and knowledge (also: management skills und team-spirit)
e) Lack of quality-consciousness and reliability
f) Lack of inclusiveness
g) Interference of party politics

All these points have to be considered in the planning stage, and proper parameters of success, (operationalised and time-framed) have to be discussed and agreed upon with all stakeholders.

Village Action Plan—Model for Replication

The essentials for all activities connected with the Village Action Plan are:

1) Assessing local conditions
    a) Unused / under-used and hidden potential and resources
    b) Assessing formal and informal power structures
    c) Assessing supportive forces/conditions—assessing adverse forces/conditions (bottlenecks, stumbling blocks, communal tensions, political influence, etc.)
    d) Compiling data (people, communities, enterprises, employment/unemployment, age structure, education facilities, health features, land, etc.), local NGOs (their impact),
    e) Assessing success and failures of development schemes in the past ("learning from the past")
2) While assessing the above facts, prospective local leaders/activists for the Village Model are identified, and

simultaneously, a qualifying programme is developed, be it knowledge and skill development, be it leadership training, or be it measures for building up self-confidence—change of mindset and attitudes. Concerning women, we have to do our utmost to involve them actively in the Model, from the start, and encourage them to take over leadership tasks. Women have to be emboldened to act on their own; husbands and (male) relatives also have to learn to respect women at the same eye-level.

Sustainable Self-employment and Employability—Job Creation

Prior to our thorough search for viable business opportunities by un-earthing unused potential and resources, we can give the following practical suggestions:

1) *Team[6]-farming (including both, agriculture and animal husbandry)*
   a) Small landholdings are no more viable. If several small landowners pool their land after a viable business plan, it can develop as a highly profitable venture. Designing the business plan and also the initial financing can be done with the expertise of the International Institute.
   b) The emphasis should be put on organic farming as there is the market of the future and also the aspects of environment protection are included. Soil testing and suggestions of feasible farm products has to be done by experts, from Government's side and also, by international experts. On this fundament, the decisions for agricultural products in view of their marketability can be taken and the training requirements decided upon. The training side and also, the assessment of suitable farmers for the team (leadership qualities, team-abilities, SWOT of personalities and potential) can be taken up by the International Institute. Here, we have a wide field of action for convergence as the elected bodies at grassroots and District level are ready and prepared

to support viable ventures (where this is not the case, ways and means have to be devised for change). The International Institute offers practice-oriented leadership training, especially for the needs of grassroots level leaders.

c) Concerning the problem of marketing, we have to design and implement the products in the first place after considering the marketability nationally and internationally—"natural" products is the market for the future!

d) A suitable IT has to be developed: software to support the farmers concerning all their activities (sharing experiences in success and failure, providing on-the-spot information, and also, for marketing purposes, The International Institute with its "Satellite System of Experts" can provide the necessary expertise in custom-made ways so to cater to the local needs. It can be closely linked with the SECE Model (see 2.)

2) *Self-Employed Change Entrepreneur (SECE): setting up an IT-based service unit for various tasks, like:*

a) Issuing documents authorised by Governmental departments

b) IT information Centre (also: Internet Café)—service for those who cannot handle the net

c) Has scope for expanding and can thus create

i) New jobs

ii) IT Training and apprenticeship

The following shows the system and potential of this model:

SECE-Model[7]

The SECE-Model is a successful concept for self-employment. It is designed in two main fields of activities: inside the village, and outside.

In Maharashtra, the Gramdoot Model shows the initial steps of the concept.

Here are the graphs to illustrate the concept:

Approaches outside the Village

External Contacts and Cooperation

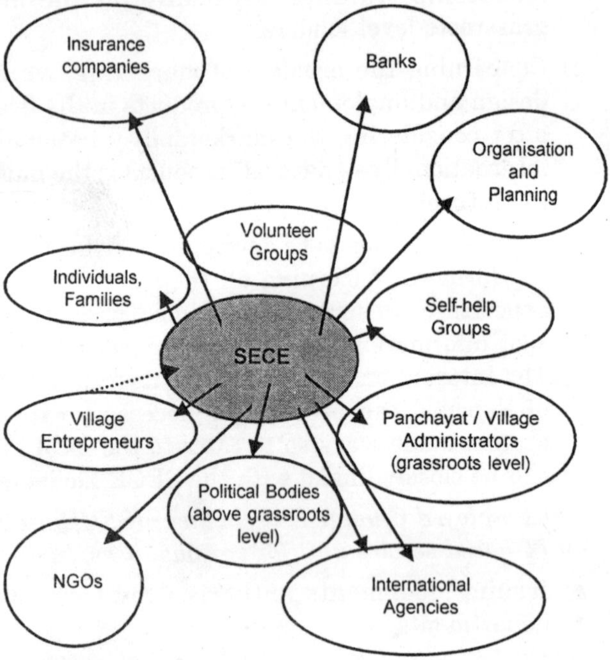

Approaches inside the Village

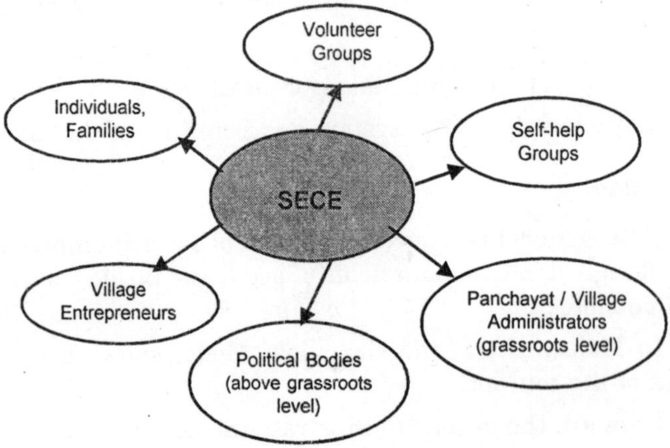

3) *Team-Service:*

a) Pooling skills and knowledge of several individuals offering "inclusive" service in various fields.

Example for "Building Unit": Mason, plumber, electrician, painter, carpenter, roof maker (+ interior decorator, horticulturist) etc. organise themselves into a House Construction Service Unit, offering custom-made "packets" for house construction, renovation and repair works. The "packet" includes proper financing and fixed time-frames for completion. Their emphasis is on quality, reliability, and time-conscious delivery. The main advantages are obvious:

i) By pooling all resources, the calculation will be much more competitive through concessions from whole sale firms.

ii) Work will be done much faster through well-organised procedures.

iii) Customers are relieved from dealing with many artisans and the problem of time-wise organising the manifold tasks.

iv) There will be guaranteed quality in material and work performance.

v) Customers have a guaranteed, reliable financial plan which gives them security in their venture.

b) The International Institute can provide necessary training in managing such a unit, especially in team-management, in project designing, and marketing skills, and also facilitate professional training for knowledge and skills if needed. We can assess the potential, trainings needed, and we offer our Milestone Monitoring System[8] to avoid mistakes in the initial phases which would invariably lead to future failure.

4) *Renewable Energies:* high potential of convergence, team-oriented, connected with other activities, preferably by clustering several villages in the venture

The setting up of a village-oriented Renewable Energy Plant is a unique example where convergence of several villages, grassroot elected bodies and other Government agencies can ideally function.

To make it a success, several villages should be clustered for the venture, and it is of utmost importance that the villagers themselves have to contribute to the plant. From many previous schemes we know that setting up a plant which is wholly financed by grants will run into failure for the (main) obvious reason: human psychology shows that there is no "identification" with a project if it comes free; when the funding is over, there is no motivation for maintenance and further development—people are just waiting for the next scheme to come. "I don't care for what is not mine." But, if people invest in a scheme, their mindset and attitude changes drastically, and a sense of responsibility prevails.

The International Institute has good contacts with one of the leading universities in Germany in the field of renewable energies where appropriate technology is highly developed and tested. They successfully developed technology which has two main features:

i) Almost maintenance-free (a big problem otherwise)

ii) Producing energy by using everything organic (from kitchen waste to all sorts of waste material, like leaves, wood waste, etc., also using specific plants which can grow on otherwise non-arable land)

The successful running of such a plant would contribute to:

i) Creating jobs

ii) Training and apprenticeship in knowledge and skills

iii) Financial gains both, for the stakeholders and also, by selling energy to outside customers

We can facilitate the contacts with the University of Kassel for constructive cooperation.

5) *Waste to Wealth:* in close connection with:

i) renewable energy (4.)

ii) water protection (6.)

iii) recycling of waste and waste raw material (4.)

All over India, we observe the neglect of environment protection, especially concerning non-organic waste. We are confronted with heaps of plastic rubbish and other products harmful to ground water and for animals that die miserably from them.

There are technologies which can recycle most of these dangerous materials, and, at the same time, produce raw material for manufacturing usable products which can be marketed.

For us, this is an example for convergence closely connected with disaster management. Setting up a recycling plant should be a village clustering scheme, like the concept for renewable energies.

At the same time, setting up such a unit would create awareness for environment protection and make people conscious about avoidable waste and the duty to contribute to nature protection in view of a liveable world for future generations.

6) *Water protection:* In India, the technology for almost all problems of water conservation is highly developed, and it is not understandable that the authorities hardly invest in these fields. Especially in rural India, where exploitation of nature in the form of destroying forests (for the sake of roads, settlements, etc.) without re-planting the lost natural habitats, and gross violation of water protecting principles and soil protection is rampant, we have to use all possibilities to change that.

In view of convergence, the grassroots authorities together with the village population can do a lot to mitigate this already abysmal condition by creating awareness and, at the same time create viable enterprises in this context.

Watershed issues have been tackled in various ways, and there are already existing schemes which are working well.

We suggest setting up a "Water Agency" in close cooperation with the village and District authorities which will implement the necessary measures, and will be responsible for maintenance and further development—technology-wise, and by continuously implementing and supervising the scheme. It will mainly include:

i) water harvesting

ii) water recycling

iii) groundwater replenishing

The International Institute can help in designing the scheme and suggest village-internal awareness activities to enlighten and motivate all villagers for support. Also, we can facilitate the cooperation with experts—from government and/or private agencies—for training and implementing initial steps.

The suggested "Water Agency" would create jobs and, at the same time, provide training and apprenticeship.

7) *Health Club:* Unfortunately, there is not much emphasis in average Indian schools (private or governmental) to create awareness for the importance of sports in view of all health issues. More so, girls and women are almost completely out of the picture when it comes to practising sports in rural areas. In this context, we like to emphasise the importance of courses in self-defence to enhance self-confidence in girls and women and also, make them capable to not longer be victims of crimes like rape and other atrocities.

Our suggestion of setting up "Health Clubs" in villages catering to all villagers would be a viable enterprise, and it is a highly convergenistic scheme.

We observed in almost all villages we visited that there is usable infrastructure, like schools which are empty in the evenings or other seldom used structures like village community halls, etc., where a health club could be run.

The health club offers services in various ways, and it should work well coordinated with the Primary Health Centre and the village educational institutions.

The following features would make the Village Health Club a viable scheme while offering:

i) Different courses in specific sports and yoga for all gender and ages (yoga can be practised by everyone).

ii) Sports practising opportunities providing workout equipment and consultancy for individually appropriate type of sports and how to exercise.

iii) Courses in pre- and post-natal exercises (midwifes + staff from Primary Health Centre could be the trainers—they will be trained by experts).

iv) Courses in nutrition and hygiene (in close cooperation with staff from Primary Health Centre).

v) Courses in self-defence for Women and girls.

vi) Courses for family planning.

vii) Awareness campaigns on HIV.

viii) Awareness campaigns on drug abuse (instead of prohibition which is solely to the benefit of black marketers who are thriving in Wardha District—very un-Gandhian!).

ix) Setting up specific sports teams: soccer, cricket, handball, volleyball, hockey, etc., for both the genders!

x) Conducting sports competitions (inter-village, District-wise, State-wise).

xi) Supporting school sport.

xii) Yoga courses for all genders and all ages.

xiii) Providing training for sports teachers (if there are none in a village school, the Health Club could be appointed for giving sports lessons).

The Health Club could be a forum for all these activities, and through specific courses for women and girls, it could be made attractive for the female population.

It is made viable through membership fees and fees for the courses. The Panchayat should support the Health Club financially by either providing the necessary infrastructure and (initial) equipment, and by paying for services in the interest of the local authorities.

8) *Professional Education Institute:* Implementation and supervising agency for Dual System of Professional Education (DSVE).

   Setting up a "Professional Education Institute" can be a viable enterprise, reaching outside the village itself by attracting young people from other areas also. It will use existing infrastructure, and the small local enterprises will highly benefit from its advantages concerning especially the quality level and also, will attract youth and employers from outside the village.

   It is highly convergenistic as it needs support from local and District authorities, and also from public-private/private enterprises.

Irmel V. Marla/Dr. Kamal Taori

All these "Models for Replication" can become viable enterprises and, at the same time, they will improve the overall living conditions. Other ideas for setting up viable enterprises will automatically evolve from the stakeholders themselves, as soon as the practicability of the initial projects is seen and understood.

For example, identification of local artisans and assess possibilities for marketing their skills (also team-producing) is to be done in the overall assessment stage.

The International Institute is dedicated to the holistic approach, and it puts emphasis on gender-neutral schemes. It is aiming at an egalitarian society where gender, religion and other ideologies, also baseless and outdated hierarchies, should be put behind in view of honouring individual abilities, merits and the preparedness to take one's life into the own hands. Self-initiative and social responsibility are the ways and means to achieve our goal.

Model for sustainable development of farms/making farmers into farm managers, against dependencies from grants and subsidies and also, from contract farming:

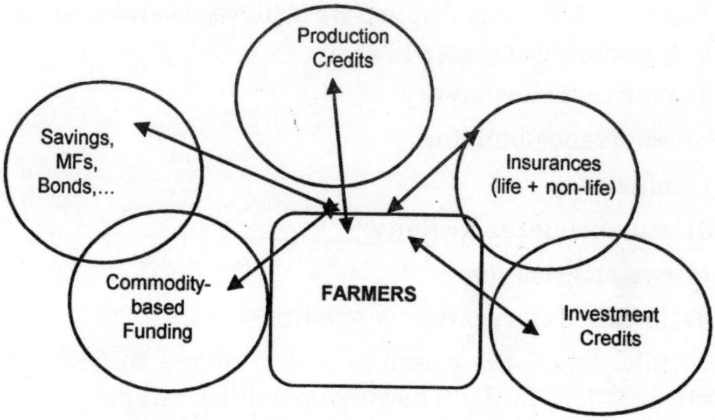

All efforts could be made easier and more efficient by tying up with appropriate research institutions, Students internships at farms, networking with service providers, cooperation with experts in monitoring and/or evaluating results after parameters for sustainability, etc.

a) Enablers for success:
b) (appropriate) technology/IT
c) (dual) education
d) Appropriate infrastructure
e) Appropriate tools for financing and insurance

Again: Contract Farming can bring all the models to zero if it follows patterns of opportunistic profiteering through exploitative measures.

Irmel V. Marla/Dr. Kamal Taori

Concept Milestone Monitoring System

The following is one of our easy-to-handle tools for making sure that a project becomes a success, provided the planning is up to expectations.

The Milestone-Monitoring-System is part of any of our initial planning processes, and it ensures that from the very beginning of any activity the parameters of success are clearly defined and monitored:

With the Milestone System we achieve several goals at one time, especially processes like:

a) clarity, transparency
b) confidence-building
c) efficiency
d) enhancing productivity
e) systematisation
f) in-time intervention possibilities

If we take again the example of the village SECE[9] we can illustrate it like in the following (simplified) steps:

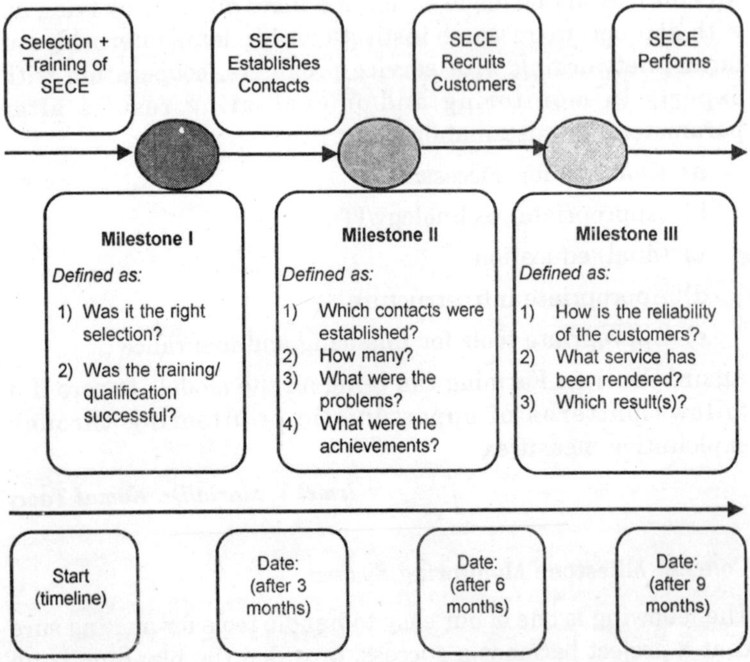

Milestones have to be defined as checkpoints by exactly describing the aim and/or fact which is to be reached/stated at a given time. At the same time, the definitions of the milestones should be restricted to the most crucial aims or facts to avoid the danger of bureaucratisation lurking on every corner. It should be clear, upfront, as simple as possible, and understandable for everybody.

Furthermore, this method helps to enhance clarity in thinking and also, forces to think in an aim-oriented manner. If the SECE is well trained, he himself is responsible for the work processes. Every milestone he reaches successfully in time will enhance his self-confidence, and thus his self-motivation.

Last but not least, it goes without saying that the SECE is to be involved in the milestones plan from the start, be it with the definition of the aims, or be it with the time-fixing. After some experiences and also, after some success in fulfilling milestones, the SECE will be well equipped with self-confidence and the necessary skills to design his programmes and plans accordingly.

For the Panchayati Raj institution to be efficient as a Unit of Self-Governance it is important that a "SECE" type of local experts are identified, trained, and supported in their efforts for self-employment, and that they receive appropriate recognition from all levels of governance and financing so that others will emulate their performance. We also emphasize that for all the "29 subjects" earmarked for the Panchayati Raj institutions, the "SECE" type of local expert, service provider and self-employed entrepreneur is the only sustainable solution.

If the People's Plan should become a replicable reality, it has to start from grassroots level, meaning bottom-up in contrary to the usual failure-prone top-down-approach which has led to an overall stalemate. The bottom-up-approach brings about the resource-convergence which is utterly needed, and it is appropriate in a democratic set-up.

After the collapse of centralised planning in all socialist countries, People's Plan as opposed to a ruthless market-driven system, should lead to a humane, dignified, civil development where all people concerned have their share of the improvement of living conditions, thus gaining happiness in a true holistic sense.

1. Defining People's Plan
   a) USP of People's Plan
   b) Defining "people"
2. Some key words:
   a) Self-reliance
   b) Viability
   c) SECA
   d) SOPP
   e) SHG
   f) Charity to CCCB
   g) Convergence
   h) Market
   i) Cluster
   j) Risk:
      i) avers
      ii) lover
   k) Productivity
   l) Investments
   m) RoI (Return on Investment)
   n) *Sarkari—A Sarkari—Asar/kari*. The combination of these three terms is deliberately done to show development, prosperity, better results, howsoever short-lived the may be. To void misunderstanding, we define these terms as follows:
      i) *Sarkari:* The Governments have become too powerful, power-wielding, and ever-present, ever-interfering in all fields.

ii) *A Sarkari:* Non-Governmental forces, can be supportive for sustainable development, but can be acting for themselves only, pursuing their vested interests.

iii) *Asar/kari:* efficient forces, impact-making.

3. Institutions in Wardha:

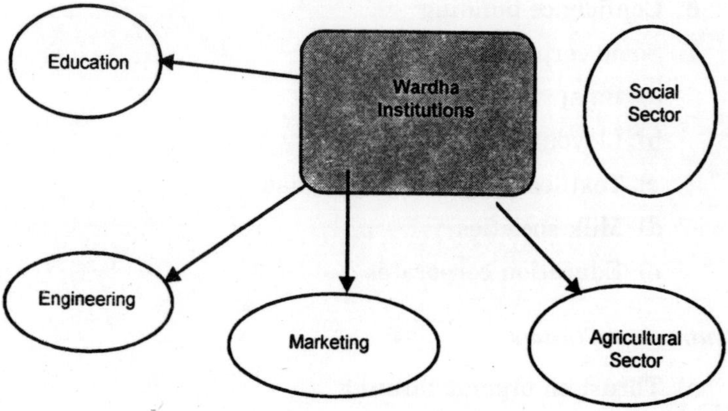

Learning from These Institutions

— Exploiters (?) All Government bodies/institutions are basically exploiters.

Lessons from Hind Swaraj

What needs to be done? How and why and for/by whom? When? For how long?

1. Value addition
2. Rural activisation programme
3. Self-reliance
4. clusters
5. Policies-enhancing frauds

How to reduce vulnerability (and feeling insecure, risk-averse)?

1. As an individual
2. As per a group
3. Organise the unorganised
4. Unused infrastructure
5. Leadership HRD–planning
6. Confidence-building
7. Some corporate sectors
    a) Bajaj
    b) Lloyds
    c) Textiles Pulgaon Hinganghad
    d) Milk societies
    e) Education corporates

Centres and Clusters

a) Thrust on organic farming
b) Mines, coals
c) Involve all political parties
d) Prohibition (role played by women)
e) Issues on farmers suicides
f) HRD of local Government bodies
g) Role of university and retired people
h) Water issues and reservoirs
i) Tinkering is not the answer

Plan of Action

1. Use villages as clusters
2. SEVIPP
3. Role of middle classes
4. Role of people's representatives

5. Wastage of funds on fertiliser subsidies, petrol, diesel, etc. (in the era of environment protection!)
6. Sensitisation
7. Shift to natural production
8. Re-define productivity
9. Brainstorming issues
10. Corruption
11. Prohibition
12. Health
13. Litigation
14. Education

Success Parameters of Wardha Plan

Statistical data

a) Self-employment
b) Women's SHG
c) Issues on happiness level

Perverted (often applied by Government bodies) Parameters of Success (compartmentalised approach with thrust only on quantities)

a) More (unused-useless) infrastructure:
b) Hospitals
c) school buildings
d) more
   i) doctors
   ii) lawyers
   iii) litigations
   iv) police stations

   v) roads and bridges (which are not used)
   vi) consumption (more junk food)

e) less
   i) biodiversity (receding of groundwater, etc.)

Wardha Plan for Action

Main Characteristics of Wardha

1. It is one of the most backward, smallest Districts.
2. It has the highest rate of farmers suicides.
3. It is the only District in the State where prohibition is in force for the last many decades.
4. It has the highest numbers of local newspapers.
5. It is one of the most unwanted places for postings of civil servants, where mostly the officers prefer to stay in Nagpur and go and come back daily.
6. The Government finds not many willing takers for senior appointments for this so-called highly politicised District where each and every nook and corner is supposed to be full of politicians. Since Gandhiji, Vinobaji and others had a solid impact before and immediately after Independence, while the legacy continues, albeit weaker and weaker, the third raters, failures and mafias seem to have taken over most of the institutions and big chunks of the civil society.
7. The so called "Wardha Plan on Gandhian Lines", composed by the Planning Commission, Government of India, two decades back, seems to have become totally rut and out of date. It is worth questioning under the Right to Information Act, about the impact, the cost and the way this Plan has been implemented, and what are the results. According to our information, nothing worthwhile has been done. There are innumerable

instances where public money has been squandered ruthlessly, with impunity, and also without any control.

8. The so-called planning process is nothing but the distribution of funds to the elected representatives for their arbitrary distribution and to a select few.
9. The whole economy of the District is around cotton, pulses, wheat, milk, and hardly any organised, public, and/or private industry except Lloyds exists in the District.

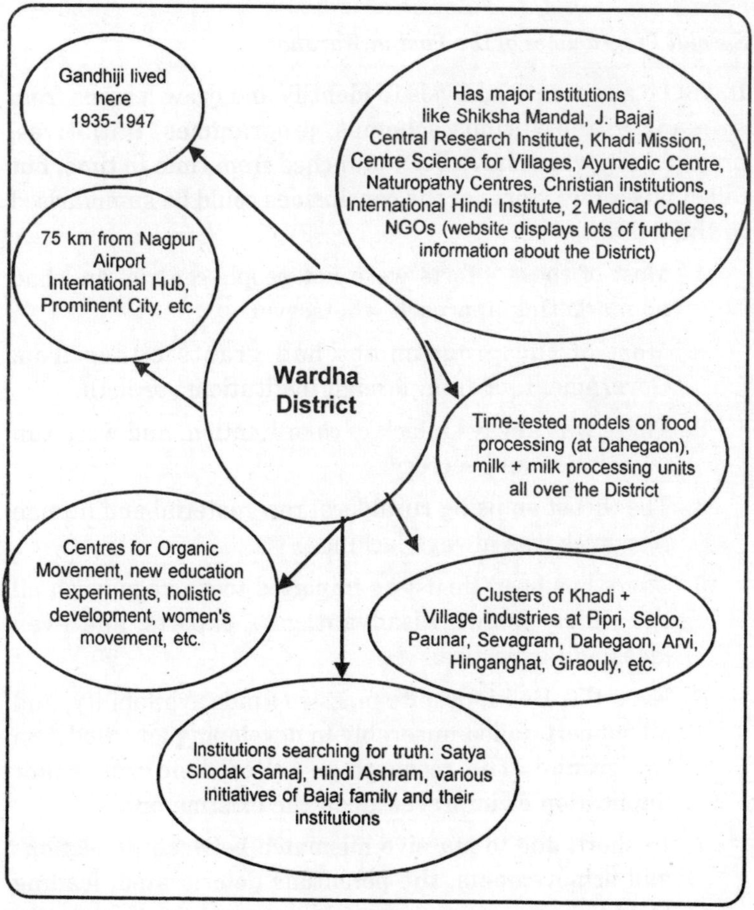

Some of the special contents of these programmes have been around holistic development, environment protection, cluster-oriented, self-employment, self-sufficiency, non-violent, and holistically oriented. It is a pity that despite many good intentions and successes, many of these programmes have not succeeded further. There is a lot of infrastructure, buildings, guesthouses, in most of these institutions, but due to lack of clarity, of proper aims and objectives, visions, and proper attention to HRD with marketing thrust, it is a District of hopeless situation and despair.

Special Programmes of the Past in Wardha

It will be a separate analysis to identify and draw lessons from so many of the various schemes, programmes, initiatives, projects, etc. which have been launched from time to time, but failed miserably. Some of the conclusions could be summarised in the follows:

1. Most of these efforts were not people-centric, and had no marketing approach whatsoever.
2. Most of the programmes had grants either from Government, or from foreign institutions, or both.
3. There was always a lack of co-ordination, and were run in isolation and secrecy.
4. The thrust on using rural/local raw material and human resources was always lacking.
5. There has been thrust on imported technology (with all the widely known disadvantages), exports, and even ideas and expertise.
6. Even IIT, Delhi, despite massive funds availability, and all support, failed miserably in developing any model on the ground. The research so called done was either duplication or improved upon the existing one.
7. In short, due to massive mismatch between projections and achievements, the potentials deteriorated, leading to more and more hypocrisy, money in the wrong

pockets, tremendous wastage of resources, and creation of infrastructure not suitable for the masses at the grassroots level. It is a pity that despite a very good connectivity of rail and road and air transport, and the rich history of the place and the con sequent goodwill of so many saints and wise people, the leadership, the financiers, the politicians, the institution holders, failed completely in showing to the nation and the world the relevant and pertinent model of development which could have been set up.

Suggested Parameters of Success for the Wardha Plan

1. Keeping in mind the unique features and characteristics, it is important that any plan develops on challenges of our time, and also of the future. It must also involve all those concerned, i.e. women, youth, all those neglected and till now not involved, so far.
   a) Hence, it must have conceptual clarity.
   b) Providing skills + skill upgradation.
   c) Must meet the challenges of market + consumers
   d) Must have replicability, self-sustainability, environmentability, and automatic upgradeability.
2. Hence, by using the unused, or marketing the unmarketed, it is possible to develop cluster-based, cost-effective, entrepreneur-realising initiatives by encouraging progressive, competent leadership.
3. There is urgent need to consider the following Plan on:
   a) Learning lessons from past efforts, investments, initiatives, and plans. This is essential to understand holistically the good and bad aspects of the past so that mistakes can be avoided from the very beginning and better planning processes are initiated.
   b) All the position- and resource-holders need to converge to understand their vision, perceived

problems, and potentials. This is to unearth hidden potentials without wasting time and resources.

c) Self-employment, viable investment, and policy packages with thrust on cluster-based, marketing-driven, turnkey consultancies, need to be evolved.

d) A cadre of turnkey consultants and self-employed change agents with a new system of professional training/apprenticeship based upon Rashtrasnt Tukadoji Maharaj Jeevan Shikhsan Abhiyan, organised by the Nagpur University, needs to be fully operationalised, by associating educational and other institutions without any delay.

e) In this process of holistic change, the "Open Letter to the Planning Commission, Government Of India, Fingers to "Fist", needs to be kept in mind, since the changing of mindset, professionalism, operationalisation of wisdom, need a radically different, unconventional approach to face the challenges of globalisation.

f) Banks, insurances, retired people, and community-based institutions (CBIs), can play a very important role in developing new models of development.

g) Hence, both bureaucrats, NGOs, market forces, IT companies, etc., all should pool their resources, knowledge, and experiences to bring out widely acceptable, functionable models of development.

h) Type of projects which can be considered include:

    i) raw-material-based,

    ii) skill-based,

    iii) marketing-based

    iv) export-based,

    v) holistic-based

steps.

i) We consider the following schemes suitable for Wardha:

1. Cotton to garments.
2. Milk and dairy-based products.
3. Herbal-based enterprises.
4. Education, training, technology- based ventures.
5. Fruit and other productivity-linked rural raw-material-based ventures.
6. Marketing-linked enterprises.
7. Tourism, clusters, technology and Gandhian spiritually-linked investments opportunity creation.
8. Since Gramdoot has already created IT-based self-employment infrastructure in rural areas, we can build upon these.
9. The ultimate test of development is the happiness-based, nature-oriented, efficient technology, and self-governance type of initiatives. So long as the planning, funding, training, and governance are done from outside and from above, the fate of all these measures is bound to be gloomy or disastrous.
10. Hence, a steering group is to be inducted in which all constructive forces will join hands and brains to bring out the best in all efforts (striving for excellence!).
11. *Preventive steps against farmer's suicides*: On the background of rising numbers of suicides among farmers it is essential that the future links for the development plan of Wardha District are able to encompass this aspect also. Many feel that by giving one lakh rupees to the deceased families, some consolation is provided. There may be some cases of drunkards, extremely mentally or

otherwise sick people, lunatics, etc. also committing suicide, or even getting murdered undetected. However, one fails to understand why this matter is not at all being examined from the holistic angle. At all levels, there seem to be allergies against examining the issue from all angles, as it would be essential. It is not only a question of non-remunerative prices for the agricultural products, but also wrong planning, training, mindset and attitudes, social pressures and stigma, and wrong prescription in dealing with the problems. Various initiatives in the sector of ginning, in animal husbandry, irrigation, fertilisers, cost reduction, organic farming, organic processing, etc., seem to have totally failed, and many of the mentioned issues have never even been implemented.

a) All these cast doubts on the motives and sincerity of all those who should matter. Many feel that the people have been baking their breads on the deaths of innocent, poor, deprived, ruralites. The entire system seems to be devoid of sensitivity and genuine concern for good governance. The so called "WARDHA PLAN on Gandhian lines" by Planning Commission has just become another fund-distributing and looting instrument.

b) It is high time that cluster-based rural activisation processes through sustainable self-employment, self-reliance, viable investment, using the un-used and massive thrust on rural galvanisation are initiated.

c) The leadership issues at the grassroots and using manpower with Gramdoot calls for innovative, creative, unconventional, future-oriented synergy-based steps. This is possible and imperative if anything at all should change for the better.

Offer by the International Institute for Holistic Research and Voluntary Action (IIHRVA):

a) As an action-oriented institution of global concern, we offer our expertise and services to converge the ongoing efforts with the Government, non-Government and also, people-based institutions.

b) The challenges of the future competition can only be tackled by ancillarisation, clusters, and timely, efficient monitoring.

c) The skill-provision, skill up-gradation, and cost-reduction combined with quality enhancement, productivity enhancement, customer orientation, and marketing strategies, have to be strongly insisted upon by involving all people concerned.

d) All students need a re-orientation for the necessary change of mindset and attitude by personality development, sensitisation, feeling responsible for the society, grassroot orientation, holistic and action-oriented view. We know very well that in the presently nearly hopeless state of the educational system this would be an uphill task, but: do we have another, better option?

e) The credit-deposition-ratio concept of the banks has to be efficiently taken care of. It is a fact that efforts made in the past were very superficial, slipshod and altogether futile. With better planning, innovative experimentation and by involving the uninvolved, why can't we have better and sustainable humane models for development?

f) A lot of resources have been frittered or squandered away in the name of so-called efficient technology. While repeating the problem over and over again is altogether futile, it is high time that the so-called reservoirs of technology are re-designed to suit the expectations of the users.

g) *On problem-solvers versus problem-creators or carriers-of doubts:* Unfortunately, those who have the capacity and also, the will to solve problems, are normally not in positions to put their ideas into practice. On the contrary, most of the time we find the problem-creators or else, the carriers-of-doubts in the decision-making positions so that either nothing moves or, even worse, good ideas are suppressed or ridiculed. The term "impossible" or the phrase "this was always done like this" is much in vogue and hinders all progress. Under this conditions, it is worth learning from the "in-spite-of"-performers with their willpower and ability to endure, the track-record-holders, and similar models.

h) *Role of efficient communication and role of Gandhian philosophy:* It is pitiable that especially in Wardha District, Gandhian principles of de-centralisation, involving all those concerned, evolving development measures from grassroot level, humane education and other values, are not at all taken up.

Summing Up

The distinct, unique position of Wardha requires a highly different approach to meet the challenges of holistic, sustainable human development in the era of globalisation. There are enough hope models being performed by ground-based doers. The mindset of the established institutions needs to be altered to learn lessons for action for the benefit of the masses. Symptoms like farmers suicides, increasing Naxalism, loss of faith in Governments and their institutions, and the overall widespread frustration within the youths indicate a cancerous disease of the whole society.

There is no shortcut for correcting the situation. It can only be done by a holistic approach to action, based upon the philosophy of Mahatma Gandhi and other likeminded thinkers.

What is required is conviction and sincere search for betterment. Unless this is done immediately, the future will not pardon all those who have knowledge and expertise to act and do not do it, but all those innocent souls who never had any ways and means to change their fate, will suffer along with. We will not let that happen!

Wardha has previously been a place of vision in action where even today many models of hope are more or less kept up. The inability of the National Planning Commission to fulfil the task of showing models of hope can be successfully done by people and institutions in and around Wardha if they see the challenges of our time and look inside it with an open mind. Hence, let us hope the poor and the deprived do not have to undergo prolonged sufferings because of the insensitivity of those in power and authority.

Irmel V. Marla/Dr. Kamal Taori

Training Modules—Train-the-Trainers (TtT)

The following graph depicts our flexible training system of "Leadership Modules", designed by and conducted through the International Institute for Holistic research and Voluntary Action:

Other (Customisable) Modules

a) Time-planning (time-management) and monitoring (milestones system)
b) Holistic Planning and Implementing (inclusive planning)
c) Evaluation of
    i) Plans
    ii) Implementation
    iii) After-surveys
d) Customised leadership assessment and trainings
e) Change of mindset and attitudes towards cost consciousness, quality consciousness, and reliability

Marla/Taori ***May, 2010***

Plan of Action for enhancing Rural Entrepreneurship: Offer for Cooperation to the Legislators of (XXX)[10]—suggestions for non-violently and sustainably solve the Naxal/Maoist issues:

Submitted to several State Governments

We came to know with great satisfaction that you are putting deep interest in holistic sustainable development, and we are looking forward to meeting you, sharing your experiences and, surely, your interest in the work we are doing, especially in view of the dire need to enhance entrepreneurship in rural areas on a sound footing, independent from grants and subsidies, and thus sustainable. In this context, we offer a Concept-cum-Action Plan to deal with the so-called Naxal/ Maoist problem, as we perceive the highly escalated violent situation as one where the people at grassroot level are sandwiched between two powerful forces. This "Sandwich situation" leads to utter misery, as, frankly speaking, both powers are only up to destroy each other without taking into account the plight of the people.

We developed various holistic "Models for Replication" which can be implemented to bring about viable changes in the village economy, and leading to an overall welfare of all and to take up successfully the challenges of our time.

Essentially, the rural areas have been neglected since Independence, and we have to pay a dire price now. Not only teachers and doctors refuse to do service in rural areas, but also our industries go to these areas only when they are lured by special incentives, like the SEZs[11]. To our opinion, the concept or SEZs is utterly wrong and highly exploitative as taxpayer's money is used to provide huge advantages for already highly profitable enterprises. No wonder that in all the areas where the local population is neglected and/or exploited, anti-democratic forces can achieve foothold, or else, they can wield power—all to the disadvantage of the grassroot people. To quote Karl Marx: *They have nothing to lose than their shackles*, and they are shackled from both the sides!

We developed "Models for Replication" aimed at developing rural entrepreneurship as against the evil system of grants and subsidies.

The International Institute in close cooperation with Rural Business Hub Foundation India as its executive partner put its emphasis uncompromisingly on Holistic Approach to Sustainable Development.

In this context, we developed a range of 'Models for Replication' to be implemented in rural areas.

We send you a selected range of "Models for Replication" which can be included into an Action Plan for enhancing sustainable development through various suitable methods. Our "Model" system has the unique feature that it can be easily adjusted to the varying local conditions without having to change the whole Action Plan.

There cannot be any doubt that it is the task of the hour to bring about viable change of mindset and conditions, especially in rural India, and that this change has to imply environment protection as one of the foremost parts of any activity.

Our suggestions contain the Following Main Features:

1. *Inclusive and convergence-led planning, taking the village as a base.* On the basis of these findings, we make it one of the most important features of our approach to include the villagers themselves from the first step of planning onwards: they know best what is possible from

their angle and also, what they are prepared to invest. We insist on 'investment' from the side of the concerned villagers as only with this pre-condition we can develop a quality consciousness and the scope for sustainability.

We researched various poor conditions in rural areas from a holistic, business-oriented angle and found that there is an overall lack of systematic planning, lack of coordination from the side of the administration in their support efforts, and the lack of future-oriented management, using suitable technology, like IT support for information and marketing approach.

2. *Assessing and identifying the potential of the village, like human resources and natural resources by the villagers:* The villagers have to assess and identify all potential available in their village, be it human resources (skills, knowledge, experiences), be it labour force, and also the natural resources: water, plantation, actual condition of all existing activities (like animal husbandry, etc.), village industries and services.

   In this context, all involved also have to assess specific problems which have to be tackled, like water resources and conservation, forest protection including support for tribal population, type of agriculture and animal husbandry, and also scope for change in behavioural patterns, education, health and productivity.

3. *Identifying un-used or under-used potentials, like buildings, equipment, etc.* Usually, in our villages we find lots of un-used, or under-used potential, mostly leftovers from earlier "development projects" which have failed. In the case of building and/or equipment, we, together with the villagers have to assess and decide if such resources can be made to good use (like buildings could be converted into sheds for animals, into godowns for products, or into halls for village industries, as workshops, for services, etc.). Normally, in the case of buildings, they are owned by the village authorities, and it is often a relatively small amount of money involved to renovate them and make them functional.

Another source of unused or under-used potential are knowledge and experiences of people having been trained earlier and, due to failure of a "project", are now without work or else, they cannot apply their knowledge and skills anymore. These can be tapped and further improved.

4. Assessing the scope for viable enterprises, like *Team Management* (for agricultural units, renewable energy plants, 'waste to wealth' units, lakes and fisheries, etc.) and *marketing opportunities.*

   By analysing the present conditions, decisions have to be made by the villagers on the type of activities and enterprises in the future: certain problems like availability of water, raw material, and fodder, have to be discussed so that either the problems will be solved or else, the type of activities has to be changed.

   We have to find out if our model for "Team Farming" can be adopted so that several farmers are managing their enterprise together, with the support of suitable IT and the proper marketing analyses and information. The idea is that several small landholders club together to make the agricultural (or any other activity) a viable venture. The "Team"Training could be taken over by the Institute/ RBHFI, and suitable villagers can be specially trained for future monitoring and keeping up a high level of quality performance.

   For example: If several villages would club together and build up viable animal husbandry enterprises, they could employ a veterinary doctor locally, exclusively for their needs, and this doctor should be well versed in natural medicines as opposed to chemical medication which is poisoning both the animals and the consumers of the goods.

   Another example: If several villages would club together in establishing a plant for renewable energy from biomass technology, all would benefit. It would be run on proper business lines with good revenues for all stakeholders; there would be sufficient and affordable energy for all activities in the villages; the plant would provide jobs for many people; training and qualification in maintaining and running the plant would be given to local people, and, last but not least, principles of environment protection would be put into practice, thus educating the whole area

5. *Plan of Action comprising the above-mentioned issues, the methods of implementation and the role players.* On the basis of the above-mentioned information, data, findings, discussions, and ideas together with the villagers and, preferably, with village and district elected bodies and administrative authorities, an Action Plan for Change would be designed.

   This Action Plan contains the steps to be taken, the investment plan, the people involved, and the training necessities. It also describes the ways and means in which the elected bodies and the administrative authorities will render their support.

   We are of the opinion that the villagers could thus establish future-oriented, viable enterprises which would make them independent from grants and subsidies, and would provide good revenues for them, and also create jobs locally.

   The Action Plan also shows the possibilities of convergence, and the cost reduction through systematised coordination and clubbing of resources. It shows further how reliability and quality consciousness concerning the work and the products are trained and monitored to keep up a high quality level and improve further. Especially in view of marketing efforts, the necessities of quality consciousness and reliability are of utmost importance. Many initially good business ventures failed miserably because reliability concerning quality level, timings and coordination destroyed marketability of products and services.

   Depending on the local conditions, needs, ideas and possibilities concerning both human and financial resources, the Action Plan will be implemented by the people and monitored by the IIHRVA/RBHFI with Government agents initially, till local people will be trained and qualified to take over the tasks. These "Change Agents" could be self-employed village persons (male or female) who are personally accepted by the villagers, who show dynamism and determination in their performance, and who are able to be qualified in the required fields, like IT and marketing issues. Thus, we can establish a "Self Employed Change Entrepreneur (SECE) [12]" who will assist the villagers in many future oriented ways.

The Action Plan will meticulously contain the different steps to be taken—after our 'Milestone Method' —, the specific phases and the parameters of success after which the reviews and evaluation is executed. The Milestone Method ensures that mistakes can be detected and changed in time so that later failures at crucial points of development are avoided.

Financial matters will be completely transparent, and involved villagers will be undergoing training in accountancy, tax and banking issues, according to their abilities. No outside power should interfere, even in the case of initial funding by government sources. Any initial funding should later turn into a revolving fund for other ventures in the village; otherwise the ventures should be financed by proper banking channels and methods.

Who will All benefit from this Scheme?

a) The entrepreneurs
b) The PRIs
c) Banks
d) Insurance companies
e) Organic farming propagators (and the people, as food poisoning is avoided)
f) IT based enterprises developers—taking suitable IT to the villages
g) Unemployed youth

h) Village and district planners and Institutions

i) 6Ps (9Ps) propagators[13]

j) A change of mindset and attitudes will take place: from grants & subsidies-led to viable, SME development.

k) A change from lethargic attitudes on the side of villagers, and attitude of negligence on the side of the administration towards action-oriented, vibrant, future-oriented, responsible mindsets

l) Transparent and self-supporting, decentralised system of accountability on all sides will be established.

m) The Government as such through increase of revenues

n) The Legislative together with the respective Ministries through viable Models for Replication and their success in the interest of the people

o) Increased export opportunities through improved quality level, reliability and, preferably, natural, healthy products

Who are going to be the Losers?

a) The inefficient and corrupt in all sectors

b) The stereotyped minds and the status-quoists

c) The exploiters on all sides: locally, District-wise, and State-wise, in Government and in the private sectors

d) The politicians and political parties who are interested in keeping the villagers dependent

e) The propagators of "urbanising rural areas" (a most deceitful concept where the villagers would be further exploited and suppressed)

f) All suppressors, oppressors, and mafias of all sorts

We are prepared to take up the implementation of an "Action Plan for Holistic Viable Rural Entrepreneurship" if the Legislators and/or the Government are willing to provide the needful support.

As an outlay, the following shows the main activities our IIHRVA/RBHFI could put into the efforts, i.e. our Unique Selling Points.:

Basic Approach

a) Un-conventional, holistic approach to research, analysis, planning and implementation

b) Uncompromisingly result-oriented (as against procedure-oriented = bureaucratic way)

c) Uncompromisingly inclusive, following cluster-approach for viable businesses

d) Against the evil system of grants + subsidies which pressed rural population into a state of beggardom, rendered them helpless and hopeless, deepened an inferiority complex, and killed all self-initiative, a pre<-condition for entrepreneurship

e) Marketing-oriented (customer-oriented, exploring markets, using IT)

f) Profit-oriented (non-exploitative)

g) Environment-oriented (incl. health issues and education).

Methods and Tools for Implementation

a) 6Ps System[14] for sustainable rural development (9Ps)

b) Module system for:
   - i) Leadership training: emphasis on holistic change
   - ii) Assessing local potential
   - iii) Entrepreneurship

c) Environment issues
   - i) Water
   - ii) Waste to wealth
   - iii) Renewable energies
   - iv) Organic farming

d) Enhancing self-employment and employability
   - i) Dual System of Vocational Education (DSVE)[15]
   - ii) Team farming
   - iii) Team service

iv) SECE (IT-oriented)[16]

v) Suitable IT for the villages

e) SoEZs[17] (as very different from the SEZ concept).

We would like to emphasize that every MLA could obtain an Action Plan for his/her respective constituency. We offer to make a presentation for further clarification, information and eventual cooperation.

Looking forward to your reply, with kind regards and best wishes, yours

Irmel V. Marla
(Sociologist/Anthropologist)

Dr. Kamal Taori
(IAS, rtd.)

Letter submitted to the KVIC Board, containing suggestions for immediate steps to improve the performance:

Dr. Kamal Taori, Vidyarthi
Member of KVIC Board

July 12, 2008

Suggestions for Activating Relevancy and Enhancing Viability of KVIs

In view of urgent need for drastic steps towards catapulting KVIC into the twenty-first century, I suggest the following for consideration in the meeting of the All India Khadi and Village Industries Board, on July 16, 2008 at Delhi:

1. Urgent need to overhaul the training centres making them into viable enterprises.
2. Urgent need to overhaul the infrastructure and customer approach of the Khadi Gramudyog Bhavans all over the country, making the outlets into viable enterprises. Personnel especially has to be trained in customer-orientation/customer-satisfaction.
3. Big KVIC institutions as centres of excellence by diversification, customer-orientation, re-orientation towards natural designs through 6Ps (Public Private Panchayat Profitable Progressive Partnership). In this context, we suggest to make part of the salary dependent on the sales skills/performance of the respective sales

person. Also, a "team premium" (yearly) should be given to the sales personnel of specific outlets after pre-fixed parameters of performance. Regularly appreciate good performance by introducing transparent, easy-to-handle parameters-cum-tools and publicise accordingly and also, document by SOPP (Series of Performer's Presentation).

4. Holistic approach by converging all existing material and immaterial (skills and knowledge, etc.) resources and also, identifying and developing hidden potentials.
5. Developing suitable IT tools for enhancing communication between local producers/consumers/ markets/outlets, researching consumer needs, and also, tools for efficient marketing strategies nationwide and international.
6. Making use of all opportunities given by globalisation by networking efficiently in international markets and sharing nature-oriented manufacturing.
7. "Waste to Wealth": encouraging renewable energy units (local and area-wise) by setting up biomass and similar technology for self-employment and job creation, at the same time living and producing cost-savingly, and actively protecting environment.
8. Introducing overall transparency and accountability by using proper tools and suitable IT at all levels.
9. Strengthening the Confederation of Village Industries through involving grassroot people and institutions in all policy and decision-making processes, making good use of suitable IT communication tools which will enhance speed and overall efficiency.
10. All programmes of this Ministry must be linked up with Panchayati Raj institutions to successfully deal with the above mentioned areas of serious concern.

Dr. Kamal Taori, Vidyarthi

Remark by the authors: It is almost needless to say that hitherto none of the suggestions was taken up in earnest, and, realistically, we do not expect serious actions. But, as is our commitment, we will develop other wake-up calls to bring about the necessary change.

India cannot afford the luxury to neglect the immense potential of business opportunities which are buried in our rural areas, lest our economy will suffer terribly—not only half the population! — and we will take a backseat in global sustainable development.

Open Letter to the Planning Commission, Government of India "Fingers to Fist"

Respected Ahluwaliaji,

We are part of various institutions who are seriously concerned about the way planning in this great country is being done and monitored. The experience of five decades of planning leaves no-one in doubt that the planning processes have pathetically made people totally dependent either on Government or God.

All established institutions which were supposed to facilitate people's self-reliant economy and self-sustained livelihood, have been destroyed. This has led to over-dependency and loss of confidence at the grassroots level. Needless to say, the signs of disaster from a holistic view are clearly visible as part of farmer's suicides, diminishing water-level, overpopulation, loss of bio-diversity and unconcerned heartless governance, leading to overall insecurity and devastating law-and-order situation.

All this, we believe, is directly attributable to the type of planning this country has experienced since formation of Planning Commission. We also feel that in-sensitised and unrealistic planning models and processes have created a situation where the whole country is bound to further dis-integrate, and polarisation on the bases of caste, creed, politics, etc., is leading to the looting of resources by the organised and those in power.

The Planning Commission of the Government of India and the States are directly facilitating the exploitation of the masses by the organised with impunity, without mercy. Many of the laws enacted for developing the country on sound democratic and civilised lines, seem to be directly or indirectly supporting the exploiters due to the inherent weaknesses of the planning processes.

All this is because the planning process has become totally outdated, insensitised, unrealistic and devoid of ground realities. There is a lot of infrastructure like, for example, schools, hospitals, guesthouses, tourist places, industrial estates, godowns, training centres, Government staff, research centres, marketing clusters, etc., which are lying underutilised or even worse, totally un-used. All the documents brought out by the Planning Commission and the Ministries seem to be repetitive, stereotyped, and do no talk of success parameters, outstanding achievements, cost-reduction efforts, properly utilising staff, and using everything which is unused, or even marketing the unmarketed.

We are offering a few suggestions which, if implemented, can definitely benefit the masses and ushering in an era of self-reliance, entrepreneurial spirit, and an overall capacity enhancement to face the challenges of globalisation.

Plan of Action

1. All Ministries and Departments must be forced to reduce at least 10 percent of their budget and also, their staff by re-structuring and re-organising the infrastructure of workforce and workplaces.
2. Ministries must be forced to identify the best and least priority program/expenditure, design it people-centric at grassroot level and involve the Public-Private-Partnership (PPP) model.
3. To shift from charity to self-reliance and confidence-building processes, training and turnkey consultancy are imperative. Encourage professional bodies like chartered accountants, all-India-change-providers, to take up the challenges and make our economy competitive.
4. Self-employment, viable investments and policy packages are the crying need of the hour. Panchayati Raj

institutions, NGOs, IT-providers, banks, all professional training institutions, and all media should join hands to powerfully converge and trigger off sustainable human development. The issues of the massive problem of credit deposit ratio and funds for small and rural enterprises as a part of viable investments in clusters, requires a new, holistic approach. By using models like "Gramdoot" of Wardha, it is possible to achieve the effect of "low cost–high impact–sustainable quality system development".

5. The planning processes must encourage vision in action, creativity, self-initiative, at the Village and Block levels. This means planning from bottom-up by the people concerned instead of top-down. The around 500 Joint Secretaries and around 105 Secretaries to the Government of India, coming from all the Services, but mostly from IAS, have to assess and put forward the problems of their assignments and seek solutions from the Planning Commission.
6. The greatest problem is the lack of coordination, corruption, low quality level of leadership in institutions and politics. This leads to the mindset and consequent work-culture of submissiveness, bureaucratised, compartmentalised, and finally totally stale performance. We need efficient, inbuilt systems in the planning and monitoring systems which encourage viable business models by involving banks and professionals and all those uninvolved till now.
7. Integration and harmonisation of organisations based on holistic approach and action compel us automatically to involve community-based, religion-based, and spiritually-based institutions to pool their knowledge and experiences to develop marketing-oriented employment programmes.
8. The total diversity of Indian conditions would require us to learn from the European Union. More and more liberalisation, free trade and movement, simplification of laws and rules combined with grassroots empowerment policies, would make India instantly

vibrant, transparent and thus, in the monger run, corruption-free.

9. In all programmes where 100 percent grant is being given, more and more thrust must be on involving the corporate sector and also, turnkey change providers. Innovative suggestions, experiments and practicable models must be recognised and encouraged.
10. Despite our over-dependency on All India Services and also, on Government bureaucracy, massive problems in the quality of education, return on investment, health, roads, bio-diversity, overall infrastructure, energy consumption and energy-losses, waste management, gender sensitivity, etc., continue to be serious. This means, MPs, MLAs, and other elected representatives of the people, together with political parties, and IT professionals, need to be made accountable and professional in a coordinated way. Planning processes must induce improved leadership performance by the elected representatives to face the challenges of globalisation efficiently.
11. Holistic approach to grassroots activisation and operationalising change requires an open and vibrant mindset. Holders and replicators of traditional knowledge and wisdom need to be incorporated into all planning processes. The Western models of planning and development are not apt to the conditions we face in India. Thus, we urgently have to design our own efficient model of planning and monitoring.
12. There is the urgent need to re-define development, employment standards, GDP, natural resources management, success parameters, and even minorities and backward status. This way, we have to re-define our reservation policy and also, the overall performance/ accountability standards.
13. Can we neglect further Gandhiji's and Vinobaji's visions of a vibrant and powerful, egalitarian India based upon de-centralisation, peace and non-violence which would offer equal and affordable opportunities to everybody?

Hence, there is the need to re-plan the entire planning based upon the basic principles of humanity, convergence, laws of nature, human shortcomings and also, their aspirations to grow.

14. NRIs, retired persons, teachers, self-help groups, professionals, etc., can play a very important role, provided the planning processes involve and encourage them to make an impact by convergence and by qualified, transparent, easy-to-handle (self)grading systems.
15. The indicators of disaster from the holistic view are very clearly visible all around us. No wonder that one-third of the Districts in India are already under Naxalite impact, other areas are under other threats and, if this continues unabatedly, the entire India will be under the threat of chaos and Mafia influence in no time. Hence, the holistic approach which encompasses all spheres of life, economy, governance, incentives, training, will bring out the best of the people and the nation on all levels. But, this would require a total change of mindset and attitudes based upon trusteeship and leadership.
16. Some programmes can be specially earmarked to be planned, implemented and monitored by local women's self-help groups. This could include latrines, sanitation, non-conventional energies, traditional medicines, education, micro-financing, animal husbandry, organic products, wholesome nutrition, etc., leading to better cost efficiency and also to more sustainability.
17. NGOs with IT and media qualifications can definitely converge in the "fingers-to-fist" approach. Self-grading and self–evaluation, self-monitoring, self-realisation, and self-reliance could ultimate lead to an improvement of the overall level of well-being and happiness. This means, all those planning processes which till now have killed people's self-initiative and have made them over-dependent either on Government or God, need to be ruthlessly discouraged and eradicated. A higher level of discussion, churning, publicity and an aggressive, transparent type of networking could kill this lethargy and bring forth vibrant activities.

18. Programmes like community policing, crime-free villages, initiatives for peace, creative planning, viable investments, environment protection, waste-to-wealth, cost consciousness and cost-reduction, de-centralisation in all spheres like planning, etc., need to be integrated with training and monitoring. The 29 subjects, earmarked for Panchayats by all the successive Governments, must be operationalised for better quality results. The real India has to empower all forces at grassroots level, and this is possible only by handing over completely and permanently, and not by delegation.
19. Many of the institutions funded to 100 percent either by the State Governments or the Centre, have long back outlived their utility and must be either closed down or else, turned over for good use to the PPP-model. Every Department must be forced to perform as good Government rather than Government in (their own) business.
20. The All India Services with all types of direct and indirect employees need to improve as real top class professionals who have taken oath to the Constitutions and not to individuals /bosses. This means a change of mindset on the one hand, and constant awareness of the original objectives for which that post or the respective position or organisation has been created. This is possible only by a qualified, functioning system of work evaluation and HRD tools in action. Those who want to try a different professional approach must be encouraged to quit or retire prematurely. Let them go on for corporate, or voluntary sector assignments or else, even study leaves or limited foreign assignments. The point is that after about 38 years of service, they have been working totally cut off from reality and from grassroots level conditions. Temporary, slipshod measures or blind activism to show off is not at all conducive and does not contribute to the welfare of the Nation. In all, there is dire need to overhaul the whole system of All India Services to make it democratically functioning and

transform it into a vibrant, dynamic driving force of sustainable change.

21. All the training centres need to be managed, run and developed on PPP basis by involving all those who have credible and active interest in this field. All productivity linked institutions must be made to perform by integrated systems capable of meeting the challenges of diverse country like India.

To sum up

We cannot neglect the pre-Independence promises, and the freedom fighters that had a clear vision of a holistic India. All the parties, people, leaders, office-bearers, have been merely talking about vibrant India, but the real challenge of operationalising a sustainable change is persistently left out. Let us share our problems of governance, planning, funding, work culture, etc. with the people. Let us ask the people for the best options and let them be closely involved in all processes of planning and implementation. The Government, whether it is Centre or State, cannot be the sole repository of knowledge, wisdom, best practices. This means the inducing of dynamics of change with broad-minded, holistic, transparent, and committed servants of the nation. Saving the nation from the looming disaster cannot be left to the disaster management centre of the Central and State Governments manned by bureaucrats or politicians. Each and everyone has to be fully involved and integrated to find lasting solutions for the problems of 120 crore people with all the (bio)-diversities. Let us act in a rationalistic, realistic, and professional way before it is too late.

The following signatories are committed volunteers to provide and facilitate turnkey consultancy, training, change, and tools for operationalising the above-mentioned suggestions professionally. The culture of repetitive mistakes, blaming each other for failures or poor/non-performance, and also justifying and finding excuses for this, need to be ruthlessly done away with at every level of Government. This is possible and also, imperative in the era of globalisation and, with it, the unavoidable necessity of localisation.

We firmly request the Hon. Deputy Chairman and all members of the Planning Commission to join hands with us in these efforts!

Please let us know if, when and what action will be taken.

January 26, 2007

International Institute for Holistic Research and Voluntary Action
Internationales Institut fuer holistische Forschung und Aktion
(India—Germany)
Irmel Marla (Chairperson)
Dr. Kamal Taori (Hon. Consultant)

Remark by the authors: This letter was not graced with even an acknowledgment. Our planners don't feel the need to improve, nor do they accept 'outside' suggestions.

Selected Training Programmes on Holistic Leadership conducted by the *International Institute for Holistic Research and Voluntary Action* in Collaboration with *Rural Business Hub Foundation India*

The International Institute conducts Workshops on Holistic Leadership in Modules. The advantage of this Module System lies mainly in its flexibility: for example, participants who are already experienced in leadership positions, can chose from the Modules those which are necessary and/or suitable for them; for others it might be important that they participate in the basic Module where key abilities for leadership development is assessed. Thus, the Module System provides customised training for the whole range of leadership levels.

Training Module on "Holistic Personality Development" (part of leadership training modules)

1. Assessing key abilities
2. Building up strengths
3. Realising and dealing with weaknesses
4. Building up overall self-confidence in identified areas of individual personality structure

Training-cum-Refresher-Workshop on Holistic Leadership for Leaders Who want to contact with Others

All good leaders who know about the moments and phases where they feel utterly alone, let down—either by their superiors or else, by their staff—and in this context, we emphasize the necessity of exchanging experiences with colleagues in an open atmosphere, and with the aims and objective of finding solutions for various problems.

Preferably, the platform for such an exchange should not be in the same workplace, and also, the colleagues should not be from the same department/company/institution.

Workshop on "Good Leadership"

1) What is your perception of "good leadership"?
   — Describe it in maximum three sentences
2) Which abilities do you have that makes you a good leader?
   — Describe maximum three attributes
3) Why do you want to be a leader?
   — Describe maximum three reasons

Questions

What makes you feeling uncomfortable (awkward, uneasy, etc.) because of other's behaviour towards you?

a) Describe your feelings, and how you deal with it.
b) Describe a practical experience.
c) What do you do / how do you behave to enhance motivation of co-workers?
d) How do you motivate yourself?

Information about the Twin Organisations, IIHRVA + RBHFI

Rural Business Hub Foundation India (RBHFI)

The concept of Rural Business Hub is very convincing and promising. It caters to the essential principles of:

a) Living and working in dignity
b) Enhancing quality of life
c) Triggering off self-initiative
d) Encouraging entrepreneurship
e) Enhancing employability
f) Bringing about sustainable rural development
g) Rendering perspectives and hope to the hitherto hopeless

The International Institute for Holistic Research and Voluntary Action (India-Germany) (IIHRVA), with its thrust on sustainable rural development independent from grants and subsidies, it is determined to contribute to the success of the RBH concept while putting all expertise and efforts into realising it.

We consider the RBH as a viable scheme, a Hope Model to be replicated all over rural India. In sharp contrast to the SEZ concept, we designed the SoEZ model.

In true holistic approach, encompassing all spheres of life while working for the necessary change in sustainably developing hitherto neglected strata of society, it brings them into the economic mainstream to successfully compete in the era of globalisation.

In order to put the concept of RBH efficiently into practice and also, to avoid previous failures with basically well designed Government schemes, we established the following:

Rural Business Hub Foundation India (RBHFI)

Which will facilitate and monitor the practical implementation of locally suitable measures.

The RBHFI puts main emphasis on:

a) action-oriented planning and processing
b) participatory, inclusive planning and action
c) focusing on grassroots level requirements
d) converging all resources available

e) assessing and evolving hidden or unused potentials
f) rendering high quality levels to professional education
g) making participatory education on all levels accessible for all
h) marketing the unmarketed

To achieve these aims and objectives, the RBHFI will use the services of the International Institute for Holistic Research and Voluntary Action (IIHRVA) which has the necessary expertise and provides the services needed, the essential preconditions for sustainability, like:

a) inclusive, aim-oriented planning
b) management-/leadership training
c) financial expertise
d) whole spectre of HRD tools

The RBHFI and also the IIHRVA, are not affiliated to any religious or political group or organisation.

Our holistic approach is uncompromisable, and we are determined to contribute to shaping a better society where religions and political opinions are not misused as tools for wielding power. They should take the place appropriate to them: as individual concerns, comprising individual beliefs and convictions, bringing like-minded people together.

In our holistic view, there is no right for imposing these individual concerns onto others. This is what makes a peaceful, humane society. This is our vision which we are pursuing with all efforts.

We forcefully strive for integrating the dis-integrated and to fight for a peaceful, egalitarian society where there is hope and scope for everybody according to potential and talents.

The RBHFI also will work on bridging gaps between hitherto estranged or uncoordinated resources, organisations, governmental bodies, NGOs, and all forces that are able to join hands in bringing about sustainable Rural Development. In this context, we developed our:

Holistic System of 6Ps

Public **P**rivate **P**anchayat **P**rofitable **P**rogressive **P**artnership which we follow in all our activities.

Shaping a liveable future for the neglected

Our networking activities are spread all over India, and are also internationally linked.

Together with the IIHRVA, we conduct international seminars, workshops, and conferences in India and in Europe, thus bringing people together and joining hands in contributing to shape an overall better, peaceful world where everybody can live without exploitation, fear and want, and where welfare for all becomes reality.

The RBHFI puts further emphasis on building up self-initiative and self-confidence in those who did not have a chance to develop these key abilities for entrepreneurship. We want all those working in the fields of Rural Development to shift from

Charity to **C**reativity, **C**apacity and **C**onfidence **B**uilding (Ch to CCCB).

and networking internationally.

Profile of IIHRVA

The International Institute for Holistic Research and Voluntary Action in Cooperation with Rural Business Hub Foundation India

Our Outlook, Holistic Approach and Practical Suggestions for Activities

Our International Institute is committed to a holistic, practice-oriented approach to development. We undertook thorough research especially on the phenomenon of lack of entrepreneurial spirit in villages and also, the contra-productive impact of dependencies from grants and subsidies on the underprivileged strata of our society. The most significant results we published in the recent book *Operationalising Holistic Human Development* (Marla/Taori, Concept Publishing

Company, New Delhi, 2007) while analysing some serious disastrous issues of the hitherto so called development, and presenting practical solutions. The farmer's suicide, loss of hope, increasing extremism, Naxalite's movement, water scarcity, loss of hope-generating models, corruption, wastages of Government funds, etc., have also been some of the areas of serious concern. We also felt that the stereotyped solution to these mind-boggling problems of our time cannot be solved by the well-known routine efforts. Hence, it is the right time to look beyond and identify potentials of networking with established performers to explore new and innovative convergence-based efforts for model building.

During our intensive work in and around Vidarbha, we have established a network with many performing institutions. They have been on their own, without any financial or even technical support from the Government, and still have established a unique position for themselves in diverse fields. Some of them have been already visited by us. We are confident that if we all network, discuss openly, frankly and fearlessly the potentials of working together, a new innovative, sustainable and urgently required mode of convergence, and cost-efficient, bankable, viable, models can emerge.

Hence, we have following suggestions as a Plan of Action:

1. *Media:* There are already networks of media persons all over Vidarbha, and, for this matter, all over India, who are either in villages or District or Block level. They have various skills of writing, visualising, documenting, interacting and marketing. They also have computer skills, know about market and marketing issues, and have a fair amount of closeness and contacts with local administration, including banks, police, market, local Panchayats, Blocks and various ongoing schemes of the Government which are well known to them They also have a good all-round communication infrastructure, and also attend frequent media and press conferences called by various interest groups. In short, they are ideal for being oriented to function as SECA, or Self-Employed Change Agents, whom we have mentioned in our book

for galvanising the rural economy. We call it a Marketing-Led Activisation Programme (in brief, for our purpose, we shall call it as MLA-P).

We also feel that the established media all over India must take a lead so that subsequent advantages could be operationalised in the same system by effective networking and lobbying for change by involving the grassroots workers and the qualified leaders.

2. *NGOs/PPEs:* We have good contacts and proper documentation of the Gramdoot model of Wardha which has been acclaimed as a great facilitator all over India, but nobody has come forward as yet to make it the tool of a Total Rural Activisation Programme (TRAP). It is high time that the expertise of them is shared with your rural press reporters so that they not only earn extra income as SECA (Self-Employed Change Agent), but also contribute to becoming a solid change agent to consolidate and activate the dormant rural economy.
3. *Finance:* We also have partners in the financial field, especially microfinancing, who have expertise in project making and evaluation for the banks. They are already approved as consultants with various banks and funding institutions. They are prepared to be our network partners in establishing relationships with funders on the one hand, and developing viable village activisation programmes on the other. We have already suggested to them to start a Rural Investment and Infrastructure Galvanisation Services (RIIGS), so that the greatest need of the rural sector could be met in the same system by following principles of sound banking and viable investment. This is very important if we want to compete and also develop replicable, transparent and viable projects for meeting the challenges of globalisation in the days to come.
4. *Coordination:* We are planning to establish a joint Steering Group under the chairmanship of a suitable volunteer. Since there are (for example) media offices in all the districts, and also a good training centre at

Nagpur, we could consider starting a training, motivation and consultancy centre on the above lines from there. The purpose is to use the under-used or, as our Company calls it, as "Marketing the Unmarketed", since so much is really unmarketed in India. We feel there is dire need to converge, properly coordinate and use all that is unused.

5. *Public Authorities/Bodies:* Since elected leaders at all levels have a lot of discretionary local developmental funds at their disposal, and often good proposals do not come, it will be our joint effort to develop convergenistic plans with the people and the NGOs. Here, ongoing programmes of the Central and State Governments could also be converged for better results.
6. *Volunteering:* Our Institute and the volunteers and experts working around it are willing and keen to offer their services and expertise at no cost, it will be our effort to bring various players on a common platform, so that we show some models of hope for others to come, examine and replicate them.
7. *Methods:* To achieve maximum success in our mission, we may operate all our programmes in viable clusters so that the monitoring of all the activities could be on a regular basis with timely correction mechanisation after a specific Monitoring Milestone Concept (MMC) developed by our Institute.
8. *Sustainability:* Programmes which have a solid investibility potential with adequate margin provision by the entrepreneurs are our priority. Our mission is to galvanise the rural economy and not waste our time and energy on duplicating ongoing programmes of the Government which are of basic priority for all important Government functionaries and, at the same time, have been utter failures in view of sustainability and viability. Anyway, by not competing and duplicating, we will achieve much in the field where the Government is not making any efforts, or these are new or untapped areas. Once activity generation picks up in the rural set-up, we

can be assured that the holistic development of the village would be a reality, which in turn benefit all the ruralites. This approach to MLA-P has not been tried anywhere in India and Vidarbha could be an ideal cluster to launch it with your active and full participation. Incidentally, our Institute has already done adequate ground level work to launch this appropriate programme which would lead to the following advantages:

a) We do not duplicate the ongoing programmes.

b) We have total convergence, and a marketing-led planning.

c) We use all unused, and implement with Public/Private Panchayat Partnership Principles.

d) We pool, "supplement" or compliment and do not duplicate.

   We do not neglect any future-oriented idea.

e) We depend upon local resources, skills, knowledge and technology by networking from grassroots level

f) Our special thrusts are on implementing the Dual System of Professional training (DSoVT), for enhancing the standards of employability and quality), environment protection, organic farming, renewable energies, value addition, local demands, clustering, cost reduction, and quality orientation (also in view of globalisation) with emphasis on self-employment.

g) Our priorities are for those disadvantaged in the society, performing Self-Help Groups, entrepreneurs, and those who have entrepreneurial spirit, and we reward performers.

h) We first present a Series of Performers (case studies) as replicable models, so that confidence is generated.

i) We network with local media, PRI, banks, trainers, so that duplication is avoided and proper coordination ensured.

j) We will document and replicate all our initiatives by training as many SECAs as possible, and by giving them functioning networks and a platform to address their grievances and eventual cases of harassment.

k) We will face the challenges of globalisation with all the means we realistically have at our disposal for saving local jobs and to save people from starvation and exploitation.

l) Our thrust is to shift from manipulative, secretive administration to transparent, participatory managerial changes, including single window services.

m) We will facilitate and encourage diversification in all sectors and build up confidence in capacity and productivity.

n) A new leadership style will be developed which is democratic, egalitarian, participatory, meritocratic, and conducive to civil society.

o) We will analyse policy, training, and networking issues in totality and design suitable models accordingly.

p) The middle classes at all levels of society have an active role to play in this context; we propagate a change of mindset and attitudes which have been neglected hitherto.

q) We will explore marketing potential with railways, airports, bus stations and seek the help of established institutions like Khadi and Village Industries Commission (KVIC) and others, so that they also shed their lethargy and become active partners in the change process for and with the masses.

r) Local schools, colleges, community based institutions, religion-based, and spirituality-based institutions are to be fully involved in our holistic, all-encompassing programme, provided they fit into our philosophy of transparency and viability.

s) Our efforts will lead to models for total, holistic reforms which no Government department can today even think of, or visualise, forget implementation altogether. This is because the whole structure of the Government is compartmentalised and bureaucratically suffocated which does not suit the developmental paradigm essentially required for sustainable, viable development in the interest of our people.

To sum up: It is high time that we network for replicable results to save the majority of our people from the imminent total, nearly unavoidable disaster. The only way out is to involve grassroots people, local institutions, include marketing-led activisation processes, and let all benefit by working hard. Let us be facilitators in this Herculean task of encouraging the rural masses to realise their true, unexplored real value, and contribute to bring them out of their beggardom, and to avoid more suicides as a first step to improvement. We are confident that there are many well-meaning and knowledgeable people in the country and abroad who would be glad to share their knowledge and skills in this national resurrection programme.

There is also an urgent need to take action on these lines because unless a programme with thrust on total transformation of villages is not launched as a part of benefit and self-reliance-led convergence, it will again fail. The SECA, and also the DSoVT as designed by us concern mostly the middle classes for their recruitment. They should be leaders of tomorrow for ensuring long-term sustainable change. As mentioned above, there is also a dire need to galvanise all the dormant systems at the district level and below by unleashing business-oriented initiatives. Hence, if you find the above outline convincing, we may organise a first brainstorming workshop on these lines at the earliest at Nagpur, Akola or Wardha as per your convenience. You may also share this letter with all those who could contribute in any way, including substantiated comments and constructive criticism with better options.

Our recent dialogues in Europe and Germany with various functionaries have also cemented our conviction that there is an urgent need to launch innovative experiments if we have to become a vibrant, humane society. Our rural areas need all attention to develop their potential into a big force, and this can be done only by the type of initiatives we have mentioned above. We suggest that you may also consider inviting volunteers for this programme propagate it. We are prepared to offer our Total Service Package to make a distinct dent in an otherwise dismal scenario.

Irmel V. Marla — *Dr. Kamal Taori (Vidyarthi)*
(Chairperson) — (Partner & Advisor)
International Institute for Holistic Research and Voluntary Action, India-Germany

Letter from International Institute for *Holistic Research and Voluntary Action* and *Rural Business Hub Foundation India* to:

To

Shri Yadav
Director of the Department of Institutional Finance
Government of Uttar Pradesh,
Lucknow

Dear Shri Yadav,

The Institutional Finance Department in a State like U.P. has a very, very important role to play in galvanising viable investment opportunities. While the credit deposit ratio of this State has laggered around 25 percent for the last many decades, it is heartening to note that in the last three years, it has moved up to around 45 percent. While various innovative and timely changes have contributed to this improvement, there is definitely need for paying attention to the points below for further improvement in this process.

Our interaction at various forums in and around the State of U.P. has convinced us that if coordinated and properly articulated policies are developed, there is scope for tremendous achievements. The following suggestions will go a long way in brining out the best of U.P.:

1. Fixed targets for each department for mobilising bank finance. The tendency to plan and implement all investment proposals only through Government departments must be discouraged, and private initiatives or Public-Private Partnerships (PPP), preferably the more efficient 6Ps (Public-Private-Panchayat-Profitable-Progressive-Partnership) must be insisted upon.
2. The mindset of public functionaries needs to be changed towards customer orientation and customer-friendly behavioural patterns as normality. At present, our bureaucrats treat customers as inferiors, almost as enemies who have to be put into place.
3. The same applies to time-wise performances of our public functionaries. As there is no proper work evaluation nor control, one can postpone work *ad infinitum*, thus creating a dependency of customers from the goodwill of the administrator, and, supports all types of corruption.
4. The overall work efficiency of the administration has to be enhanced by re-structuring the salary system. At present, a good or excellent bureaucrat is not appreciated against those who do their work deficiently, or even try to avoid proper working altogether. This is a highly de-motivating factor leading to frustration and lack of commitment (suitable models of pay structures linking performance and salary can be implemented by our Institute, adjusted to the possibilities within the given framework—by laws and otherwise - of payments).
5. Good leadership is widely missing. We consider this fact again as an issue of mindset which has to be changed and also, an issue of assessment of proper personnel selection.
6. The outdated (colonial) system of IAS/IPS/IFS has to be completely overhauled to cater to modern-times necessities. It is basically undemocratic and lacks all required flexibility. In the same way, in our highly specialised fields of administration, it is unthinkable that Officers can switch from one field of work to a completely different one and perform properly, not to speak of anything near excelling. Thus, a lot of harm is done in

both ways: to the officers who cannot keep their knowledge and skills updated for high performance, and to the people concerned who cannot get the service they deserve and pay for.

7. Banking institutions have a very difficult role to play. On the one hand, they have to satisfy the depositors at all times, on the other hand, the viability and the recoverability of the advances have to be always ensured. This is like tight-rope walking. By developing suitable packages or modules, and learning from successes and failures, suitable policy packages can be evolved to find appropriate ways and means for sustainable success.
8. Our contribution in the meeting held with the bankers, and the civil servants, also clarified our doubts regarding potential of developing bankable projects by involving all the departments of the State Government. The massive inefficiency, so obviously noticeable, can also be done away with by involving the departments in this exercise.
9. The head office of the bankers and their sensitivity in involving the borrowers in viable project-making, and marketing-led investment, can definitely enhance the credit-deposit-ratio.
10. The NRIs and the entrepreneurs of other states, having interest in the development of Uttar Pradesh, can play a very important role in bridging the gaps between the bankers and the ground realities. Suitable rewards and incentives, and recognition by independent evaluatory bodies, like our Institute, can enhance its credibility.
11. Cluster-oriented investment policies with backward-forward linkages have the potential of absorbing massive viable investments. To meet the challenges of globalisation also, this is the only option.
12. A training programme for Self-Employed Change Agents (SECA) and Self-Employed Organising Entrepreneurs (SEOE) will go a long way in developing efficient and easily accessible delivery mechanisms. Our Institute has developed special modules for these special training programmes, and, in collaboration with the Directorate

of Institutional Finance, we would like to launch these modules on self-study basis.

13. Panchayati Raj institutions, rural media, IT service providers, local infrastructure holders, and even community-based institutions, can play very important roles in enhancing c-dratio of a region.
14. Unused and highly under-used infrastructure needs to be made operationalisable by involving a blend of innovative, non-conformist, flexible policies.
15. With thrust on non-gender-biased, but focused on the underprivileged, environment-friendly clusters should be developed.
16. Our Institute has a panel of experts from banking and insurance sectors who, if given an opportunity, would like to network for achieving excellence on a very cost-effective basis.
17. There are many more areas which have to be taken up on a turnkey consultancy basis, provided suitable tie-ups, reliable coordination and support are ensured at District and State levels. It has been a great experience for us to interact with diverse groups for enhancing c-dratio.
18. We offer our services to organise training programmes for qualifying selected personnel in the above-mentioned fields and also, conceptualise schemes for turnkey consultancy including follow-up monitoring, assessing and evaluating viability of schemes, train-the-trainer courses for sustainability of change.

We thank the Director of the Department of Institutional Finance, Government of U.P., for giving us the opportunity to interact and learn from them. We look forward working with you on a long-term basis.

Irmel Marla
Chairperson

Dr. Kamal Taori
Partner & Advisor

International Institute for Holistic Research and Voluntary Action (India-Germany) in collaboration with *Rural Business Hub Foundation India*

March 6th, 2007

The following document gives information about the evaluation of a Workshop-cum-Brainstorming for Senior Officers of one of the State Government's departments, conducted by the Chairperson of the IIHRVA:

Notes

In Medias Res

1) *Areas of serious concern* mentioned by all participants (remark by one of the participants: "Everybody here is a PhD in problems,":
   a) Ideas cannot be realised because of lack of input.
   b) Time pressure when proper planning could avoid that.
   c) Frequent fluctuation of DGs creates void of orientation/perspectives.
   d) Lack of coordination with other departments.
   e) Work problem: propaganda instead of information.
   f) No work evaluation.
   g) No appreciation of work—no incentives for good/above average work, no consequences for under-performers.
   h) No targets, lack of orientation.
   i) No IT facilities (no computers, no internet access!).
   j) Decision-makers are not approachable.
2) *Need expressed for:*
   a) IT facilities—very much needed in view of work efficiency, and in view of globalisation
   b) Regular upgrading of knowledge + skills
   c) Orientation Programmes in: up-to-date communications (all media)
   d) Coordination of work with all authorities concerned
   e) Work appreciation, incentives
   f) Training in individual communication skills (negotiating, etc.)
   g) Setting target groups

h) Easing time pressure by timely planning wherever possible

3) *Analysis:*

a) An overall commitment to the work is to be stated. The Officers are:

i) concerned and serious about their work but, at the same time,

ii) they feel quite "left alone", mainly by their superiors, or

iii) by having to struggle with many adverse circumstances, like

iv) lack of electronic equipment,

v) lack of simple equipment for dealing with mass media (comm. technology),

vi) lack of coordination between different Departments or Ministries, or else,

vii) by the lack of orientation to target groups, and their

viii) feeling of lack of appreciation by their superiors.

b) These above-mentioned facts and feelings lead to under-performances, frustration, de-motivation, and finally to the mindset and attitude of relative passivity, thus harming efficient productivity.

c) A change of work conditions and also, as a consequence, changes of mindset and attitude is necessary to enhance the productivity of the Department and make it a dynamic, modern, powerful, convincing, viable enterprise with lots of potentials for the concerned State authorities.

4) *Solutions:* The International Institute for Holistic Research and Voluntary Action (India-Germany) offers to conduct the following Seminar Modules:

a) For the officers:

i) Self-motivation,

ii) Quality control,

iii) Training in communication skills (dealing efficiently with media),

iv) Information skills via all media (convincing strategies),

v) Cost consciousness,

vi) Change of mindset and attitudes.

b) For superiors:

i) Selected leadership issues (work appreciation, motivation, incentives, upgrading personnel skills, etc.)

ii) Organisation development (building up capacity pools, etc.)

5) In addition to the above-mentioned Training Modules, the analysis shows that an upgrading of the technical equipment is a must. In the era of globalisation, the ... department has to be linked up globally via Internet to continuously benchmark its own work and develop upgrading strategies if the State Government should be credibly inform the people and efficiently connect with them. Also, sharing experiences and information with colleagues in other States is quickly and efficiently established.

In the same way, the workplaces have to be modernised electronically so that valuable time and energy can be used for efficient production, thus reducing overall costs. In this context, comparatively simple equipment like proper recording and filming systems should be provided.

Concerning the infrastructure of the department, the DG should go into re-structuring the present organisational set-up with the aim of giving responsibilities for planning and co-ordinating to the officers within an appropriate framework. This would enhance motivation by a high level of job satisfaction. Work appreciation and also, dealing appropriately with under-performers should be done in view of good leadership.

Document of evaluation of a second Workshop-cum Brainstorming for Senior Officers of a State Government department, conducted by the Chairperson of the International Institute for Holistic Research and Voluntary Action:

Notes, Analysis + Solutions

In Medias Res

1) *Areas of serious concern* mentioned by all participants:
   a) No aims and objectives (no proper guidelines, i.e. no job description, but infrequent circulars and orders which are day-to-day reactions on external demands)
   b) Government gives this department lowest priority
   c) Problems with DMs
   d) Field officers have to cover too large areas—lack of transport facilities
   e) No infrastructure: local offices have no skilled staff
   f) No decision-making power for the officers ("no jurisdiction,
   g) No coordination with other department or Ministries
   h) No IT facilities (no computers for reports, etc., no internet access!)
   i) Problems of dealing with various different authorities at one time: local bodies, Forest Dept., Heritage Dept., Transport + Road department, Temple/Shrines/Mosques authorities, etc.
   j) No appreciation of work—no incentives for good/above average work, no consequences for under-performers.
2) *Need expressed for:*
   k) Regular upgrading of knowledge + skills (example: responsible for construction works, but lack of expertise, etc.)
   l) Orientation Programmes in: Planning, implementing, quality controls, information to tourists, tax/revenue issues (no appreciation of cost-conscious performance, and no consequences when money is squandered)

m) Coordination of plans/work with all authorities concerned

n) Responsibilities / decision-making for officers

o) Work appreciation, incentives

p) Training in communication skills (negotiating, etc.)

q) Setting aims and objectives

r) IT facilities missing or deficient: no suitable software, not linkages within the department, nor to external departments or other agencies.

3) *Analysis:*

a) An overall commitment to the work is to be stated. The Officers are:

i) concerned and serious about their work but, at the same time,

ii) they feel quite "left alone", be it in the field as such, or

iii) by having to struggle with many adverse circumstances, like

iv) lack of electronic equipment,

v) transportation problems,

vi) under-skilled field staff,

vii) lack of coordination between different authorities, or else, by the

viii) lack of orientation via aims and objectives and their

ix) feeling of lack of appreciation by their superiors.

b) The fact that all participants are of the firm opinion that the .... department has lowest priority in the Government, is deplorable.

c) These lead to under-performances, frustration, de-motivation, and finally to the mindset and attitude of relative passivity in the sense that visions and ideas are not developed which should be essential for proper functioning of the ..... department.

d) A change of work conditions and also, as a consequence, changes of mindset and attitude is necessary to enhance the productivity of the department and make it a dynamic, future-oriented, viable enterprise with lots of potentials for the welfare of the State.

4) *Solutions:* The International Institute for Holistic Research and Voluntary Action (India-Germany) offers to conduct the following Seminar Modules:

a) For the officers:

i) Planning, implementing,

ii) Quality control,

iii) Information skills via all media (to tourists),

iv) Cost consciousness (tax/revenue issues),

v) Training in communication skills (negotiating, etc.)

vi) Change of mindset and attitudes

b) For superiors:

i) Setting aims and Objectives (by involving all concerned)

ii) Selected leadership issues (work appreciation, motivation, incentives, upgrading personnel skills, etc.)

iii) Organisation development (re-structuring existing setups, work flow, coordination issues).

5) In addition to the above-mentioned Training Modules, the analysis shows that an upgrading of the technical equipment is a must. In the era of globalisation, the ... department has to be linked up globally if these fields in the State should be continuously developed as it could be.

In the same way, the workplaces have to be modernised electronically so that valuable time and energy can be used for efficient production, thus reducing overall costs. Concerning the infrastructure of the department, the DG should go into re-structuring the present organisational setup with the aim of giving responsibilities and decision-making power to the officers within an appropriate framework. This would enhance motivation by a high level of job satisfaction, giving opportunities to develop and implement new ideas, thus creating a multitude of driving forces for a booming, future-oriented tourism industry in the State.

6) There is urgent need to understand the challenges of globalisation. For a challenging and in many aspects difficult State like ..., we would like to provide turnkey consultancy services where the true performers can excel, and the non-performers can be motivated to perform or else, start performing. The challenges in the same system are to bring out the best in every individual and in all resources.

The Document Shows the Work and Ideas of the IIHRVA + RBHFI in Cooperation with Like-minded Institutions

MoU Between International Institute for Holistic Research and Voluntary Action (India-Germany) and Institute for XXX (entrepreneurship & development, in one of the State's capital)

In the era of globalisation it is imperative to view entrepreneurship from a global, holistic angle. Thus, our efforts should be linked up and performance-cum-impact enhanced by joining hands in our efforts, wherever it is feasible and viable to render support by our respective expertise.

The State XXX in particular and India in general, require a new, holistic approach to development, based upon self-employment, genuine entrepreneurship, modern marketing tools, and use of all IT facilities. Stereotyped repetitiveness of compartmentalised approaches can no longer be upheld as they are no solution for the challenges of competitiveness in view of the strong impacts of globalisation.

Genuine entrepreneurship can only be evoked and made sustainable by bringing forward self-initiative in individuals, building up self-confidence and customer-oriented behavioural patterns-cum-products, coordinating and converging resources and expertise, and also, creating independence from grants and subsidies. This way, all like-minded individuals, institutions and even Government bodies should join hands in these efforts.

Especially in rural Uttar Pradesh, where we are facing widely the lack of future-oriented activities, all efforts should be taken to overcome the present weaknesses in self-employed, sustainable development.

The Institutes cover similar fields of action, like capacity building, identifying and developing hidden potentials, and training in HRD issues, triggering off sustainable entrepreneurship in rural areas, to name only the main topics. Expertise and experiences should be clubbed in conducting joint seminars + workshops and also, regular meetings should be held to share experiences and exchange and agree upon future plans of action.

At present, we suggest the following as a Joint Plan of Action:

1. National convention on entrepreneurship both at State and regional levels
2. Recognising and documenting series of successful performers as entrepreneurs
3. Organising self-financing training programmes for training of trainers on Self-Employed Change Agent basis
4. Research competition, technology, policy and hidden resources/potentials via standardised HRD tools and parameters in view of the performance in the same system as these are the most important aspects of any network and management
5. Identifying possibilities of direct involvement of experts from both the Institutes for jointly conducting trainings, seminars and workshops.

By working together on a systematic, self-financing basis, we expect that activisation at the grassroots level in Uttar Pradesh and, via replication of good performer models, will be successful.

Irmel V. Marla
Chairperson (IIHRVA)

Dr. Kamal Taori, IAS (rtd.)
Hon. Consultant (IIHRVA)

February 15, 2007

The following letter is a reminder to the then Principal Secretary, Government of XXX, on follow-up activities to earlier verbal agreements:

September 4th, 2007

Dear Shri ...,

We were surprised to hear that you had not received our "XXX Plan for Action", or all the other material for activities and models we sent to you.

The "XXX Plan" which was researched, analysed, and developed by us, has some distinct new features as opposed to other, more or less stereotyped concepts.

We have tried to look at the relevant issues both, from historical and also from the grassroot people's angle, and of course, our approach is uncompromisingly holistic and action-oriented.

Again, I am enclosing a copy of our "Plan for Action", along with our model "Dual System of Professional training". The latter could provide big scope for self-employment and employability, together with a high quality level of skills and knowledge.

As I have mentioned to you, our Institute is prepared to make a presentation to all interested, so that the newness, the non-conformist approach, and the implementability of our concepts can be shown and discussed.

I do hope that this time, our material will reach you so that it gets the attention it deserves.

Regards and best wishes,

Dr. Kamal Taori

On behalf of International Institute for Holistic Research and Voluntary Action, Chairperson: Irmel V. Marla.

Remark: This letter, too, was not graced with any response.

Excerpts from a letter to Chief Justice Mumbai High Court, describing experiences in a District Court

March 20, 2009

To:

Hon. Chief Justice Mumbai High Court
Bhaurao Patil Marg
Mumbai

Hon. Shri Kumar,

I am a German Social Scientist and Anthropologist (Magister Artium, University of Heidelberg), and I live in India several months a year, to continue various initiatives, research and analyses, started by my late Indian husband, Dr. Sarma Marla, Professor of Sociology at the University Heidelberg. I am working with my own "International Institute for Holistic Research and Voluntary Action" (India-Germany) in Rural India to contribute to enhancing entrepreneurship, self-employment and employability towards self-reliance, especially independence from grants and subsidies, and also analyse policy issues (for details please see my website).

I am also the co-author of the book *Operationalising Holistic Human Development—Food for Thought and Ideas for Action* (Concept Publishing Company, New Delhi, 2007) which I wrote together with the Indian partner to my Institute, Dr. Kamal Taori, (IAS rtd).

At present, I am researching for assessing and analysing burning issues concerning the life of "normal" Indian citizens to be published in an Indian magazine, and in this context, I also stumbled upon the Wardha District Court. As I am straight-forward by nature (German?), and also, cannot perceive that Indian Judiciary System should, considering the doubtless wonderful Constitution of India, operate with such severe flaws, I decided to inform you directly to draw your attention.

I enclose my article on the Indian Judiciary System, a result of extensive research and studies, focusing on provincial District Courts, High Courts, their judges, lawyers, and procedures, which will be published soon. I take great care to not to rely on gossip and rumour-mongering, but try to get proper background information, studying the respective documents available, as is good journalist's research approach, and moreover, I have no personal interest whatsoever.

I found that there (in Wardha) are specific serious shortcomings which I categorised in the following:

a) Time: delays and timings which are uncomprehensible
b) Witness issues: witnesses and evidence neglected
c) Decisions: not comprehensible

The facts:

To a.:

a) In spite of the fact that a litigant applied for getting an earlier Court date fixed, a long date of three months was fixed.
b) Several cases were not processed at all for a long time with the excuse that documents are missing whereas all the documents were delivered. After more than one year, the case was accepted—on the basis of the same set of documents which were at hand from the beginning.

I refrain from stating the overall delay in processing cases as this seems to be a disease which is not specific to the Wardha District Court but to courts all over the country. (My suggestion: Computers should not be used as sort of electrical typewriters, but as efficient tools for speeding up procedures, for coordinating and creating necessary transparency.)

To b.:

Litigants made the experience that evidence crucial to their cases was not taken into consideration at all after the opponent's lawyer had intervened. For example, there is the case of an obvious impostor giving witness statements in writing in spite of the fact that the person in question is dead since 20 years, and thus cannot possibly give evidence in a case which concerns situations happened after the demise of the "witness". Documents of this had been provided to the Judge but he bluntly dismissed them, again, after the opponent's lawyer had intervened. Referring to this example, I was informed about several similar cases.

To c.:

There is an admittedly very blunt proverb in German: "God's decisions are made in heaven, but Judge's decisions are made in hell." Now, we could think that the German Judiciary System is functioning the same way as in India, but I cannot fathom procedures like I came across in Wardha could happen there.

Judges dismiss pleas for no comprehensible reasons and, significantly, at least in the cases I was informed about, only and miraculously, after the opponent's lawyer had clandestinely intervened.

There are many other strange incidences which I won't mention here as I had no opportunity to verify them—but you would have the power to do so! — and also, they are of minor importance in this context, albeit not for the people concerned; nevertheless, your attention should also be drawn to these.

The matter of fact is that not everything goes well which should be well, and I feel compelled to quote Shakespeare: "Something is rotten in the state of Denmark", i.e. in the Court of Wardha, and I am of the opinion that the Mumbai High Court should take a closer look into the state of affairs.

I do hope that you won't take offence for my outspokenness, but India is the country I love and cherish, and have never kept quiet in the face of injustice done in the name of justice.

Concerning the above-mentioned observations and descriptions of facts, I do hope that I could draw your attention: within the next two weeks, I will send a few documents, real-life case studies (with the consent of the litigants) for your perusal which will establish the facts.

With due respect and high regards, I am awaiting your response.

Irmel V. Marla

Quote from the Actual Website of the District Court of Wardha

"Paragraph containing the Historical information of the District Court, Wardha: "The District Wardha is a Historical Place. The Sewagram Ashram is at a distance just 5 K.M. from the court. Sewagram is the place from where Father of Nation Mahatma Gandhi guided to the Freedom fighters." (My own remark: It came to my mind: What would the Father of the Nation think and say about all these things?)

Letter to the then Private Secretary to a State Minister

January 27, 2009

My dear Shri .....,

You will kindly remember my meeting with you and the Hon. Minister when we discussed problems of increasing crime, suitable IT, development, and issues of HRD.

Our Institute is working focussed on holistic sustainable development against the evil system of grants and subsidies, which includes action-oriented studies in policing and policies. Our analyses have brought out that the pre-condition for reducing crime rates sustainably, lies in actively involving all grassroots potential, introducing suitable IT and identifying progressive, accountable leadership in action.

We all know that in the era of globalisation, and often using "Globalisation" as an excuse, stereotyped, insensitive, and inhuman means of functioning are prevalent, which are indifferent to the ground realities, thus completely counter-productive in view of supporting a truly civil society. In this context, we think it is important to propagate a non-conventional approach to the burning issues we are facing, taking up challenges like self-employment, employability through enhancing quality consciousness, and fighting the economic dependencies and stalemates caused by continuous artificial "help" through grants, subsidies, and the like.

To trigger off unconventional practicable ideas, a holistic brainstorming will be conducted by the International Institute where we intend to evolve guidelines for all-encompassing, participatory and integrative positive development which is so dearly missing in our compartmentalised society.

We would be very glad if you could kindly request the Hon. Minister to be with us in Wardha/Sevagram on either of the dates from 7 to 9, February, 2009, to contribute his visions and also, share with us our ideas for action. Please inform us, preferably via mail.

Regards and best wishes, yours

Dr. Kamal Taori, also on behalf of Mrs. Irmel V. Marla, Chairperson of the International Institute for Holistic Research and Voluntary Action in collaboration with Rural Business Hub Foundation India.

Letter to: Administrative Judge Nagpur High Court in connection with obvious fraudulent procedures in the case of a charitable educational institution in the jurisdiction of Wardha Charitable Commission

23 July, 2009

Subj.: Specific case of mis-interpretation leading to fraud of justice, ...

Dear Sir,

Our Institute has already sent an exhaustive letter a few months back to you regarding the above-mentioned cases which we intend to thoroughly study—especially in view of Mahatma Gandhiji's supposed to be impact on Wardha District. As yet, I was not graced with even a reply of acknowledgement. As you are informed, we are compiling case studies on the grassroots functioning of the Indian Judiciary, and Wardha has unexpectedly proved to be a source for quite interesting material.

In the meantime, I got even more substantial information on the cases I mentioned in my earlier letter, which I don't want to withhold from you. Below, I am giving the gist of dates and contents to clearly show the obviously fraudulent goings-on within the setup of the judicial machinery in the District which boasts of Mahatma Gandhi.

May 3, 2008: complaint submitted to the Court of first ad-hoc District Judge, on which the Judge passes the following orders: "Read application. Since complaint is against bailiff call remarks of bailiff and AS concerned within 3 days, this application be regd. as MJC.", signed: 3 May, 2008.

Nothing happens till 6th December, 2008 (!). Then, suddenly, on this date, a notice is issued to the bailiff and the AS to give reply within three days.

On 11 December, 2008, the bailiff replies without answering the specific questions, but tries to save his skin by accusing the complainant that they have tried to bribe him.

The AS replies on 11 December, 2008, that he does not know anything about the case because he was not the concerned AS.

On 15 December, 2008, Mr. ..., ad-hoc District Judge-2, to Wardha, passes the order which is inconsistent, non-factual, and full of concoctions, cooked-up fantasies, and biased jumping to conclusions, defying all logical thinking.

As we are intending to publish a thorough analysis of the functioning of the judicial system in India with emphasis on Mahatma Gandhi's District Wardha, and, we will conduct an international Workshop for Action on Human Rights issues end of October, 2009, in Sevagram itself, it would be appropriate for the machinery of jurisdiction in Wardha to get their act together.

Our team has thoroughly investigated the issue, and we came to the following conclusions and questions:

1. Why was no notice issued by the Hon. Judge as per his orders dated 3 May, 2008? Why suddenly, after a gap of about seven months, a notice was issued to the bailiff and the AS?
2. When the AS says that he was not the right person to explain, why was the explanation from the right person not sought?
3. When the bailiff talks of efforts to bribe him, why has this accusation not been taken seriously?
4. Why has the complainant not been called to give evidence and also been given the opportunity to be heard and to make it clear that no bribery was ever there in the picture?
5. The inconsistencies in the order of the Hon. Judge, and the basis of the inferences as to the statement of the bailiff, call vehemently for a detailed, thorough inquiry. For example: the bailiff had nowhere mentioned that the complainant was sitting inside the office of the Trust while the Judge has concluded and mentioned in the order that the complainant was there. The proven fact is that the complainant was nowhere even near the Wardha District that day, but the Judge was obviously not interested in finding the facts.

6. The sequence of events and the way these miscellaneous judicial issues have been summarily disposed of, the main clumsily issues sidelined—to my opinion: obviously hushed up—show the malafide intentions hitherto inexplicable to our analyses.

If these facts (exemplified at random) would not be so depressing, we would just be happy, as researchers, to find ample information of deviations from the path of justice. But, we would have preferred to find "Justice done" in the District of Gandhiji rather than "Justice bent" or at its best, "neglected". We feel sorry and, at the same time, we still have not lost all faith in the Third Power in the Democracy of India.

We could proceed like all researchers: evaluate our material and publish it, for the whole world to read and relish. But, we feel it a matter of fair play to inform you and give you the opportunity to set things right.

Looking forward to your reply and, if possible, to an appointment with you.

Greetings and regards,

Irmel V. Marla (Sociologist/Anthropologist, Univ. of Heidelberg, Germany), Chairperson: International Institute for Holistic Research and Voluntary Action

Letter of Dr. Kamal Taori to Shri N.R. Narayana Murthy, Chairman: Indian Institute of Management, Vastrapur, Ahmedabad-380 015

No. DG/1
12th April, 2006

Respected Mr. Narayana Murthy,

As I had mentioned in IIM Ahmedabad meeting, the National Productivity Council (NPC), was a pioneer in formulating the Memorandum of Association of IIMs and that is the reason probably why in IIM Calcutta, Bangalore and Ahmedabad, NPC has been included as a founder member.

I have attended meetings of IIMs in Bangalore and also Ahmedabad in the last four months and feel that there are some basic issues which need to be taken up. I had also mentioned these issues in the IIM Bangalore meeting which have been duly recorded in their minutes.

The basic objectives of IIM, as mentioned by the Comptroller and Auditor General includes the following:

a) to provide educational facilities for youth for careers leading to management responsibility;
b) to contribute towards improvement of decision-making skill and administrative competence of practicing managers;
c) to develop teachers and researchers in different fields related to management; and
d) to assist organisations in solving their management problems by providing consultancy services.

The elaborate functions of the IIM society are mentioned in the Memorandum of Association and the Rules, by and large, it is to serve the needs of business and industry by providing professionally competent and continued management education with incidental actions.

I think a time has come when not only IIM but even NPC is facing similar challenges of governance, autonomy, accountability etc. which require restructuring to suit the challenges of our time. In the last two decades, NPC has also reduced its dependence on the Government funds and Government has already intimated that in future NPC must become totally self-sufficient. IIM Ahmedabad has already become self-sufficient though others still are not so lucky. However, the issues of salary structure, promotion of the staff, incentives along with flexibility, autonomy and leadership issues for quality requires definitely a different work culture and mind set.

Towards nation building, either through productivity or management training, the following are few of areas which need to be seriously considered:

i) There are many unexplored and may be unknown areas where bigger vision of the nation and its competitive strength have still not been explored and utilised. India as a unique nation with so much diversity probably has to be understood holistically. Due to lack of this holistic vision, whether it is productivity or management or quality or administration probably full justice is not being done. Hence, individuals and individual institutions may be performing exceedingly well but as a nation definitely it is highly under performing.

ii) In the nation building process, compartmentalised, sectarian excellence is not bound to be sustainable. Whether it is outstanding leadership or policy support, there is a need for identification with clarity of success parameters. IIM Graduates, being the highest income earners may command respect but the needs of management in the poorly performing areas of economy cannot also be ruled out. What are the other success parameters? Can we say that States where IIMs are located have benefited from the multidisciplinary expertise of these institutions of excellence? Similar problem is very much in the NPC also because in cluster or in focused areas, there is lot which requires to be done.

iii) The areas of Public-Private Panchayat Partnership, unutilised infrastructure, value for the money, neglected areas of economy etc. requiring excellent management and productivity enhancement have not received the type of excellent management or administration or training which they deserve.

iv) There are many policies, systems, control mechanism which have miserably failed in a democratic system like ours. There are many institutions who have comparative advantage and still there is a compulsion to set them at liberty to explore full potential where best of capacity could be utilised. Hence in NPC, we are exploring productivity enhancement in the same system by identifying and correcting mindset, work culture, change of attitude where in the same system success can be achieved. Of course, there are requirements of collaboration, understanding and commitment.

Hence, despite excellent reputation and profit earning capacity of IIMs like Ahmedabad, I have raised even in NPC the following questions:

i) Do we have areas of weakness, potential, unexplored capacity, demand, identified as a part of holistic excellence of the nation? This has to be based upon aspirations of the nation, charter of the duties of the institute and compulsion of excellence in totality.

ii) Emerging challenges of globalisation and compulsions of localisation require repositioning and restructuring of all institutions. Do present structures of governance including autonomy, monitoring and evaluation have the capacity to fulfil the above objectives?

iii) The best of the students trained by IIMs are serving which category of the economy and the employers? While everybody would like to have the best of salaries, position and status, are the management issues really applicable only for top corporate organised sectors or there has to be enough thrust on management issues of probably unmanaged areas and organic sectors?

iv) While globalisation throws many more opportunities, the threat perceived areas and disaster potential areas need to be understood with lessons of the past and threats of the future that means a holistic or broad-based understanding of multi-disciplinary management teams. Has any work been done on that?

v) For developed models of excellence cluster based, IT-led investment policies with thrust on viability as employment and policy correction would require constant education. I have done some work on this which is available in some literature enclosed. But the thrust is on convergence, IT for masses, decentralisation, organic systems, transparency and marketing led investment policies with clarity, productivity and brevity and speed. These can also be presented so that a network of institutions and neglected sectors could be taken up for action-driven market-oriented training, capacity enhancement for full potential exploration.

The above are few of the points I think require more detailed action-oriented convergenistic thinking. May-be-some of these issues could be taken for action research or further discussions.

In the meantime, I shall be grateful to have your views so that a policy paper on the above lines could be taken up for further discussion.

Regards,

Yours sincerely,

(*Dr. Kamal Taori*)

CC: *All GB Members of IIM Ahmedabad.*

Letter to the Speaker of the Legislative Assembly, U.P.

October 2nd, 2007

Respected Shri Sukhdev Rajbharji,

It was a great pleasure to hear your very matured, balanced, visionary views. The subsequent meeting at your residence today gave us an opportunity to understand the undercurrents of sustainable development for U.P. in particular and India in general.

Kindly accept our heartiest congratulations, and we hope that you as the Chairman of the U.P. Legislative Assembly, and as people's representative from Azamgarh, can facilitate and lead a new movement for India's potential realisation.

We have asked the Chief Development Officer, that we would like to facilitate a replicable, transparent, competitive model for the backward areas of your constituency. This will involve our role as facilitator, coordinator, turnkey consultants, and an overall vision-in-action-ability provider. It can be done only with full cooperation and support of all those who matter.

We will need the following basic data from the District/ Development Officers.

1. Details of the most backward Blocks with potentials as perceived by bankers, local leaders, PRI institutions, entrepreneurs, and the people.
2. Credit deposit ratio with efforts in the past to improve the same.
3. Unused/under-used infrastructure in the Block/in the villages.

4. Potential of Public Private Panchayat Profitable Partnership (PPPPP) in the Block and the villages.
5. Position and activities of Self-Help-Groups.
6. All information about population specifics, like number of people in the respective villages, sex ratio, schools and educational institutions, etc.
7. Law and order situation (statistics) and crime-free villages as per register No. 8 of the Police Stations. (The most crime-prone villages and the less crime-prone villages.)
8. List of NRIs—village-wise, and also, persons from the villages living and working in Mumbai, Delhi, Lucknow, etc.
9. Retired Army and Civil Servants—village-wise.
10. Failed or succeeded projects and schemes in the villages, like family planning, education, agriculture, water, etc.
11. Currently running projects and schemes in the Block and villages.
12. Quality of leadership at Block and village levels.
13. Local media in the respective villages, like reporters, part-time journalists (teachers), etc.
14. Private investments in the villages, like village industries, water pumps, shops, small and medium enterprises, educational institutions, transport, dairies.
15. Any other information or data which can be provided by local functionaries and/or the District Administration, including Panchayats.

Once we get these information, we would like to camp there for about three days in the most backward area/Block of your constituency, analyse further and give an overall training-cum-consultancy Plan for Action. We are confident, this will be a very unique, unconventional approach to development by involving the local leadership actively.

With profound regards,

Irmel V. Marla
(Chairperson)

Dr. Kamal Taori
(Hon. Consultant)

IIHRVAction in Collaboration with RBHF

P.S. Based on the above, we had a thorough group discussion at Sultanpur on 01st October, 2007, with all the officers of the District Administration, where the following additional points emerged. This has enhanced our confidence that we are in a position to give turnkey consultancy and effective training for developing replicable models for bringing out the best of all potentials in the District, which hitherto are lying dormant. The DM and CDO also, agreed to offer five economically most backward Blocks for total turn-about on effective parameters and turnkey measures. It was also agreed that to draw lessons from past failures and successes, a conference of ex-CEOs, DMs, will be organised to learn from past experiences and evolve viable future plans for action.

This area has been a VIP area for the last many decades leading to a mindset and attitudes adverse to entrepreneurship. It is high time to involve all the uninvolved so that we use all the resourceful sectors for developing replicable models with thrust on future-oriented, sustainable, non-exploitative entrepreneurship to face the challenges of Globalisation.

To : *Shri Sukhdev Rajbharji, Hon. Speaker of U.P. Legislative Assembly*

Copies to: Shri Sanjaykumarji, DM, Sultanpur
Shri I. D. P. Rai, CDO, Sultanpur
Shri Amit Goel, Adviser, Ministry of Panchayati Raj,
New Delhi

Marla/Taori: Selected Project Proposals for State Governments and Central Government— "Capacity Development through Change Management Processes with emphasis on Convergence for Integrated District Planning"

Aims and Objectives

Change management as a decisive factor for holistic sustainable rural development has always been our top priority. In the last three years, based on our individual four-decades-long experiences, we have tried to converge all resources at the Village and District Plan level, putting special emphasis on heterogeneous groups and also, bridging the gaps in our adverse compartmentalised infrastructures.

In this process, we have re-defined many terms which are hindering sustainability of development through maligned, distorted use, most prominent among them is "planning". First of all, we found that "planning" is very often used as an excuse for doing nothing. Furthermore, "planning" is executed by administrators and authorities who have no:

a) Stakes in development issues
b) Accountability
c) Experiences of grassroots level conditions
d) Sensitivity for problems of sustainable development
e) Present-day data which would be necessary for any positive result
f) Commitment for action-oriented efforts
g) Quality consciousness combined with determination for performance.

We are already working on implementing our "Wardha Plan for Action"[18] which we can present if necessary.

We are propagating and practicing international cooperation with holistic outlook and approach on all issues related to rural development through unconventional "models for replication", workshops, seminars, research, and turnkey consultancy for all stakeholders. The institute is actively promoting international networking, supporting all efforts for global peace and understanding.

Our Institute has a number of decisive USPs based on our holistic approach differentiating us from the usual business of consultancy:

a) Internationality (both, Chairperson (German) + Partner/ Advisor (Indian) as main representatives are networking internationally with emphasis on exchanging/sharing knowledge and skills.
b) Holistic approach: Emphasis on improving overall living conditions in rural India through enhancing entrepreneurship (self-employment, job creation) and employability against the grants and subsidies.

c) Unconventional approach towards sustainable, holistic development through our "6Ps"- Model (overall inclusive, Identifying/assessing and developing hidden potentials, both human potentials, and also all other resources (natural resources, all infrastructural un-used local potential, "using the unused", "marketing the un-marketed").

d) Expertise in developing highly flexible "Models for Replication" by including all stakeholders, experiences in working together with government agencies by using our unconventional approach.

e) We developed an unconventional, very efficient tool for analysing potentials of employment and investment, the "Hippoo-, Kippoo-…"-Model[19].

f) Emphasis on inseparably combining knowledge and skills in all stages (see Model: "Dual System of Professional Education"[20] as part of bringing about change in the educational system).

g) Unique features of closely connecting different markets and cultures in an efficient way, thus bringing about better understanding, constructive and non-exploitative economic cooperation, and sustainable growth to the advantage of both the sides.

h) We have expertise and vast experiences in organisation development, building up self-confidence, assessing hitherto unused potential and give utmost importance to action-oriented, inclusive planning.

i) Unbureaucratic, highly flexible set up of the Institute after our "Satellite" system: Planning, Implementation, Monitoring, and Training are performed without bureaucratic office infrastructure: both the leaders work through electronic media, and are connected with independent experts who cooperate if and when needed. At the same time, we use hitherto unused local infrastructural facilities, and also local skills and experiences.

j) The Institute functions with its two leaders as decision makers and has no hierarchical patterns.

k) Specific qualifications and experiences of the leaders:

   i) Twenty-eight years of practical experience in all HRD areas in a private company plus 40 years frequent research in rural India, active involvement in activities of holistic rural development.

   ii) Forty years in Indian Administrative Service, author of more than 30 books on issues of sustainable rural development, active involvement in activities of holistic rural development.

Main Activities/Priorities of the International Institute

1. Establishing close international cooperation with companies, NGOs, Panchyats, academic institutions and persons working on the same lines.
2. Exchanging findings of respective research activities and also, evaluate them ("aims & objectives": workshops and seminars), exchanging practical experiences with all cooperating partners and others interested.
3. Propagating holistic approach to research and action and all other activities; offering trainings on methods of holistic approach.
4. Conducting international seminars in Germany and India, inviting grassroots experts to share experiences and to learn from each other.
5. Conducting research on holistic rural development in India, also: developing holistic methodology, and synergise activities.
6. Develop "grant-less" concepts for self-employment, enhancing productivity by applying eco-friendly ways and means and/or producing eco-friendly goods, efficient marketing strategies, environment protection.
7. Offering professional turnkey consultancy for holistic: self-employment, enhancing productivity, environment protection, educational and professional training systems, identifying hidden, unused, unmarketed potential, institution building.

Evaluation, References and Quality Issues

Reputation of Organisation and Staff (Competence / Reliability): The International Institute is registered in Stutensee, Germany as Pvt.Ltd. Company in 2006

Chairperson is the founder, Mrs. Irmel V. Marla, Sociologist/ Anthropologist, Partner and Advisor is the Indian Counterpart Dr. Kamal Taori (IAS, rtd.), Economist and experienced Trainer.

The Institute is organised as a model for unbureaucratic efficiency, using all suitable electronic media and having the "Satellite"-system for special expertise, an infrastructure.

The representatives of the Institute qualify through their respective decades-long practical work on sustainable development, analyses and implementation activities, and the whole range of HRD methodology and tools.

The Institute is free of any liabilities, and the same applies to its representatives.

Litigation and Arbitration History: NIL

General Organisational Capability which is likely to affect implementation: As already mentioned, our organisational infrastructure has a flexible, IT-supported set-up which allows to short-time reaction to any requirements, like special expertise, increased number of field workers, and evaluation tools. We have close contacts with experts in various fields of development issues, and we cooperate closely if needed. Salient features of our management setup is inclusive planning and organisation and a highly decentralised infrastructure combined with uninterrupted milestone-monitoring[21] from planning stage to all follow-up measures.

Extent to which any work would be subcontracted: As described in our "satellite"-system, we are cooperating with experts and/or field workers if and when the need arises on work-oriented, limited contract basis evolving from our planning. We have sufficient and qualified experts and field workers at our disposal.

Quality assurance procedures, warranty: The quality assurance evolves from our specific planning and our control mechanisms.

Warranty issues should not arise due to our quality and time-related surveillance and flexible corrective mechanism through our milestone-monitoring system.

Our specialised knowledge covers the overall requirements through our holistic approach which has as work-base the convergence of all resources available (see our 6Ps-system[22], our work platform).

We have worked with several State Government departments on various issues, like enhancing leadership qualities, preventive disaster management, "Self Employed Change Agent"-system in various villages in XXX, workshops and training seminars on holistic sustainable development in XXX.

We are convinced that the described project is of high importance and also, a highly challenging task. The change management process fostering convergence for integrated District Planning has to attend to some very difficult development phenomena. They include the following:

a) The 73rd and 74th Constitutional Amendment Acts have accorded a constitutional status to Panchayats.

b) These bodies and their leaders have to undertake planning, implementation, and monitoring of services delivery.

c) These were the prerogative of bureaucracy at different levels.

d) To strengthen de-centralised governance in general and integrated District Planning in particular is challenging and difficult because it involves change in attitudes and working of all the key players in District Planning.

e) Apart from local officials, banks, the private sector, the marketing forces, the political parties, and civil society have roles in District Planning and monitoring. But for a good plan, the multiple service providers and role players have not been made stakeholders.

f) The traditional systems of compartmentalised planning, funding, evaluation, monitoring, and overall supervisory systems through a highly bureaucratised infrastructure presupposes development as process of spending through grants from the Government.

g) The self-propelling, transparent and sustainable enabling factors of development have made a mockery of District Plans as they highly depend on the pattern of State and Central Plans which is nothing but allocation of funds without catering for the merit and for the local needs. The grassroots stakeholders are hardly involved with the result that there is no control, nor accountability, nor consideration of and for the local people.

The Important Aspects of the Task

a) An analytical understanding of the local conditions.

b) Involvement of all the stakeholders.

c) A replicable development model has to be evolved which means this model has to be cost-efficient, convergonistic, based on local knowledge, skills and resources, and conclusions from learning lessons of the past.

d) This model has to be highly flexible so that it can be quickly and successfully transferred to other areas (after our module-based models).

e) Unused resources (or under-used) need to be identified and handed over to the stakeholders for equity-based partnership and finally ownership and unconditional use. His implies unobstructed, and unhindered use by the stakeholders in view of the usual interference from governments and/or administration

f) the role of IT, marketing through value-addition, reliability and quality in the era of globalisation, global competition, is another important aspect which has to be addressed

The different components of the Project have to be adequately vetted through suitable IT, leadership upgradation, transparency, accountability, financial viability, and management skills for change to be successful, sustainable and replicable.

These are based upon our various analyses as shown in the enclosed "Action Plan for Wardha District"[23]. Also, we refer to the following publications by the Partner and Advisor of the International Institute, Dr. Kamal Taori for clear outlay of the concepts and practical measures of introducing change management[24], and joined authorship of the Chairperson of the International Institute, Irmel V. Marla/Dr. Kamal Taori[25]

The Outcome of the Project

a) To come out with the obstacles and stumbling blocks hindering integrated District Planning.
b) To develop a model based on the above mentioned findings for integrated Change Management.
c) To foster convergence at District level through integrated District Planning.
d) To evolve pilot and test model methodologies for Change Management.
e) To finalise and develop methods of Change Management.
f) To develop and institutionalise systems and capacities of different stakeholders of Change Management.

The salient points of our conceptual framework include the following:

a) People know best what is best for them (total inclusiveness).
b) There is a lot of duplication on the side of the Government and, what is even worse, a highly compartmentalised set-up.
c) The 73rd and 74th Amendment to the Constitution have to be operationalised by raising the quality of leadership, building up leadership skills from grassroots level, support of local policies from the top, and a radical shift from Charity to Creativity-, Capacity-, Competence- and Confidence building at the grassroots level[26]

d) The training institutions have to be given incentives for the staff based upon turnkey consultancy and profit sharing.

Since integrated Change Management at the District level is a highly complicated and complex process, countering powerful vested interests of political, judicial, entrepreneurial, administrative forces, it seems to be an uphill task. A number of institutions and organisations, both national and international, have worked on this sort of assignments, but all have miserably failed. The main reason is the utter lack of a holistic approach because it is very difficult to understand and also, extremely difficult to implement in view of the vested interests especially at the District level, and the lack of support from the decision-making authorities. The coordination we are trying to establish within the scope of this Project, is counteracted from almost all levels[27], one of the main evils is the all-pervading parasitic and loot-based approach.

In this Project, we intend to focus on an uncompromising holistic approach comprising the following methods and measures:

a) Involving the grassroots level stakeholders from the very first step of planning throughout the implementation (after our milestone model) and all the follow-up monitoring and feedback measures.

b) Conduct "Workshops for Action" for grassroots stakeholders, and all groups at District level, including government officials, administrators, banks, and all local communities to design roadmaps for practical steps towards holistic approach to sustainable development and inclusive growth.

c) Train the above-mentioned groups in Change Management, based upon our "6Ps"[28] model, and present success cases for better acceptance and overall acting accordingly.

d) Our intended "Workshops for Action" include, as necessary for the Holistic Approach, environmental issues like water conservation and replenishing, recycling systems ("Waste to wealth"), renewable energies and an overall awareness of necessity of using natural resources instead of destroying them. For this, our Institute has valuable contacts with German academic research institutions and organisations in the above-mentioned fields.

e) Our International Institute also has close contacts with municipalities in Germany working very efficiently in integrated decision-making, citizen-oriented, inclusive planning and practised environment protection. These experiences could be transferred to Indian conditions while adapting suitably and by avoiding initial mistakes.

We intend to implement the following steps:

a) After signing the agreement for the Project, we would start to implement the Pilot Phase for a few villages in the agreed upon District immediately (i.e. within two to three weeks of preparation)

b) Identifying resources and potential (open and hidden[29]) available in the pilot villages and analysing them for efficient use with the aim of designing business opportunities and perspectives for self-employment and enhancing employability.

c) Designing a "Plan for Action" subject to appropriate alternatives according to our system of monitoring modules ("milestone" system).

d) Re-defining the resources for village planning, i.e. people's skills, unused lands and infrastructure, banking experiences, knowledge, skills and experiences of retired persons, NRIs, ex-Army persons, schools and college infrastructure, quantity and quality of education.

Technical Proposal Evaluation Form 3 (Task Manager)

General Qualification of the Team Leaders:

Suitability for the Project:

a) International Experience—Yes

b) Training Experience—Yes

c) Professional Experience in the area of specialisation—yes
d) Knowledge of the region—partly, but: due to long-time experiences the abilities for quick indepthknowledge are more than sufficient
e) Language qualifications: English, Hindi, Marathi, French

Senior Experts

The Project Team will be twofold: Chairperson of the Institute together with the Partner and Advisor. In addition to the Project leaders, a senior and a junior assistant (officer) will be employed, depending on the size of the Project.

Both, senior and junior assistants will be carefully selected among already known.

Experts/field workers. Selection criteria will be on the basis of:

a) Qualifications
b) Performances

Excerpt from Proposal to GoI—(Proposal to produce a Concept & Action Plan for a Centre of Excellence/Think Tank for Local Governance)

"Service Provider Consultancy"

> What is productivity but making the most of one's time and talent, and energising the whole surrounding environment so that men and women are inspired and motivated: that is make the most themselves, both as individuals and as members of society on all planes of living, thinking and acting: whether it is politics or economics or home, village or factory, life at the ground level or life of the spirit.
>
> *(Mahatma Gandhi)*

Team Member: Dr. Kamal Taori

a) Four decades of experience in Public Administration with particular experience in the areas of decentralised governance.

b) Retired from IAS in 2006 as Secretary to the Government of India and, as the enclosed detailed bio data brings out, has written and implemented, and made intensive policy studies about local governance.

c) His various writings and researches bring out issues in strengthening institutions and mechanism, so as to enhance the capacity of elected representatives for human development-oriented, inclusive planning, implem-entation, and improved accountability in local governance.

d) As Director of State Institute of Rural Development (SIRD), Lucknow (with 50 District Training Centres for local bodies and rural development), and other similar assignments containing training and research for capacity building of grassroots stakeholders, these issues have been one of his deep-founded special fields.

Team Member: Irmel V. Marla (Sociologist/Anthropologist (from Univ. of Heidelberg, Germany), expert in Socio-Psychology as described in detail in the bio data, Mrs. Marla is highly experienced in diverse:

a) methods of research and evaluation
b) organisation development
c) leadership development
d) grassroots level confidence and competence building
e) capacity development (bottom-up).

Both the experts work through the International Institute for Holistic Research and Voluntary Action towards holistic sustainable development, and they are determined to apply unconventional ways and means because the conventional methods—after our research and evaluation—have proved failures or, at its best, were not satisfactory nor sustainable.

In this context, we developed our non-hierarchical model of functioning units which function as driving forces for continuously striving for excellence and identify and evolve all local potential to achieve improvement of living conditions and coordinated efforts at the grassroots level. Thus, we would develop an holistic inclusive Action Plan for Research and Capacity Development on local governance issues.

One of our main aims and objectives we are following is especially setting up efficiently.

The Institute is organised as a model for unbureaucratic efficiency, using all suitable electronic media and having developed and implemented successfully the "Satellite"-system for special expertise, an infrastructure which is highly cost effective.

The representatives of the Institute qualify through their respective decades-long practical work on sustainable development, analyses and implementation activities, and the whole range of HRD methodology and tools.

The Institute is free of any liabilities, and the same applies to its representatives.

Model of Analysis for Employment, Investment, Warning and Policy (EIWP):

a) HIPPOO Hidden Investible Potential Power of Organisation

b) KIPPOO Known Investible Potential Power of Organisation

c) PIPPOO Practised Investible Potential Power of Organisation

d) TIPPOO Threatening Investible Potential Power of Organisation

e) FIPPOO Frightening Investible Potential Power of Organisation

f) GIPPOO Globalisationally Investible Power of Organisation

g) DIPPOO Disastrously Investible Potential Power of Organisation

Model for Holistic Approach to Sustainable Rural Development

After our field analyses, the root cause forthe lack of an entrepreneurial spirit and successful rural businesses is the rampant system of grants and subsidies, 'help' schemes and the like.

With these, self-initiative and self-confidence had been literally killed as is clearly to be seen in the fact that rural business opportunities are hardly taken up.

All these mainly Governmental measures, but also 'help' projects from national and international NGOs, UN, etc. are keeping the rural masses in dependency, factly holding them in the bondage of beggardom.

If a sustainable solution should come about, we have to do away with futile measures, and bring about a change of mindset and attitudes at all levels towards entrepreneurial spirit and building up competency and self-confidence.

Our holistic approach means:

"Shift from

a) Charity to
b) Creativity
c) Capacity
d) Competency and
e) Confidence building."

Proposal to GoI: "Monitoring Convergence Between NREGS & Ongoing Schemes of other Ministries"(IIHRVA in close collaboration with RBHFI)

Profile of Organisation

> What is productivity but making the most of one's time and talent, and energising the whole surrounding environment so that men and women are inspired and motivated: that is make the most themselves, both as individuals and as members of society on all planes of living, thinking and acting: whether it is politics or economics or home, village or factory, life at the ground level or life of the spirit.
>
> *(Mahatma Gandhi)*

Our Institute has a number of decisive USPs based on our holistic approach differentiating us from the usual business of consultancy:

— Internationality (both, Chairperson (German) + Partner/ Advisor (Indian) as main representatives are networking internationally with emphasis on exchanging/sharing knowledge and skills.

— Holistic approach: Emphasis on improving overall living conditions in rural India through enhancing entrepreneurship (self-employment, job creation) and employability against the grants & subsidies, also converging potential, resources (material & immaterial), and infrastructure hitherto compartmentalised.

— Un-conventional approach towards sustainable, holistic development through our "6Ps"- Model[30] (overall inclusive, Identifying/assessing and developing hidden potentials, both human potentials, and also all other resources (natural resources, all infrastructural un-used local potential, "using the un-used", "marketing the un-marketed")

— Expertise in developing highly flexible "Models for Replication" by including all stakeholders, experiences in working together with government agencies by using our un-conventional approach to suit local conditions

— We developed an un-conventional, very efficient tool for analysing potentials of employment and investment, the "Hippoo-, Kippoo-..."-Model[31]

— Emphasis on inseparably combining knowledge & skills in all stages (see Model: "Dual System of Professional Education"[32] as part of bringing about change in the educational system)

— Unique features of closely connecting different markets and cultures in an efficient way, thus bringing about better understanding, constructive and non-exploitative economic cooperation, and sustainable growth to the advantage of all stakeholders

— We have expertise and vast experiences in organisation development, building up self-confidence, and capacities, assessing hitherto un-used potential and give utmost importance to action-oriented, inclusive planning

— Un-bureaucratic, highly flexible set up of the Institute after our "Satellite" system: Planning, Implementation, Monitoring, and Training are performed without bureaucratic office infrastructure: both the leaders work through electronic media, and are connected with independent experts who co-operate if and when needed. At the same time, we use hitherto un-used local infrastructural facilities, and also local skills and experiences.

— The Institute functions with its 2 Leaders as decision-makers and has no hierarchical patterns ("2-Heads Leadership Team")

— Specific qualifications and experiences of the Leaders[33]:

  — 28 years of practical experience in all HRD areas in a private company plus 40 years frequent research in rural India, active involvement in activities of holistic rural development

  — 40 years in Indian Administrative Service, author of more than 30 books on issues of sustainable rural development, active involvement in activities of holistic rural development

Main activities/priorities of the International Institute

— Establishing close international cooperation with companies, NGOs, Panchayats, academic institutions and persons working on the same lines

— Exchanging findings of respective research activities and also, evaluate them ("aims & objectives": workshops and seminars), exchanging practical experiences with all cooperating partners and others interested.

— Propagating holistic approach to research and action and all other activities; offering trainings on methods of holistic approach.

— Conducting international seminars in Germany and India, inviting grass root experts to share experiences and to learn from each other

— Conducting research on holistic rural development in India, also: developing holistic methodology, and synergise activities.
— Develop "grant-less" concepts for self-employment, enhancing productivity by applying eco-friendly ways and means and/or producing eco-friendly goods, efficient marketing strategies, environment protection
— Offering professional turnkey consultancy (for holistic: self-employment, enhancing productivity, environment protection, educational and professional training systems, identifying hidden, unused, un-marketed potential, institution building.

We have shown through the USPs of our Institute why we could be the best service providers for the project Monitoring Convergence Between NREGS & Ongoing Schemes of other Ministries".

We are well acquainted with the shortcomings of the existing infrastructural set-up, especially in view of lack of coordination due to the overall totally compartmentalised functioning of the administration at District, State, and Central levels, and we would be glad to realise our future-oriented, holistic concept, especially at the District level.

Through our international cooperation, like the contacts with the Municipality and Lord Mayor of the City of Stutensee, Germany, we had the opportunity to study a well-organised local administration, working efficiently and citizen-friendly with lots of voluntary impact from the citizens and also, a very un-bureaucratic set-up. These experiences we included in our practice-oriented approach to our activities.

We are convinced that our unconventional approach will lead to success in the venture, and that it will also bring about acceptance from the grassroots level stakeholders as it would lead to a distinctive improvement of existing conditions.

Our capacity to fulfil the task is highly satisfying as we work very flexible with our "Satellite"-System so that we have support in personnel and in expertise exactly as and when we need it.

Working on issues of rural development programmes

The team Leaders of the IIHRVA have worked in the fields of sustainable rural development since more than three decades, as is shown in their respective biodata.

We have worked on issues of policy changes, training and HRD, planning, science and technology, marketing and overall convergence for rural development programmes.

The Team Leaders have worked on and documented various issues of rural development programmes.

Our holistic approach is all-encompassing so that issues of hitherto compartmentalised dealing with problems will be converged, coordinated and thus put to utmost efficiency by making best use of the inter-dependency and inter-connectivity. For example, financing and viable investments are seen closely with building up capacity for entrepreneurship which again is inseparable from educational issues, and so forth.

Thus, all our activities are:

a) holistic in methods, analyses, and action
b) inclusive (see our 6Ps model[34])
c) scientifically founded and future-oriented

Network

Our International Institute has strong ties with various organisations on national and international levels, including academic institutions (mainly in Europe), and also places for organic farming, waste recycling, and various educational institutions for sharing expertise. One of our main networking activities is on issues of administration with thrust on streamlining bureaucratic processes, citizen-friendly set-ups, participatory administration, and balancing the powers and influences in these fields. For this, we are networking with various municipalities in Europe, and the formal and informal exchange of administrators to share experiences and learn from each other is high on our agenda.

On the national level, we worked with several State Governments on leadership trainings, issues of rural development and disaster management. The Rural Business Hub Foundation India which is headed by one of the Team Leaders, Dr. Taori, and is closely connected with the IIHRVA, has intensified contacts and cooperation with governmental and private institutions all over India, at present mainly on issues of environment protection, like water conservation, waste recycling ("Waste to Wealth" for rural enterprises), and overall policy changes concerning rural development.

As our *Rural Business Hub Foundation India* has District level connectivity through NGOs, the elected bodies and administration, and civil society institutions, we can bank on these experiences and contacts.

Experience in the subject area

Both the Team Leaders have extensive experiences in processes of convergence as it is an integral part of our holistic approach and also, in view of our emphasis on cost efficiency.

"Monitoring and streamlining convergence between NREGS and the ongoing schemes of other Departments/ Ministries for creation of durable assets, value addition, and strengthening the livelihood resource base for the rural poor".

Our Institute is already working on these issues: we put emphasis on coordinating efforts, especially to enhance the efficiency of measures by fusing them together and build up new infrastructures for success and sustainability. We analysed success and failures of various projects and schemes, and our findings concerning the widespread failures come to essentially five results:

a) Lack of inclusiveness in the planning stage and compartmentalised approach

b) Lack of proper assessment and use of local potential and resources

c) Lack of accountability at all levels

d) Lack of timely monitoring[35] and follow-up measures

e) Lack of efficient communication and transparency

On this background, we published our book *Operation-alising Holistic Human Development—Food for Thought and Ideas for*

Action in the Rural Context[36] which not only describes in detail all the issues mentioned in the required experiences for the Project, but also shows methods, ways and means and all possibilities to successfully tackle the stumble blocks hindering sustainable rural development.

Explaining our Project

"Convergence" is a term highly misunderstood and misused, leading to failures and mis-perceptions, and that is why it has to be clearly defined here:

We understand "convergence" as a continuous activity to:

a) efficiently connect,

b) co-ordinate and

c) fuse

   i) energies,

   ii) potential,

   iii) resources (material + immaterial)

d) into viable,

e) functionable,

f) sustainable infrastructure (unit, organisation, enterprise, etc.).

To achieve these, we developed our four essentials:

a) to learn from past experiences,

b) to avoid repeating the same mistakes (unfortunately this is happening over and over again),

c) to attentively adjust to the present conditions, and

d) to include future scenarios into our schemes.

We provide constructive-critical alternatives to local problems. With our RBHI which follows as one of its models for replication the "Self Employed Change Entrepreneur"-scheme (SECE)[37], closely connected with the scheme "Self Employed Organising Entrepreneur", which we implemented in various villages in Maharashtra so far.

True to our principle of minimising bureaucracy as far as possible, we developed our "Satellite"-System: it is organised like satellites around a planet—which is the International Institute/Rural Business Hub Foundation India — and we seek and contract their services as and when required. Otherwise, the "satellites" are independent individual experts, or organisations with the necessary expertise, they keep close contact with us and also, they have the same outlook and approach to activities.

These are only a few of our unique features which should give us a unique position in justifying our seeking this assignment.

Description of Team

One of our unique features is the principle of "Team Leadership" which enhances efficiency and, at the same time, avoids hierarchical bottlenecks.

Our Project could be implemented in any of the Indian States

Since we have connectivity all over India with local partners, we are used to adjust fully to local conditions and also to establish open communication with grassroots level people and the authorities.

Our emphasis will be on skill-building and moving towards sustainable employment through convergence as is shown in the "aims and objectives" of our Institute.

Also, the necessity of creating awareness amongst the NREGS beneficiaries and those on other Governmental schemes and services will be taken care of. Besides the main tasks formulated in the project description to bring about convergence within the scattered landscape of different schemes, we would, at the same time, analyse and identify all possibilities to bring about and/or enhance entrepreneurship leading to independence from grants and subsidies.

Concerning the "target groups of intervention", we are of the opinion that, after our inclusive approach, our priority should be on the grassroots level population. The NREGS is supposed to reach out for the BPLs, so that our main task would be to find out the obstacles leading to poor performance of delivery.

All other people and authorities involved in the process would be included in our concept after we defined the system of approach and research. The latter may be different from region to region.

Expected outcome of convergence as per convergence guidelines issued by the Ministry resulting in creation of durable assets, value addition and strengthening the livelihood resource base of the rural poor.

All these aspects, as outcomes of convergence are persistently missing as yet, will be efficiently tackled by our holistic approach, especially with our practical tool of "6Ps"-Model[38].

The question of value addition is directly linked up with quality consciousness and quality performance, competition, and marketing issues. In this context, we have to stress the importance of suitable IT in rural areas which is, in a practical and functionable sense, highly neglected as yet. Our model for replication "SECE"[39] is a very valuable measure to counteract unnecessary, useless "IT-obsessions" (and the subsequent waste of money) in a practicable, successful manner.]

Deliverables/results (documents on innovative good practices, highlight issues of concern, i.e. planning, training, etc., and any procedure or mechanism for regular monitoring of convergence, impact of convergence on increase in cultivable area, irrigation potential, ground water recharge, efficient use of irrigation system and productivity).

We have already worked on deliverables/results through our Series of Performer's Presentations, and highlighted our issues of concern in various presentations.[40] We have been frequently writing, and voicing our opinions in various fora, and we were very often confronted with utter insensitivity of those on power and authority. Above, we mentioned "repeating the same mistakes over and over again", and this is what has been detrimental to sustainable development, and, unfortunately, it is still continuing. We are determined to work against and fight this evil, and we are prepared to put our fingers in all these wounds.

One of our great assets, beside our expertise, our experiences, our combination of scientific methods and outlook with practice-oriented tools, is our independence from authorities, employers, parties, politics, community- and/or religious-based affiliations, any type of lobbies, etc.; our outlook is sustainability and merit based (especially important in the context of our future team members), holistic in nature, and truly international.

Time schedule with milestones/performance targets of monitoring.

•

Technical proposal containing detailed methodology of monitoring.

As described in detail in our "Milestone"[41]-System of planning and monitoring, we do not differentiate between the very first steps of a project/scheme and the following steps. Our holistic approach is encompassing all elements and also, leads to coordinated measures with the utmost cost efficiency. Thus, we consequently do not differentiate between targets of monitoring as our system covers all activities and participants in a way which allows transparency and comparing at all stages.

Our methodology of monitoring is described in our Milestone-System, and the persons responsible for carrying out the tasks locally will be local partners trained by us in proper performance.

Workshop for Action: Human Rights in India

We will conduct the first of our series "Workshops for Action" under the umbrella theme of "Human Rights" with emphasis on the conditions in India, but with international participation. Our workshops for action are designed to show alternatives to the usual conferences, lectures, and other functions where many stereotyped speeches are delivered, memoranda and intentions are voiced, but practical results are not achieved or else, hasty agreements are blown up disproportionally while no actions are following.

The Human Rights Issues can only be analysed and brought to action in the spirit of International Solidarity and commitment to World Peace, irrespective of affiliations to countries, gender, "race", religions, ideologies, or politics.

In view of the fact that the gap between the haves and the have-nots in our country widens day by day and, in view of the fact that we find convincing ideas for solutions in Gandhiji's Philosophy, we dedicate this workshop to the more than 100 years-old "Hind Swaraj" treatise by venturing into transporting the wisdom and suggestions it contains into the Twenty-first Century.

We will be a small group of around 25 international participants who are committed to find practical, implementable answers. There will be two different workshops on the following topics:

1. Human Rights in 'Hind Swaraj'—what are the practical suggestions and how to implement them in the present-day society? - 'Living and working in dignity'—how can we bring about change towards an egalitarian society?
2. Human Rights versus 'Reservation' and 'Minority Protection'—what must be changed?—What went wrong with originally good intentions? What policies should be implemented to avoid our society becoming further fragmented (by "substituting one injustice with another").

The workshops will design "roadmaps for change" which will be discussed and agreed upon in plenum sessions, where the implementation plans are laid out. The participants will receive short theme papers beforehand to prepare for the workshops, and we invite short theme papers from the participants, too.

We are determined to avoid all "speeches for speeches sake" and other paraphernalia of the usual conference/seminar-tourism, and make the best use of the time we have to come to practicable results.

All deliberations will be videoed; we intend to publish the findings.

Please apply for participation by an informal e-mail, or use the form for postal delivery.

We accept participants in time-wise range, and we will inform you immediately.

Looking forward to a fruitful Workshop for Action, greetings and best wishes,

Conveners: Irmel V. Marla and Dr. Kamal Taori

Document for Press Conference in Sevagram/Wardha: Press Note

Workshop for Action: Human Rights in India

From October 30 to November 1, at Sevagram, Wardha District, Maharashtra

The first of a series of "Workshops for Action" under the umbrella theme of "Human Rights" with emphasis on Rural India took place with international participation as well as various Indian experts from Industry, academic fields, social work, and representatives from Gram Panchayats shared their ideas.

Our workshops for action are designed to show practical alternatives to the usual trodden paths of "development" where we observe overall failures. The Human Rights Issues can only be analysed and brought to action in the spirit of International Solidarity and commitment to World Peace. The Workshop took up the following topics with the aim of evolving a practical, implementable.

Roadmap for Action

1. Human Rights in 'Hind Swaraj': What are the practical suggestions and how to implement them in the present-day society on Gandhian lines? - 'Living and working in dignity'. How can we bring about change towards an egalitarian society?
2. Human Rights versus 'Reservation' and 'Minority Protection': What must be changed? What went wrong with originally good intentions? What policies should be implemented to avoid our society becoming further fragmented (by "substituting one injustice with another").

1. After the Gandhian principle of "Living and Working in Dignity", it was agreed to implement a holistic "roadmap for change" by establishing Models for Replication in selected Districts, Wardha foremost among them. The roadmaps for change should lead to an overall improvement of living conditions, independence from grants and subsidies, enhancing entrepreneurship, self-employment and employability, by identifying and converging local resources (material and immaterial), using hitherto unused potential, and stressing on holistic sustainable development for all. Other places where we will establish our Models for Replication will be: Rajnandgaon (Chhattisgarh), Vadodara area (Gujarat), Parbhani (Maharashtra), Imphal (Manipur), and a tribal area in Kerala. Salient features of our holistic approach to sustainable development are involvement of all stakeholders at grassroots level and convergence wherever possible, transparency, capacity and confidence building and leadership training. It will lead to an overall change in mindset and attitudes towards self-responsibility and self-reliance and also, to the necessary attitude of fighting corruption and high-handedness from the side of the authorities and/or power circles, like Mafias and other illegal pressure groups.
2. The reservation policies were unanimously considered as an evil in society, outdated, and as an instrument of injustice. Also, it became clear during the deliberations that the intended goals of reservation policies from Independence time were not realised. More so, the system is misused for widespread fraud, it is perverted, and it is still ballooning out of all proportions.

Above all, the present reservation system is adverse to integrating our tension-ridden society. It is persevering and further deepening the rifts and segregation due to caste and community, and thus a force tearing the society more and more apart. Besides various other serious adversities, this fact alone would compel all policy and other decision-makers to drastically change or abolish such a system but, it is also used as convenient tool for achieving political gains, that means, one cannot rely on the policy makers to join hands with. It was also stressed upon the fact that the consequences of the reservation system are harming the economy of the country as it is generating incompetency of human resources.

There is no ready-made solution to "reform" this deep-rooted evil, as it can only be abolished altogether: the essential flaw in a gender or community-based system is the fact that it is substituting one evil or injustice with another.

The reservation system has to be substituted with a just system of supporting those below and around the poverty line, irrespective of gender, caste, creed, community, etc. And the most important measures which are more than overdue (after six decades of Independence!) is to provide full access to education for every child in this country, from primary level onwards. The Human Right to Education which was recently launched via a new legislation with big fanfare (as if it was not already essential part of the Indian Constitution!) is nothing than eyewash if it is not practically established.

Realistically, one should be aware that fighting the evils of the perverted reservation policies is an uphill task, and that it has to be fought positively: creating awareness about what has to substitute the system, and convince the people to fight **for** another, a better system which will deliver the goods, as against an evil system which is hiding the facts and functioning for certain vested interests only.

The Workshop for action concluded with the agreement that the participants will meet regularly once or twice a year, and meantime stay in close contact via electronic media. The implementation and progress of our Models for Replication would be monitored closely.

Conveners: Irmel V. Marla and Dr. Kamal Taori
November, 2009

The 12-Modules-System for Leadership Training

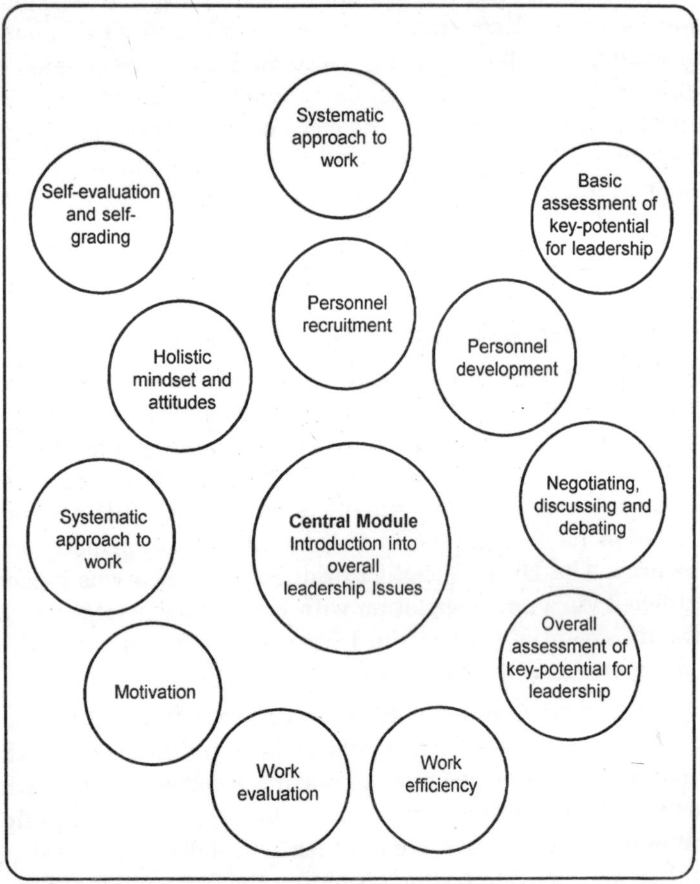

Excerpts from an unpublished article which will grow into a book

On Reservation Issues

In one of his famous songs Leonard Cohen has the line "there's war, a war between the rich and poor...", and here, we refer to the line in the context with the Reservation System in India which creates, perpetuates and multiplies war-like conditions in our society.

It is not easy in present-day India to criticise reservation policies and connected issues, mainly because of the all-pervading tabooisation of topics which should be discussed in the open in a matter-of-fact manner, without the stupid and stifling "political correctness" which is nothing than a cheap excuse for non-committal wavering, and for evading any responsibility or action. Furthermore, there is the danger of being applauded from the wrong side, of being misused as instruments for very different aims and objectives than ours.

As we discussed these dangers, we finally found it one of the most burning issues to be taken up publicly and analysed for all the evils it has perversely developed in our society.

We went into the subject with a cool, rational mind, shedding emotions and biased approach, and we try to contribute to an improvement of the very desolate present condition.

Especially in view of the pre-election frenzies, we are determined to awaken those who might be misled by vested political interests and power-conscious manipulators.

"Positive discrimination" always means, at the same time, also negative discrimination", too. So, consequently and logically, it is merely substitutes one injustice with another instead of tackling the root cause of the problem.

It is the method of taking the second or third step before the first and crucial step is made. The root cause of the problem lies in two main factors:

1. Lack of equal chances (with special efforts for the weaker sections necessarily) in all fields of education, especially starting from primary education where not much emphasis is put on as yet (poor infrastructure, poor quality of teachers training, lack of pressure on parents for non-gender-biased school attendance from the very early age, etc.)
2. Outdated, vested-interests-prone overall mindset in the non-merit-oriented system of education and all professional infrastructure.

3. Community- and/or caste-oriented policies and mindset and attitudes of the people (see, for example, the still raging war between Meenars + Gujjars in Rajasthan, and many other communities who want to avail of the many advanta͜es of certain reservation status): resulting in war-like situations, and easy to exploit atmospheres within the society.
4. Anti-harmonising, tearing society apart.
5. Inviting misuse and fraud for availing the advantages and benefits.
6. It is substituting one injustice with another.
7. It is tearing society apart.

Why we have to fight

The main reasons for uncompromisingly[42] fighting the Reservation System

The Constitution of India is one of the finest among the democratic nations in the world. Here, we quote from the original and, at the same time, we put the finger into a wound which was clearly not intended by the authors of the Constitution but developed into a Pandora's Box as a perverted system of "all are equal—but some are more equal than others."[43]

Here, we illustrate what we analysed:

> *Right to Equality*
>
> 14. Equality before law.—The State shall not deny to any person equality before the law or the equal protection of the laws within the territory of India.
>
> 15. Prohibition of discrimination on grounds of religion, race, caste, sex or place of birth.—(1) The State shall not discriminate against any citizen on grounds only of religion, race, caste, sex, place of birth or any of them.

So far, we totally agree. But alas, the articles following these are in clear contradiction to what is intended, as these provisions open the door for what we consider "substituting one injustice with another".

In fact, the machinery of reservation and quota, and the subsequent fights between the respective groups, has become a gigantic self-service octopus whose poisonous tentacles creep into all spheres of life.

> 16.Equality of opportunity in matters of public employment.—(1) There shall be equality of opportunity for all citizens in matters relating to employment or appointment to any office under the State. ...
>
> (4) Nothing in this article shall prevent the State from making any provision for the reservation of appointments or posts in favor of any backward class of citizens which, in the opinion of the State, is not adequately represented in the services under the State.
>
> (4A) Nothing in this article shall prevent the State from making any provision for reservation in matters of promotion, with consequential seniority, to any class or classes of posts in the services under the State in favour of the Scheduled Castes and the Scheduled Tribes which, in the opinion of the State, are not adequately represented in the services under the State.

From the Constitution of India

Fundamental Rights

> 16. (4B) Nothing in this article shall prevent the State from considering any unfilled vacancies of a year which are reserved for being filled up in that year in accordance with any provision for reservation made under clause (4) or clause (4A) as a separate class of vacancies to be filled up in any succeeding year or years and such class of vacancies shall not be considered together with the vacancies of the year in which they are being filled up for determining the ceiling of fifty per cent. Reservation on total number of vacancies of that year.
>
> (5) Nothing in this article shall affect the operation of any law which provides that the incumbent of an office in connection with the affairs of any religious or denominational institution or any member of the governing body thereof shall be a person professing a particular religion or belonging to a particular denomination.

Right to Freedom

19. Protection of certain rights regarding freedom of speech, etc.—(1) All citizens shall have the right—

a) to freedom of speech and expression;

b) to assemble peaceably and without arms;

c) to form associations or unions;

d) to move freely throughout the territory of India;

e) to reside and settle in any part of the territory of India; and

* * * * *

g) to practice any profession, or to carry on any occupation, trade or business.

Right against Exploitation

23. Prohibition of traffic in human beings and forced labour. 1) Traffic in human beings and beggar and other similar forms of forced labour are prohibited and any contravention of this provision shall be an offence punishable in accordance with law.

2) Nothing in this article shall prevent the State from imposing compulsory service for public purposes, and in imposing such service the State shall not make any discrimination on grounds only of religion, race, caste or class or any of them.

24. Prohibition of employment of children in factories, etc. No child below the age of fourteen years shall be employed to work in any factory or mine or engaged in any other hazardous employment.

Right to Freedom of Religion

25. Freedom of conscience and free profession, practice and propagation of religion.

1) Subject to public order, morality and health and to the other provisions of this Part, all persons are equally entitled to freedom of conscience and the right freely to profess, practice and propagate religion.

2) Nothing in this article shall affect the operation of any existing law or prevent the State from making any law.

a) regulating or restricting any economic, financial, political or other secular activity which may be associated with religious practice;

b) providing for social welfare and reform or the throwing open of Hindu religious institutions of a public character to all classes and sections of Hindus.

Explanation I.—The wearing and carrying of kirpans shall be deemed to be included in the profession of the Sikh religion.

Explanation II.—In sub-clause (b) of clause (2), the reference to Hindus shall be construed as including a reference to persons professing the Sikh, Jaina or Buddhist religion, and the reference to Hindu religious institutions shall be construed accordingly.

26. Freedom to manage religious affairs.—Subject to public order, morality and health, every religious denomination or any section thereof shall have the right—

a) to establish and maintain institutions for religious and charitable purposes;

b) to manage its own affairs in matters of religion;

c) to own and acquire movable and immovable property; and

d) to administer such property in accordance with law.

27. Freedom as to payment of taxes for promotion of any particular religion. No person shall be compelled to pay any taxes, the proceeds of which are specifically appropriated in payment of expenses for the promotion or maintenance of any particular religion or religious denomination.

Directive Principles of State Policy

38. State to secure a social order for the promotion of welfare of the people.

1) The State shall strive to promote the welfare of the people by securing and protecting as effectively as it may a social order in which justice, social, economic and

political, shall inform all the institutions of the national life.

2) The State shall, in particular, strive to minimise the inequalities in income, and endeavour to eliminate inequalities in status, facilities and opportunities, not only amongst individuals but also amongst groups of people residing in different areas or engaged in different vocations.

39. Certain principles of policy to be followed by the State. The State shall, in particular, direct its policy towards securing—

a) that the citizens, men and women equally, have the right to an adequate means of livelihood;

b) that the ownership and control of the material resources of the community are so distributed as best to subserve the common good;

c) that the operation of the economic system does not result in the concentration of wealth and means of production to the common detriment;

d) that there is equal pay for equal work for both men and women;

e) that the health and strength of workers, men and women, and the tender age of children are not abused and that citizens are not forced by economic necessity to enter avocations unsuited to their age or strength;

f) that children are given opportunities and facilities to develop in a healthy manner and in conditions of freedom and dignity and that childhood and youth are protected against exploitation and against moral and material abandonment.

39A. Equal justice and free legal aid. The State shall secure that the operation of the legal system promotes justice, on a basis of equal opportunity, and shall, in particular, provide free legal aid, by suitable legislation or schemes or in any other way, to ensure that opportunities for securing justice are not denied to any citizen by reason of economic or other disabilities.

40. Organisation of village panchayats. The State shall take steps to organise village panchayats and endow them

with such powers and authority as may be necessary to enable them to function as units of self-government.

41. Right to work, to education and to public assistance in certain cases. The State shall, within the limits of its economic capacity and development, make effective provision for securing the right to work, to education and to public assistance in cases of unemployment, old age, sickness and disablement, and in other cases of undeserved want.

42. Provision for just and humane conditions of work and maternity relief. The State shall make provision for securing just and humane conditions of work and for maternity relief.

45. Provision for free and compulsory education for children. The State shall endeavour to provide, within a period of ten years from the commencement of this Constitution, for free and compulsory education for all children until they complete the age of fourteen years.

48. Organisation of agriculture and animal husbandry. The State shall endeavour to organise agriculture and animal husbandry on modern and scientific lines and shall, in particular, take steps for preserving and improving the breeds, and prohibiting the slaughter, of cows and calves and other milch and draught cattle.

48A. Protection and improvement of environment and safeguarding of forests and wild life. The State shall endeavour to protect and improve the environment and to safeguard the forests and wild life of the country.

Fundamental Duties

51A. Fundamental duties. It shall be the duty of every citizen of India—

a) to abide by the Constitution and respect its ideals and institutions, the National Flag and the National Anthem;

b) to cherish and follow the noble ideals which inspired our national struggle for freedom;

c) to uphold and protect the sovereignty, unity and integrity of India;

d) to defend the country and render national service when called upon to do so;

e) to promote harmony and the spirit of common brotherhood amongst all the people of India transcending religious, linguistic and regional or sectional diversities; to renounce practices derogatory to the dignity of women;

f) to value and preserve the rich heritage of our composite culture;

g) to protect and improve the natural environment including forests, lakes, rivers and wild life, and to have compassion for living creatures;

h) to develop the scientific temper, humanism and the spirit of inquiry and reform;

i) to safeguard public property and to abjure violence;

j) to strive towards excellence in all spheres of individual and collective activity so that the nation constantly rises to higher levels of endeavour and achievement.

The protection of 'minorities' (and often, locally, they are no minorities at all but are bullying others around) is like a so-called deadly embrace: you die of suffocation. In our opinion, the "deadly embrace" is more the fact that due to the privileges and special rights and so forth, the abilities to self-initiatives are killed. That means, either there is no air left to breath or else, there is another disease which leaves the human being immovable, almost lifeless. And for staying alive—we purposeful avoid the plain and wonderful word "living"— he is dependent on all sorts of life-preserving gadgets (like in an ICU), and above all, he has to be permanently grateful!

In all, Reservation Policies and the so called Minority Protection are racist concepts, they don't bring harmony but rifts, and they provide privileges for the cunning and do harm to the honest.

Let there be the same laws for all citizens, let religions don't play any role in the whole context of a secular, democratic society, the government not be blackmailed by the self-styled "guardians of culture and values", but let us fight for egalitarian conditions, for equality before the law, and for equal chances for all from childhood on.

The new development: new Census is decided that it will have caste based information. That means: a fallback into sinister ages! Detrimental to all efforts to abolish or, at least, ease the caste distinctions, it is a sure way of deepening the already existing rifts and disharmonies in our society.

Excerpt from an article on injustice done to homosexual citizens, by Dr. Kamal Taori

***An appeal to fight hypocricy in our society food for thought in the context of homosexuality* (§ 377 - fight it through!)**

July 2, it was one of the days which could redeem some of worries we have concerning our Judicial system. The headlines which captured my attention:

a) Homosexuality legalised in India

b) Thursday July 02 2009

c) A court in New Delhi has overturned a 148-year-old law criminalising the act of gay sex.

d) The groundbreaking ruling allows gay sex between two consenting adults.

e) Sex between people of the same gender can be punishable by up to 10 years in prison there.

f) In 2004 the Indian Government overturned a petition that sought to legalise homosexuality but rights groups and the country's HIV/AIDS control body have lobbied for this new law change.

g) The National AIDS Control Organisation has said that criminalisation was forcing people underground and hampering efforts to battle the virus.

July 2, 2009, will be a positive landmark in India's not-so-good fields of Human Rights, better: Human Rights corner because you get the feeling that the question of establishing and assuring Human Rights for everyone is not high on our public agenda, mostly twisted and sacrificed on the altar of power and money, of superstition and leniency towards the wrong, the narrow-minded, fundamentalist, the self-styled moralists, demands.

One of the abysmally violated Human Right to live one's own life is that of "sexuality" as whole, and the plight of homosexuals in particular.

Here, I don't go into the scientific angle, as there is enough solid research done to show that one's sexual orientation is not "abnormal" in the first place, but that we are born with it, not matter what society expects us to be. And, if we are extremely unlucky, we are born in India with a *natural* orientation towards the same sex—men and women alike. As far as we know, there is the subject "Biology" obligatory in all our schools. Then, what is taught there? The same way the issue of sex education in our schools which should go without saying in modern society, the fact that sex orientation is determined by the hormone structure we are born with, does not deter even educated people—teachers of all people!—to pretend the opposite, thus depicting a narrow-minded moralist attitude, and also, twisting the facts of Indian "culture".

In sharp contrast to what we know about certain periods in Indian history, our societal patterns, the norms and regulations, have developed into a most oppressive, tabooized scenario.

> Recently, a foreign friend asked me about the statistic data of incidence of homosexuality in India. He explained that there must be a much higher incidence than anywhere else, as he observed that male youths are constantly holding hands, hugging, etc. publicly—I explained that they are the victims of a sexually extremely suppressed society where young people neither have the opportunity to develop natural relations with each other, nor can they make experiences or live their sexuality. Society and social pressure don't allow it. They cannot develop a holistic personality. Their, for foreign observers, strange behaviour, shows nothing than want, substituting a very natural set of feelings with the only way out open for them. Further, perverted notions through the present-day influences of TV, not to forget the artificialities of our

> average film productions, create a pathetic image of sexuality. "Love" is perceived as something you are craving for, but, at the same time, they have no idea about how to deal with their craving.

The recent incidences of rapes, gang-rapes, prove clearly that there are hardly natrual and sound perceptions of sexuality in this country. Our youth is deliberately deprived from developing a healthy, positive, joyful sexuality which should be the normalcy in a balanced social set-up. Our media handle the problem very conveniently: rapists are criminals (true!), they have perverted minds, they might have been abused in their childhood, they might be encouraged by group dynamics, by alcohol and drugs, but nowhere did I find thorough critical, reasoned analyses about the fact that our highly suppressive society leads to the boiling over of sexual violence.

Now, where do we have the issue of sexual orientation here?

"Homosexuality" has always been very much a part of our society, like in all societies all over the world, from ancient times. Fundamentalist perceptions of what is "right" and "wrong", and human psychology which unfortunately tends to ostrasize and punish those who deviate from the majority's dictate, have created an overall guilt complex towards sexuality. An abysmal feature in times where we have to deal with HIV, which is much more rampant in heterosexual relations, and increasing by the day. If openly discussed, enlightened people would know how to avoid it and also, how to deal with it, especially youth. A foreign friend told me that she met several youths both, male and female, who were worried that kissing might lead to pregnancy. These in the age group between 15 and 20! (Here, we have to question the actuality of our educational system.)

Moreover, suppressing naturally given sexual needs are reduced to procreation alone. No joy without guilt, no fulfilment without fear of punishment (by humans or gods)! This phenomenon is not confined to our pathetically narrow-minded pundits of morals (all creeds!), but we find it all over the world in communities with suppressive power structures; it is a mighty tool for keeping clout on people through oppressive measures and fear. Examples are abundant: Catholic dogmas, Muslim dogmas, all sectarian dogmas; there is nothing more powerful than successful suppression of natural needs, among them sexuality as the most powerful.

In India, you find "sex doctors", "sex therapists" everywhere, promising worried parents to "cure" homosexuality. As if it is a disease! We don't go into their "thearpies" here, but we can be sure that the patient is left with misery and desperation. Just imagine homosexuals being pressed into marriages: it creates not only lifelong misery for themselves, but also for their spouses!

The issue of sex education received a very mixed echo in our society. Whereas in more enlightened societies sex education goes without saying, here, we experienced an outcry of sorts from all our self-styled shepherds of morals:

a) Sex education promotes promiscuity (enlightened youths would know how to deal with their sexuality).
b) Sex education "evokes sexuality" in students (as if were not a natural feature in all humans).
c) Sex education creates rapists and killers (as if we are not having them).
d) Sex education undermines our Indian culture, it is un-Indian (no sound historian would agree to that: our ancient Gurus very responsibly dealt with the issue).

We are convinced that there is dire need of changing the societal mindset and attitudes towards sound, reasoned approach to sexuality, and this can be achieved mainly through education. Our education ministries (Central and State) should make sex education obligatory from 1st standard onwards. They should interact with parents for their support and, most important, the teachers should be trained well to do their job: after all, they are victims of the all-pervading hypocricy the same way as everyone else.

During my visits in Europe, I met three-four year olds who tell you proudly that they grew for some-time in the womb of their mother, and they came into being because his/her parents loved each other so much that they wanted to physically become as close as possible. They tell you frankly the proper names of genitals, and they know how a body is functioning, according to their ability of perception. There is no false shame, no hiding. Thus, they develop the ability to deal with their sexuality as it changes with growing older, and they have all the chances to deal with it responsibly. They are also able to understand the "opposite" sex better, as female sexuality has the same value as the male one.

True, there is sexually motivated crime in Europe, too. As with all violations against humanity all over the world, it has nothing to do with sexuality as such. It has to do with violence alone, male violence is penis-oriented, and violence is administered to those who seem to be weaker than the violator.

This leads to another demand from our education authorities: make self-defence an obligatory subject in all our schools! It will create self-confidence in girls—yes, we can! We are not subjects but we can defend ourselves!

Gandhiji was of the firm opinion that a society can only be changed by (enlightening) the children. We have to give them the prerequisites for it, the opportunities to develop into whole human beings, holistic entities where body, mind and soul are in balance. Good leadership requires strong, humane personalities. At present, there are not many around.

The verdict of the Supreme Court is a very important step towards a more enlightened society, but it is only the first step. Let us support the humane cause!

Authentic Case Study, with Dr. Taori in the midst of the case

The Speed of Justice—from 1983 to 2010
with no end in sight...

When I was Managing Director of UP State Road Transport Corporation with HQ at Lucknow in 1983, an event took place which I do think is interesting and revealing in many aspects.

The said event happened way back on 2 June, 1983 at Atrolia bus stand of district Azamgarh in UP.

Now, you might say that such an incident might be interesting as an anecdote, perhaps even as a satirical one, but in our India, long-forgotten incidences suddenly crop up again, and many people become—again and/or for the first time—involved in it, even after 27 years!

The gist of what happened is described as follows: Our group consisting of myself, the then Chief Security Officer who was a DIG rank IPS officer and, was passing from Atrolia to Azamgarh, when we noticed a new bus coming at very high speed from the opposite direction. We also noticed that this bus had written on its board some other destination. Both these observations caused immediate suspicion, and we decided to check this bus. We turned and went after the bus, horning and showing clearly that we wanted it to stop.

But, instead of stopping, the driver tried to give us a pass from the left side, which obviously was meant to create confusion and to put us in a most disadvantageous, dangerous position, and even to throw us sideways. This chase continued for about 6 km, and finally, as soon as the bus stand of Atrolia was reached, the bus suddenly stopped. Now, the driver, the conductor, and other staff of UPSRTC of the Station came out with sticks and bamboos and started beating us from all sides while shouting the most vulgar abuses in the world.

Realising the seriousness of the assault, I shouted back and tried to save at least my head as best as I could, but this assault continued for about two minutes longer. Probably, the mob did not expect a counter from our side at all, hence, one by one in these few minutes, they disappeared altogether.

Needless to say that our own driver also had disappeared in the meantime.

Finally, we did what we thought the usual and necessary: going to Police Thana for recording the FIR, going to the local Primary Health Centre for medical examination, trying to gather some witnesses, etc. To our great astonishment, we were advised by almost everyone that I MD and the DIG rank Officer should not take over such checking duties, that it does not "behove good" upon persons like us; implicitly, they meant that we should not wonder if we get beaten up in the course of events. All these trials to influence me adversely were finally topped when one of the local leaders tried to solve the problem while suggesting that he would call back all the culprits so that they could apologise because they didn't know who they were attacking. Again implicitly, he accused us of having led our poor attackers into an error as they would have never imagined people like us doing this type of checking duty.

That means: the victims are in the wrong because they would not have been attacked if the criminals had recognised their superior status. That means also: people of inferior status can be beaten up with no consequences. That means further: if persons of superior status take their responsibilities seriously and act accordingly, they need not wonder to be punished. What a perverted justification by a hypocratic world!

I felt as if the world and its logic had suddenly tilted from feet to headstand.

The story continued in the usual manner in which situations like this are handled in order to avoid any "difficulties" and finally, to hush up everything. All these well-known mechanisms started: the District Officials together with the Police Officers suddenly had to attend a meeting with the Commissioner, so that they could not meet us. Our Senior Officers rebuked us and wanted us to be more careful and dutiful in future, while by "dutiful" they meant to stick to our own narrow, compartmentalised specific tasks, and not taking over responsibilities for the whole SRTC, if and when a specific situation arose.

When we met the Chief Minister, the Chief Secretary, the Director General of Police and others, they all admired our spirit to do responsible work, but they also advised us to be careful and to carry arms with us. The seniormost Police Officer of the State even continued to boast of the best governed State in the nation from the police angle, and how safe it was to work here, except for some aberrations.

To sum up: now 27 years later, the Azamgarh Police Station rang up one day and requested me to come there, all the way from Wardha, and give evidence on this incident in the Court of the Judicial Magistrate.

I am still flabbergasted: I had completely forgotten about the incidence, and I was convinced that things would have long been buried in some files as nobody was willing to follow up the case when it happened. During all these years, during my more than 30 years of professional career in IAS, there were so many assignments in and outside the country that I could hardly remember.

But, by concentrating on all the events, I could remember clearly, as such an assault only happened once to me. Not because I had left my principles for holistic thinking and acting, but only because I was lucky not to fall again into the hands of violent criminals.

Now, once again, I am going to give evidence as we had filed the FIR.

The file in the court is yellowish, some pages are wrinkled and torn. I have no idea what happened to the file in the last 25 years. At least, the culprits are still alive, so I was told.

In the meantime, one of the senior officers who is still in service and enjoys a good reputation as performer, advised me to be a 'genuine Gandhian' and as such, should 'forgive and forget', because "after 27 years, what is going to come out?" He justifies this course on the simple and convenient 'reason' that so many criminals of more serious nature are moving openly in the society, and hence, realising the pitiable condition of police, judiciary, administration, politics, it is better to pardon them with large-heartedness and save oneself from humiliation and frustration.

I did reply to him with my genuine conviction that giving up and 'pardoning' criminals who have taken public funds for granted with impunity, and have given the message that you can always get away with blunder, cheating, and raping the system of its roots. No wonder, UPSRTC officials then, and even now, in all these 27 years, quite considerate and generous in accommodating all sorts of criminals, boosting their morals instead of disciplining the staff in the interest of the customers, and in the interest of the taxpayer who finally has to finance all these criminal activities.

And all these happenings and my musings triggered off some basic questions:

a) How do I look back to what happened then?
b) Have times changed or else, could the same thing happen again?
c) Did it happen to others, too? How often?
d) Was justice done to the victims?
e) What was the role, in all these incidences, of thje UPSRTC officials, the Unions, the Transport Commissioner's Office, the unauthorised operators, the Police, and the judicial system?

It all leads me to analysing holistically the state of condition of governance, obvious corruption, administrative high-handedness, delays, hushing up things inconvenient to some people or only for reasons of avoiding work. It is about the whole unprofessionalism of our highest administrative elite, the failure of the All India Services in general and IAS in particular.

Why is the mindset of accountability and responsibility so abysmally underdeveloped? Why should the "Boss" take decisions (or else, avoid to take decisions which comes logically to failures in decision-making), give orders, and all the work is to be done by the subordinates? Really, a very convenient mechanism to always be on the safe side: if anything comes out as failure, it is always the person who acted to blame.

Is it not the very duty of every senior officer to set an example as efficient, competent top professional, or is it just to issue circulars and expect the subordinates to do justice, to function properly? In an atmosphere like this, we can expect nothing from our senior officer who are afraid of stepping out of their AC rooms and see for themselves what is really happening in their fields of decision-making? Would they ever consider the risk of a beating or even death as part of true professional commitment and thus a hazard of the occupation for which they are well paid for? Would they ever view their way of functioning in view of their oath to the Constitution? Do they even contemplate their bondage with the Constitution?

Our citizens, the taxpayers, the policy makers, the professionals in all fields, the writers, the media persons and those in permanent Civil Service of our nation have to develop a new way of looking at professionalism in this country, and they have to derive decisive expectations and demands. Perhaps, with this radical change of mindset and attitudes at all levels, we can detect a thin silver line of "India shining", but far, far away!

The following describes the practical necessities for changing from un-professional, wrong governance—at all levels—to good governance.

It is easy to cry for "Leaders"—we have to learn to lead ourselves first, then we can understand what "good leadership" and "good leader" means and requires.

The cry for "Leaders" at present just means that others should do the job, and that it is very convenient to be led, by whomsoever, just someone to put the blame on for all failures, and as an excuse for doing nothing.

Ultimately, if one tries to find conclusive answers, there is a big void. After my analyses, there is a structural deficiency in the basic setup of our Public-Private Enterprises and logically, the subsequent functioning cannot be realised. Hence, it is high time to run them on professional lines, which means:

a) Put professionally skilled personal in charge, so that our "Public-Private Enterprises" can function properly as "Public-Private Partnerships" where not one side is exploiting the other.
b) Change the infrastructure towards transparency, accountability and cost-efficiency which would require proper monitoring and modern controlling mechanisms.
c) Analyse weak points where corruption is flowering and eradicate them.

Further developments

On the scheduled date of hearing evidence in Court, the Judge in charge was 'on leave', without having given any information to anyone. The Prosecutor, too, was not informed. Now, we tried to get another date within our short stay in Azamgarh, and this was supposed to be 29, March, 2010, for cross examination. It turned out to be partly cross examination, and finally ended clueless due to the fact that our original FIR is suddenly 'missing', as already mentioned above.

In the meantime, staying in Azamgarh, Lucknow, and Allahabad, I could talk to various people who are either involved in the case or else, can render information on how the case was handled, I also could get a copy of the original file: not only is this file in an extremely bad shape (torn and tattered, partly burned), but I found that at least on two occasions, the file was "missing" altogether: once from the police archives, and once from the judiciary.

Now, there is serious suspicion of foul play—how else could the normal procedures and normal justice be bent and perverted like in this case?

What appals me most is the fact that the culprits are comfortably re-instated in the service of UPSRTC, and that no consequences whatsoever were taken towards their criminal acts. It makes me wonder about the way our Government departments are dealing with employees who are blatantly violating the essential code of conduct, and, commit criminal offences.

The logical message would be: you can do whatever you want as long as you have the ways and means to bent the laws.

Further developments: (from 29 March, 2010, onwards):

a) Not only is the original FIR missing, but also both the personal files (of driver and conductor) are suddenly missing from the Personnel Dept. of UPSRTC.

b) During the court hearing in Azamgarh on 29, March, the accused's lawyer triumphantly pointed out that there is obviously no FIR, whereas the then CSO Roadways, Mr. Naseem, himself had lodged the FIR in June, 1983, together with me.

c) The Judge fixed the next date on April 29, 2010, and again, she was 'on leave' without prior information to anyone.

Time-wise, we have the following overview for the scheduled Court dates:

1.	21-01-2010	Evidence
2.	25-03-2010	Judge is on sudden leave
3.	29-03-2010	Partly cross-examination (FIR is suddenly missing from the file)
4.	29-04-2010	Judge is on sudden leave
5.	01-06-2010	Remaining cross-examination (the missing FIR might have been 'found')

As far as I am informed, the missing FIR has not re-appeared as yet, but this case is so full of miracles that I won't lose hope.

This story will be continued after the Court date on June 1, 2010.

The Court date on June 1, 2010, was again not graced with the presence of the Judge, she was again "on leave". One reason which was given: the 'lawyers were on strike' but, as we saw with our own eyes, the District Court Azamgarh was full of lawyers, and the lawyer of the defendants was very much there in the court room, including the defendants. Thus, it would have been perfectly possible to proceed with the case.

And again: I came all the way to attend the scheduled date, and I have to come again. Concerning the next 'scheduled date', see below.

To sum up

a) Out of five scheduled Court dates, the Judge was 'on leave' for three of them, i.e. around 64 percent absence by the decisive person in a judicial procedure.

b) The missing FIR has still not re-appeared as yet (but: the dismal file is still existing—hope for the future?)

Meantime, I was informed that the next scheduled Court has been fixed for July 7, 2010, in spite of the fact that I informed the Court that I'll be on a lecture tour in universities and other academic institutions in Europe from end of June onwards.

I requested the Prosecutor in charge to deal with the case in my absence.

(This story will be continued after new developments)

(June 7, 2010)

The next date was fixed for 25, October, 2010.

This time, another Judge had taken over. His way of firmly dealing with the procedures was very commendable. Dr. Taori could conclude his cross examination the same day, despite all efforts of the lawyers of the accused persons to have to have two cross examinations. But the sovereign and firm stand of the judge made the proceedings efficient, and so the cross-examination could be completed.

We are hopeful that the second victim, former CSO Roadways, Shri Naseem, will be cross-examined soon, and that after some time, the case can possibly be decided.

Remark: So far, we have no further news on the Speed of Justice in District Court, Azamgarh, UP, but we all know: This story could happen in all our Courts in India.

Letter to the Editor of a Maharashtra daily, *Deshonnati*, with whom we had an extensive discussion on Holistic Sustainable Development

July 20, 2007

Dear Shri Prakashji Pohare,

It was a great surprise and a happy beginning for our institute in Maharashtra that the release of our book *Operationalising Holistic Human Development* (which gives abundant thought and ideas for action in the rural context of India in general and for backward pockets like Vidarbha in particular) was released on your birthday at a simple function at Nagpur in your office by your hands.

While complimenting you on your birthday, we also took the opportunity of sharing with you and Mrs Konwar, member of National Women's Commission, Government of India, and some serious disastrous issues of so-called development. The farmer's suicide, loss of hope, increasing extremism, Naxalite's movement, water scarcity, loss of hope generating models, corruption, wastages of Government funds, etc., have been some of the areas of serious concern. We also felt that the stereotyped solution to these mind-boggling problems of our time cannot be solved by routine efforts. Hence, it is the right time to look beyond and identify potentials of networking with established performers like you to explore new and innovative convergence-based efforts for model building.

As you are aware, during our intensive work in and around Vidarbha, we have established a network with many performing institutions. They have been on their own, without any financial or even technical support from the Government, and still have established a unique position for themselves in diverse fields. Some of them have been already visited by us. We are confident that if we all network, discuss openly, frankly and fearlessly potentials of working together, a new innovative, sustainable and urgently required mode of convergence, and cost-efficient, bankable, viable, models can emerge.

Hence, we have following suggestions as a Plan of Action:

— You have a network of reporters all over Vidarbha, who are either in villages or District or Block level. They have various skills of writing, visualising, documenting, interacting, and marketing. They also have computer skills, know about market and marketing issues, and have a fair amount of closeness and contacts with local administration, including banks, police, market, local Panchayats, Blocks and various ongoing schemes of the Govt are well known to them They also have a good all-round communication infrastructure, and also attend frequent media and press conferences called by various interest groups. In short, they are ideal for being oriented to function as SECA, or Self-Employed Change Agents, whom we have mentioned in our book for galvanising the rural economy. We call it a Marketing-Led Activisation Programme (in brief, for our purpose, we shall call it as MLA-P).

— We have good contacts and proper documentation of Gramdoot model of Wardha which has been acclaimed as a great facilitator all over India, but nobody has come forward as yet to make it the tool of a Total Rural Activisation Programme (TRAP). It is high time that the expertise of them is shared with your rural press reporters so that they not only earn extra income as SECA (Self Employed Change Agent), but also contribute to becoming a solid change agent to consolidate and activate the dormant rural economy.

— We also have partners in Mr XXX, and Mr XXX, both ... have expertise in project making and evaluation for the banks. They are already approved as consultants with various banks and funding institutions. They are prepared to be our network partners in establishing relationships with funders on the one hand, and developing viable village activisation programmes on the other. We have already suggested them to start a Rural Investment and Infrastructure Galvanisation Services (RIIGS), so that the greatest need of the rural sector could be met in the same system by following principles of sound banking and viable investment. This is very important if we want to compete and also develop replicable, transparent and viable projects for meeting the challenges of globalisation in the days to come.

— We may have a joint Steering Group under the chairmanship of a suitable volunteer. Since you have offices in all the districts, and also a good training centre at Nagpur, we could consider starting a training, motivation and consultancy centre on the above lines from there. The purpose is to use the under-used or, as our Company calls it, as "Marketing the Unmarketed", since so much is really unmarketed in India. We feel there is dire need to converge and use all that is unused.

— We also feel that established media like yours must take a lead so that subsequent advantages could be operationalised in the same system by effective networking and lobbying for change by involving the grassroots workers and the qualified leaders.

— Since elected leaders at all levels have a lot of discretionary local developmental funds at their disposal, and often good proposals do not come, it will be our joint effort to develop convergenistic plans with the people and the NGOs. Here, ongoing programmes of the Central and State Governments could also be converged for better results.

— Our Institute and the volunteers and experts working around it are willing and keen to offer their services and expertise at no cost, it will be our effort to bring various players on a common platform, so that we show some Models of Hope for others to come, examine and replicate them.

— To achieve maximum success in our mission, we may operate all our programmes in viable clusters so that the monitoring of all the activities could be on a regular basis with timely correction mechanisation after a specific Monitoring Milestone Concept (MMC) developed by our Institute.

— Programmes which have a solid investibility potential with adequate margin provision by the entrepreneurs are our priority. Our mission is to galvanise the rural economy and not waste our time and energy on duplicating ongoing programmes of the Government which are of basic priority for all important Government functionaries and, at the same time, have been utter failures in view of sustainability and viability. Anyway, by not competing and duplicating, we will achieve much in the field where the Government is not making any efforts, or these are new or untapped areas. Once activity generation picks up in the rural set-up, we can be assured that the holistic development of the village would be a reality, which in turn benefit all the ruralites. This approach to MLA-P has not been tried anywhere in India and Vidarbha could be an ideal cluster to launch it with your active and full participation. Incidentally, our Institute has already done adequate ground level work to launch this appropriate programme which would lead to the following advantages:

a) We do not duplicate the ongoing programmes.

b) We have total convergence, and a marketing-led planning.
c) We use all unused, and implement with Public-Private Panchayat Partnership Principles.
d) We pool, "supplement" or compliment and do not duplicate.
e) We do not neglect any future-oriented idea.
f) We depend upon local resources, skills, knowledge and technology by networking from grassroots level.
g) Our special thrusts are on implementing the Dual System of Professional Education (DSPE), for enhancing the standards of employability and quality, environment protection, organic farming, renewable energies, value addition, local demands, clustering, cost reduction, and quality orientation (also in view of globalisation) with emphasis on self-employment.
h) Our priorities are for those disadvantaged in the society, performing Self-Help Groups, entrepreneurs, and those who have entrepreneurial spirit, and we reward performers.
i) We first present a Series of Performers (case studies) as replicable models, so that confidence is generated.
j) We network with local media, PRI, banks, trainers, so that duplication is avoided and proper coordination ensured.
k) We will document and replicate all our initiatives by training as many SECEs as possible, and by giving them functioning networks and a platform to address their grievances and eventual cases of harassment.
l) We will face the challenges of globalisation with all the means we realistically have at our disposal for saving local jobs and to save people from starvation and exploitation.
m) Our thrust is to shift from manipulative, secretive administration to transparent, participatory managerial changes, including single window services.
n) We will facilitate and encourage diversification in all sectors and build up confidence in capacity and productivity.

o) A new leadership style will be developed which is democratic, egalitarian, participatory, meritocratic, and conducive to civil society.

p) We will analyse policy, training, and networking issues in totality and design suitable models accordingly.

q) The middle classes at all levels of society have an active role to play in this context; we propagate a change of mindset and attitudes which have been neglected hitherto.

r) We will explore marketing potential with railways, airports, bus stations and seek the help of established institutions like Khadi and Village Industries Commission (KVIC) and others, so that they also shed their lethargy and become active partners in the change process for and with the masses.

s) Local schools, colleges, community based institutions, religion based, and spirituality based institutions are to be fully involved in our holistic, all-encompassing programme, provided they fit into our philosophy of transparency and viability

t) Our efforts will lead to models for total, holistic reforms which no Government Department can today even think of, or visualise, forget implementation altogether. This is because the whole structure of the Government is compartmentalised and bureaucratically suffocated which does not suit the developmental paradigm essentially required for sustainable, viable development in the interest of our people.

To sum up: it is high time that we network for replicable results to save the majority of our people from the imminent total, nearly unavoidable disaster. The only way out is to involve grassroot people, local institutions, include marketing-led activisation processes, and let all benefit by working hard. Let us be facilitators in this Herculean task of encouraging the rural masses to realise their true, unexplored real value, and contribute to bring them out of their beggardom, and to avoid more suicides as a first step to improvement.

We are confident that there are many well-meaning and knowledgeable people in the country and abroad who would be glad to share their knowledge and skills in this national resurrection programme.

There is also an urgent need to take action on these lines because unless a programme with thrust on total transformation of villages is not launched as a part of benefit and self-reliance-led convergence, it will again fail. The SECA, and also the DSPE as designed by us concern mostly the Middle Classes for their recruitment. They should be leaders of tomorrow for ensuring long-term sustainable change. As mentioned above, there is also a dire need to galvanise all the dormant systems at the district level and below by unleashing business-oriented initiatives. Hence, if you find the above outline convincing, we may organise a first brain storming workshop on these lines at the earliest at Nagpur, Akola or Wardha as per your convenience. You may also share this letter with all those who could contribute in any way, including substantiated comments and constructive criticism with better options.

Our recent dialogues in Europe and Germany with various functionaries have also cemented our conviction that there is an urgent need to launch innovative experiments if we have to become a vibrant, humane society. Our rural areas need all attention to develop their potential into a big force, and this can be done only by the type of initiatives we have mentioned above.

We suggest that you may also consider inviting a few volunteers for this programme by suitably writing about it in your popular newspaper. We are prepared to offer our total service package to make a distinct dent in an otherwise dismal scenario.

Regards and good wishes,

***Dr. Kamal Taori* (Vidyarthi)**
Irmel Marla
IIHRVA (India-Germany)

Youth Forum for Peace and Understanding—Indo-German Forum for International Relations in Action

The International Institute establishes a Forum for the younger generation in Germany and India which will facilitate/provide personal contacts and practical cooperation on Gandhian lines. The thrust will be on:

a) Educational issues at all levels
b) Environment protection including renewable energies
c) Appropriate IT for the needs of the yet to be developed rural masses
d) Empowering grassroot level confidence building including local policy making, leadership issues and rural entrepreneurship
e) Transporting Gandhi's philosophy into the twenty-first century

We invite all youth to join in this venture. We are resolved not to get involved in any Party-related politics. Our expectations:

a) Thinking beyond boundaries
b) Commitment to social causes
c) Hope generating mindset
d) Multiplicators for the cause
e) Active involvement in change processes

As a first step to provide proper infrastructure and also, facilitate the exchange of youth we offer our network connectivities all over India for realising the international coming together and learning from each other with a holistic, unconventional approach.

We do not intend to establish a bureaucratic setup but a lively and creative platform which will take up the burning issues at present and develop into a continuous vibrant, self-motivating and self-organising exchange forum.

Our appeal:

Please get into contact with us so that we can give you our suggestions and also, for example, share our opinions on:

a) spending some time in an appropriate institution in India.

b) getting more information about our work and also, about the burning issues in India.
c) giving us your ideas and suggestions for spreading them to like-minded youth and to further enhance the impact and connectivities.
d) giving us your experiences which you have already gathered for sharing them with like-minded youth.
e) facilitating mutual contacts with youth worldwide sharing interests and expertise leading to pro-active ventures.

We refer to our book *Operationalising Holistic Human Development—Food for Thought and Ideas for Action"* (published by Concept Publishing Company, New Delhi, 2007). At present, we are working on related issues like "Transporting Gandhiji into the 21st Century", "Impact of Indian Middle Classes on Development Scenario", and a reference book on the issues concerning the above mentioned Youth Forum, with thrust on the hitherto un-marketed, unexplored solid potential of Indo-German (European) relations.

We are looking forward to actively network with you and invite your ideas!

Irmel V. Marla and Dr. Kamal Taori

Letter by the Chairperson of IIHRVA, Irmel V. Marla, to the DG SRTCUP (will be published in our series of authentic case studies on the state of leadership competency in our country)

March 27, 2010

To DG SRTC UP, XXX
H.Q. Tehri Kothi, M.G. Marg
Lucknow—226 001
Uttar Pradesh

Dear Shri XXX,

I feel it necessary to inform you about a very strange incident within your Department, a case happened 27 years ago (!), and still dragging along. It concerns a former MD in the SRTC, Dr. Kamal Taori (IAS rtd.) who is Partner and Advisor to my International Institute. In this context, I could gather all information on the above-mentioned case—details will be given below—and, as I am researching functioning of Government agencies and also, the Judiciary, I do think that the Top Management should be informed so that "fishy" collaboration and goings-on detrimental to the proper functioning of an important Department can be identified and wiped out.

The case as it evolved:

2 June, 1983	Dr. Taori, MD UPSRTC, together with Chief Security Officer, Shri Naseem, IPS, went from Faizabad to Azamgarh via Atrolia by car. The whole incident is described in the enclosed document "The Speed of Justice". Same day, an FIR was registered at Atrolia Thana by CSO, Shri Naseem, IPS. Our medical examination was carried out and documented.
7 June, 1983	Second statement of Dr. Kamal Taori was recorded at Lucknow.
5 August, 1983	A wireless from CB CID, DIG Natulal, needs to be explored further, as it is not clear what it said and what triggered it off.
9 Sept. 1983:	Some correspondence from Police.
17 Nov, 1983:	Some correspondence from Police.
15 June, 1989:	Some correspondence from Police.
Between 1983&1988	Out of five persons accused, the Police investigating officer acquits three on his own.

Others were granted bail by the Judicial Magistrate, but subsequently, the DJ cancelled the bail, and thus for around 41 days, the remaining accused stayed in jail. Subsequently, they were granted bail by the High Court Allahabad.

We do not know what all happened during this period, and also, we do not know if all the five originally accused were identified, nor do we know if an identification parade took place in jail. The records are vague in this context. After some time, the Section 7 of Criminal Law Amendment Act was applied in view of the severity of the case.

On 26 July, 1983,	probably the CID was to take over this case, but what really happened is not transparent; fact is that obviously nothing happened. In the Police Record, the chargesheet or a final report is not recorded at all.
19 September, 1988	SSP Azamgarh writes a letter—contents not known (should be investigated into).
27 September,1988	The present DGP of U.P., Shri Karamvir Singh, who then was SSP Azamgarh, wrote a note for expediting this case. He also wrote a letter to SP Bhallia for tracing a certain Mr. Mishra, Inspector, who had retired and had not handed over the papers of this case. It is not clear what prompted the then SSP, Shri Karamvir Singh, to ask for the documents and for expediting the case.
7 November, 1988	Some report about 'missing file'.
15 April, 1989	Chargesheet No. 16 was sent to the concerned Court against 2 accused persons.
18 January, 1999	Probably, the chargesheet was framed.
12 July, 2001	Judge Anupathi Rao Yadav writes to DJ Azamgarh (contents not known, detailed have to be found out).

14 July, 2000	2nd Addl. CJM, Azamgarh, writes to SO regarding 'pendancy in the absence of evidence or witnesses', or so.
18 June, 2001	Fixed for evidence: whose or when is not known.
18 July, 2001	DJ writes by hand, explaining complaint or so.
5 October, 2001	Information to DJ (not known, should be examined).
8 October, 2004	Some note about 'missing documents' was issued by the PP.
26 March, 2009	Senior PP gives a note regarding action to be taken to trace the missing FIR.
13 July, 2009	The statement of Rajesh Bajpayee, the then peon of MD UPSRTC, Dr. Kamal Taori, was recorded in the Court.
21 January, 2010	The statement of Dr. Kamal Taori was recorded partly by the Hon. Judge.
26 March, 2010	Dr. Taori came all the way from Wardha to give evidence, but at the scheduled date, the Hon. Judge preferred to stay away from Court. No notice was given in time. Next date is fixed for March, 29, 2010.
29 March, 2010	After recording the evidence of Dr. Kamal Taori, during cross examination, the opposition Lawyer triumphantly stated that no FIR is in the file. The case is adjourned to 29 April, 2010, for further cross examination and also, for tracing the FIR in the meantime (after 27 years!).

As it looks like this case will become a type of 'never-ending story', I would like to put some basic questions to possibly speed up the whole thing:

a) Where is the missing original FIR? What was done to trace it? What was done to make it disappear? Was it sent to CJM within 24 hours by the police station as is warranted? If not, why not? If so, what happened in the CJM's office?

b) Where are the bail papers? Especially: acceptance, rejection, and granting by the High Court?

c) Why is the existing file in such an abysmal condition: partly torn, partly burnt so that whole pages are not legible at all, an overall very sad state of affairs? One feels that many things might be missing without a trace.

d) Why were three of the original accused not brought to book? Why is nothing in the file to explain their acquittal?

e) Why were the remaining accused re-instated as driver and conductor respectively, with full payment and "lucrative" routes?

f) What would have happened to the case if the then SSP would not have sent the notes in 1988?

g) Would it not be compulsory to lodge an FIR against the seemingly lost original FIR? There cannot be any doubt that someone within the Police/Judiciary has removed it from the file.

From a neutral point of view, the whole case—during the 27 years of its not-to-be-solved existence, is full of contradictions, suspicious procedures, non-availability of evidence which was clearly available at a certain stage of procedures, miraculous disappearances and re-appearances, that one can only assume that it was foul play from the very beginning.

I do admire Dr. Kamal Taori and his stamina to withstand all adverse actions, and to try to get justice at last. And I am sure that you will also support this noble cause—mainly in view of taking to task everyone in your Corporation who might be or might have been involved in foul play. It is not about vengeance and such petty-minded reasons, but it is about doing justice and making it clear to all that violating law and citizen's rights won't be tolerated.

Looking forward to action and to your reply, greetings ands best wishes,

Irmel V. Marla, Sociologist/Anthropologist
Chairperson: IIHRVA (India-Germany),
Vice Chairperson: RBHFI
Enclosed: Case study "The Speed of Justice" (see Appendix)

Remark: To my knowledge, nor was there any response, nor any action taken from this side.

Dr. Kamal Taori (IAS rtd.), Vidyarthi
Chairman: Rural Business Hub Foundation India
Partner & Advisor: IIHRVA(India-Germany)
6 March, 2010

First Letter by the Chairperson IIHRVA, Irmel V. Marla, to the Commissioner Charitable Trusts, Mumbai

25 July, 2009

To: Commissioner Charitable Trusts—confidential

Subject: Case studies for analyses and publication, here: application against the Government. Advocate who appeared in the Court of DJ Wardha, case "Trust Application No. 1/2008", and related issues around the Trust Act with special reference to Maharashtra

Dear Sir,

I am working on research and practical implementation of holistic development in rural India with my above-mentioned *International Institute*. As holistic approach is all-encompassing, the educational fields play a very important role on all our activities. While compiling resource material, especially case studies for our analyses of the most burning problems in the Indian educational system, we came across a most absurd case which we describe in the following. We are of the firm opinion that you should be informed about such most bizarre and incomprehensible goings-on, so that you can take the necessary steps for preventing future repetitions and, if necessary, punish the guilty:

The case as it developed:

1. The ACC Wardha had accepted a Change Report inquiry no. 212/05
2. In this CR, by giving a clear detailed order, the learned authority of ACC clearly stated the CR was to be implemented.
3. After a gap of about eight months (!), the opposite Party went to the hon. JCC Nagpur with Revision Application No: 10/2006, on 27 April, 2006. The hon. JCC passed a reasoned detailed order upholding the above mentioned order of the ACC Wardha.
4. With the Trust Application No 1/2008 (!), the DJ - 2 Wardha, was approached by the opposite Party, and he passed an order on 5 May, 2009, remanding the CR 212/2005 to ACC Wardha for holding fresh inquiry.
5. It is in this order that we noticed some glaring anomalies. There is repeated mention of the procedural mistakes in the systems followed by the hon. ACC Wardha.
6. By reading the order it appears that the office of the ACC Wardha, due to presumed legal and procedural mistakes by the State officials have become a laughing stock.
7. It suggests that because of the mistakes of the State Pleader who, on behalf of the ACC Wardha, and the JCC Nagpur, did not take proper precautions, and make appropriate, adequate representations to the hon. DJ-2 Wardha, that an order not based on legal footing could have been passed so that the duly elected present Governing Body of the Trust headed by Dr. Kamal Taori is, as a result, now seriously suffering.
8. Although the order speaks about a "fresh inquiry" preferably within three (!) months, the complexity of the case and the different locations of the members at various and faraway places, a fact well known by the DJ-

2, make it a mockery of the judicial pronouncement and also, call for a high level inquiry.

This case is especially interesting for us in view of the fact that the legal representative of the State did not take any step to represent the case properly, finally resulting in the miscarriage of justice and the irreparable loss of credibility to the State and the Offices concerned.

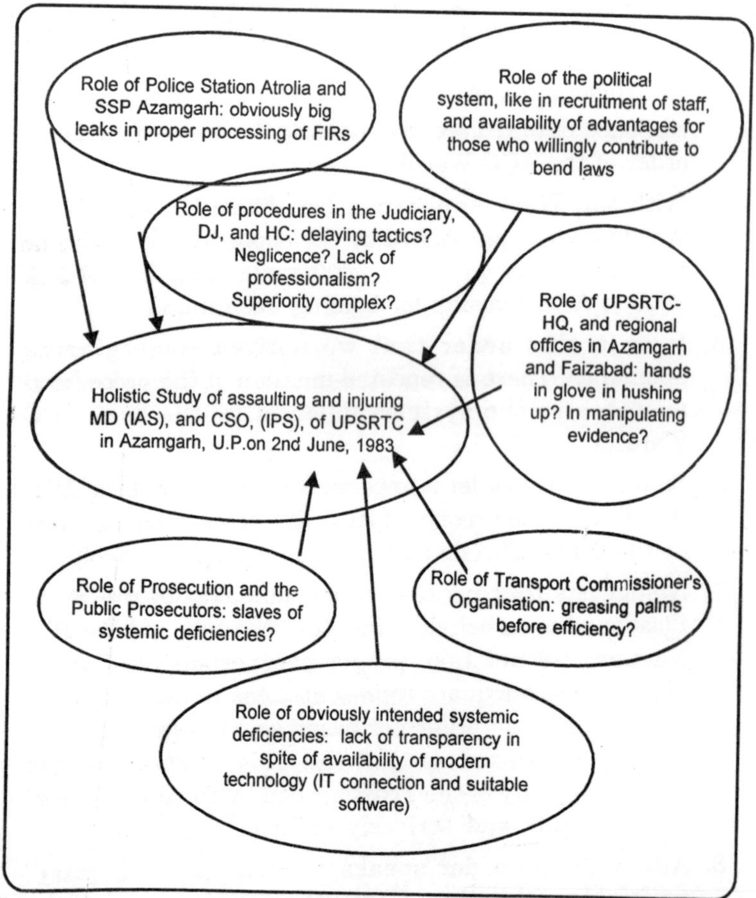

Incidentally, while going through the above-mentioned order and also, the system of interpretation of the Bombay Public Trust Act, we found innumerable flaws and weak points in this

Act, like: that it can only lead unnecessary litigations at the cost of public money, and the real purpose of the TRUST embodied in the Act, becomes a casualty. The danger of innumerous litigations, and battles for supremacy in the whole set-up of the Act, can thus create havoc, and the good, well-meaning trustees can never function properly in this system.

In the following, we are describing some of the most glaring anomalies in this Act and also, phrase the necessary questions concerning a proper functioning:

a) What exactly are the duties of the advocate or the official who represents the Charity Commissioner in the courts of the judiciary?

b) What is the role of ACC as a judicial officer and also as a custodian of the Public Trust?

c) What are precisely the procedures followed in accepting or rejecting Change Reports?

d) What are the abilities, capacities, and competencies of the staff working in the offices of the trust to fulfil the role and the expected duties in the area of trusts?

e) The Act has the entire voluntary sector under its purview. The Khadi & Village Industries, and the medical, social, educational, religious, philanthropic sectors of the society, are covered by this Act on Charity basis. But the complexity of the modern society makes them fallible and gullible to contradictory compulsions of our time. On the one hand, there is the growing commercialisation and on the other hand, the expectations or responsibilities in the amorphous areas of so-called social compulsions.

f) This situation is extremely advantageous for massively evolving corruption, harassment, and the rape of philanthropic issues concerning the conduct of the affairs in Charitable Trusts.

We are of the firm opinion that the case study of the XXX is especially suitable to be analysed in view of sound or good governance, anomalities in the present-day functioning of Govrnment Institutions, and the trustworthy, healthy development of an egalitarian civil society.

The questions we postulate (above and in the following) should, if sincerely answered and dealt with which we expect from your respected Office, lead to an overall improvement in

— the functioning of the Office of the Charity Commissioner, and

— serve as model for replication for other, similar institutions.

Our decisive questions are the following:

1. Why did the advocate representing the state, i.e. ACC and JCC, did not put down in writing all the submissions which would have helped the cause of justice and prove the facts?
2. Why are the procedures followed by the ACC and his office, not designed properly to show the facts clearly which would have shown beyond doubt the manipulative nature of putting up false statements by the opposite parties?
3. When the earlier members who:
   i) had resigned voluntarily,
   ii) presented themselves before the ACC,
   iii) given no-objection certificates to the induction of the new members,
   iv) wrote letters to the banks about the operation of the accounts by the new body, and
   v) also took back the advance payments they had earlier made to the society then, how on earth could a fresh inquiry in this matter be ordered at all? (All these facts, from a. to e., are proven through written documents, and they are part of the application of the XXX Trust!)
4. The problems of managing a rural educational institution with quality and excellence, by people of experience and determination, need to be viewed from the angle of social responsibility, but not from the aims and objectives of those who consider an educational institution an easy opportunity to amass wealth, to loot, and to make

education a business like any other, where you have a free-for-all and can exploit the weakest and most vulnerable. If properly investigated, this case would bring out the various dimensions of corruption, delay and the mindset of greed which are the driving forces behind all these obstacles, as we found out.

5. The quality of the procedures, and the need for clarity and transparency, for example the question:
   i) Are the Change Report procedures judicial or quasi-judicial?
   ii) Concerning quality and competency of the ACC:
      a) Are they personally responsible for their decisions?
      b) Can they be taken to task in case of poor performance?
      c) Are there areas of confusion and misunderstanding in the laws, the regulations and procedures?
      d) Is there too much space for contradictory judicial interpretations in the Act of Trust matters?
      e) Can trustees give rights and even their power of attorney to a criminally dismissed clerk from the judiciary and expect him to look after all the litigation and other works of the educational society? (as is the case in our case study of XXX Trust)
      f) Can former trustees after having officially and with all written legal procedures and documentation resign, then, after some time, out of the blue, decide on their own, without any documentary proof, to be members and office bearers again? This absurdity was, in the case study of XXX Trust, taken serious by the DJ-2 Wardha.
6. In our civil society with its vast discrepancies, the role of Charitable Institutions becomes more and more

crucial, especially in view of the deprived and poorer segments in the rural areas. Not too many experts and resourceful people are working in these difficult areas, and they hardly have the competency to run and manage trusts. They might have expertise in their professional fields, but when they have to run and manage a trust, they too often rely on so called experts, in reality manipulators who work only for money and have no genuine interest in quality and diversity. The issue of successful quality management in trusts need training and regular updating not only of the trustees, the lawyers, but also of the entire office of the Charity Commissioner. It also means updating of knowledge, legal systems and judiciary procedures, but also present-day requirements and demands for the charity sector and its legitimate role in our society. At the same time, the Government policies in this context seem to be highly insensitive, bureaucratic and even more exploitative than the forces we described above, that means, the continuous updating process has to be introduced in Government offices the same way.

7. The Khadi and Village industries sector is not functioning well because the legitimate element of profit has not been implemented properly so far. It is a grave misunderstan-ding to think that "profit" is something which should be seen as a negative force: as long as proper production in healthy surroundings, accompanied by job creation, training for skills and knowledge, and non-exploitative infrastructure-cum-marketing strategies are applied, "profit" is most conducive for an overall positive development. Only this way, we can be sustainable and competitive in the era of globalisation and liberalisation. How else can we meet the conflicting compulsions of change and value systems in our never-changing demographic profile?

8. While analysing the above-mentioned procedures, cases and behavioural patterns, we found it extremely important to improve the whole situation by appropriate

practice-oriented training measures. It need to be developed as a flexible system of training modules which can be undergone after specific needs at of a certain office and in a certain setup. Our International Institute is prepared to take up this task with its expertise and make the Trust sector a vibrant and moving-ahead tool for positive development. We learn on an international platform, sharing experiences and working internationally, adjusting implementable models to the Indian conditions.

9. Our International Institute works for holistic development of the society and has close working relationships with the above mentioned XXX Trust. This way, and through our transparent communication patterns, we could observe the goings-on first hand, and we know that the facts brought forward by the XXX Trust are proven facts.
10. From the information in our website, you might know that we feel close to "modern" Gandhian principles, especially concerning a code of behaviour, mindset and attitudes, simplification of procedures and transparency and efficiency of bureaucratic and judicial processes. The existent Trust Act does not meet the requirements of modern society: we observe good, determined people trying to dedicate themselves into the charitable sector in setting examples for good performance, but they are harassed by all sorts of obstacles, as shown above. It should not be possible that convicted criminals, dismissed employees of the judiciary, can interfere and disturb the efficient running of deserving institutions. It is the lack of transparency and clarity which makes it easy for fraudy manipulators to interfere and profit for their own good.
11. In this "Gandhian" context, as we prepare for a wider analysis of the social structure and significances of the Wardha District, we have already prepared a set of documents for publication, among them an analysis of the functioning of the judiciary in "Gandhiji's" District[44], the same as we will deepen our analyses of the educational sector.

We are convinced that we could evoke your genuine interest, and that you will actively deal with the matter. Please feel free to contact us if anything needs to cleared and/or verified, or if questions have to be answered. Our main purpose and expectations are that you will be ignited enough to investigate from your angle and also, get your competent staff to overhaul the Trust Act so that it will fit in our present-day society. From the latter, the whole country would benefit greatly.

We are looking forward to your reply, especially to hear from you which actions you have taken.

Warm regards and best wishes, yours

Irmel V. Marla (Sociologist/Anthropologist)

Second Letter by the Chairperson of IIHRVA, Irmel V. Marla, to the Charity Commissioner, Mumbai, concerning an authentic case study and my observation how the case was (mis)handled so far:

Stutensee, Germany, 31, December, 2009

To: Charity Commissioner Mumbai,
83, Dr.Annie Besant Road, Worli,
Bombay—400 018.

Respected Sir,

I am a German, and "Person of Indian Origin" (PIO Card Holder), settled in Kerala and working for Holistic Sustainable Rural Development in India with my own International Institute. At present, I am also writing on various burning issues of Indian Society, emphasis on Judicial System, and related topics. Also, I refer to my earlier letter dated April, 2009, in which I already tried to put your attention on the strange goings-on in Wardha ACC Office.

I am convinced that your Office should be informed about the very strange way cases are handled in ACC Office Wardha. I studied the relevant laws in the "Bombay Charitable Trust Act" and, especially from these, I just cannot fathom that things could go so obviously wrong. This is the reason why I feel compelled to inform you as the Superior Authority. A copy of my letter to you will go to Joint Charity Commissioner Nagpur, and of course, as a matter of fairness and in good Gandhian spirit, to the Wardha ACC, too. The copies will be delivered by hand.

I am referring to the case of the Charitable Trust "XXX" in Paloti/Wardha, where a group of former members, after having resigned with all proper procedures, came forward after nearly 8 months to declare their resignations as faulty and pretended to be still rightful members—documents and other evidence show clearly that their claims are fraudulent.

This is the case in a nutshell as I personally studied and analysed it. My reasons for informing you are in connection with the work of my "International Institute for Holistic Research and Voluntary Action" where Dr. Kamal Taori, the present President of XXX, is Partner and Advisor.

This special case cannot be viewed without linking it with the vested interests of Dr. Taori's self-estranged relatives in order to understand their motives and put the motives behind into right perspectives.

I tried to clarify this with your ACC Wardha, Smt. YYY, but met with utter disinterest, if not contempt, and I am convinced that this cannot be in the interest of the Charity Commission in Maharashtra.

I am very much disturbed by the goings-on in the Wardha ACC Office. I could follow the proceedings very closely and, as I am a trusted friend of Dr. Taori and his family, I could study all documents, and was personally present at several occasions when so called hearings were conducted or else, just cancelled without notice as the Smt. YYY, ACC Wardha, suddenly went on leave, this without informing at least the Taoris. I don't know about the opposite Party. If I had slightest doubts about the rightfulness of the claims of Dr. Taori and family, I would definitely discuss it with them frankly, as is my nature.

The following are my personal experiences and analyses which I am convinced would give you an insight on the reasons why ex-members of a Charity Trust i.e. XXX try at all costs, even at the cost of committing acts which are punishable according to Indian laws, try to destroy a highly successful educational institution or else, bring it under their—incompetent—possession with no other aims than money and/or vengeance. Throwing sand into the eyes of the authorities, erecting smokescreens to hide their fraud, influencing office staff, defaming and cheating are the weapons used.

Points for consideration

1. A certain Mr. PPP who is a dismissed clerk from Judiciary in (Wardha District), has been given Power of Attorney of XXX by ex-members who had previously voluntarily resigned from their membership with appropriate resignation documents. According to my various personal observations, Mr. PPP is "at home" in the Office of ACC Wardha, happily chatting away with the staff there, obviously on very close terms with them. It felt as if he is determining the situation, and I wouldn't have been astonished seeing him occupying a desk, taking out files and dealing with them. Considering the reasons why he was dismissed from his job, i.e. dabbling, removing, and manipulating Government records, this is highly alarming! To support my point, I attach the dismissal order so that you might understand my point: while in service, he removed documents or dabbled with them! The dismissal is proof enough to underline my worries.
2. I had the opportunity to talk personally to Smt. YYYY, an appointment I had sought as I couldn't fathom that she should not be aware of what is happening—after all, if at all she is present in her office, everything happens in clear sight of her.

   I might inform you that I have been Head of the Department of HRD in a German insurance company for nearly 30 years, and from that I can well analyse competences and motivations of people at work. Two main things were very clear: The Smt. YYY conveyed to me that she was "on deputation only", that gave the impression she is not at all happy with her job. Also, job motivation was not discernible in all she said, but only deep boredom, to say the least. This explains her frequent absences, I think.

To sum up: she wasn't interested in what I was trying to convey to her, and also, she seemed to be oblivious of the fact that the above mentioned Mr. PPP was behaving like taking over the running of her office, together with his "clients", the self-estranged relatives of Dr. Taori and opposite Party in the case—all this in her clear view!

3. As I understand from the "Bombay Charitable Trust Act", the ACC has to give "directions" how to proceed. This is very much missing in Smt. PPP's orders, if at all her deliverances can be called "orders". At the best, it is delaying, time-consuming and confusing (exactly what the opposite Party wants), at the worst, it is biased, almost completely yielding to Mr. PPP and Friends which seem to have all the attributes of a "gang".

   So, there is great danger that you as Superior Authority might be mis-informed and also, as long as the gang of 'Mr. PPP and Friends' come and go in the ACC's Office as they do in clear sight of everyone, I am not convinced that documents there are safe and are not in danger of being tampered with.

Main Conclusions

There is a quite strong local "informal power infrastructure" functioning Wardha District Court and ACC Office, an informal influential power structure directed against Dr. Taori and family. After serving in IAS for around 40 years, he came back to his roots, naively thinking that he could contribute to the development of his Home District. Exactly this was extremely inconvenient for his relatives, as they had to be afraid of his presence due to the following reasons (I only name the most relevant, as there are a lot of minor back-biting instances).

During his absence, a fairly big land deal has been done by forging his signature and photo (cases are now pending in Court), and his coming back would mean disclosure, the blowing off the lid of criminally cheating the brother and uncle of his lawful inheritance. There are several other frauds to his disadvantage. What is important in analysing the situation is the fact that only after it became clear that Dr. Taori sincerely would come back and then claim what is rightfully his share in the ancestral property, they had to drive him away, on the one hand to avoid him claiming his share, on the other hand to avoid punishment for having committed criminal acts, like serious fraud. From the chronology of events, it is obvious that:

1. The ex-members of the Trust resorted to revoke their voluntary resignation around eight months (!) after their proper resignation, at exactly the time when Dr. Taori was about to claim his family shares. The validity of the resignation documents of the ex-members are beyond a shadow of doubt. Here, the timing of events make the whole actions of the resigned members especially suspicious: all of them are family members who have to lose not only the property they tried to cheat, but also face criminal charges against them if Dr. Taori and family would stay on in Wardha!
2. Now, they could be confident to throw as much difficulties as possible in the way of the present management of the XXX by building up a smokescreen of blunt lies concerning their resignations, even going to the extent to fake an impostor of a long-dead former member of the Trust. All this with the intent of fighting the threat the return of Dr. Taori and Family to Wardha meant to them. They could be quite confident considering the snail pace of bureaucratic and judicial procedures. Also, they could be confident that, with their local influence, by defaming him and his family, he would soon be so demoralised and worn down so that they could keep the upper hand. In this, they underestimated the determination of Dr. Taori to see to it that justice prevails. In this spirit, he is voluntarily working as Partner and Advisor to my International Institute which is dedicated to fight unjust conditions in society wherever they might occur.

3. Dr. Taori and family could not have become part of these "informal local power structures" as he was stationed in various places outside Maharashtra during his professional career. Thus, he had no idea about the fraud and cheating, or about the well-established, well-oiled links between criminals, cheaters, frauds and the bureaucracy at local levels.
4. In such conditions, it is very easy to create evil rumours of "misusing donations" (nothing proved) and the like, all to throw suspicions on honest citizens who do their best to serve the country, be it by managing a well-established educational institution—in the case of Dr. Sheila Taori, be it as Partner and Advisor for a renowned International Institute, dedicated to improve the living conditions of rural poor and working towards holistic sustainable development. These attempts of character assassination are clearly to be observed.
5. The chronology of the Charitable Trust in question also shows that nothing at all was established and functioning prior to the arrival of Dr. Sheila Taori in 2002. She has built up the institution, and under her leadership it became a very valuable asset of Primary Education up to College level in a rural area. It is not fathomable that anyone of the opposing Party would be able to run an educational institution successfully for utter lack of competence in the first place. To my knowledge, they are hardly educated enough for such a task. Also, they are interested only in making money out of it, as is clearly to be seen in their fraudulent acts concerning their trying to cheat Dr. Taori of his ancestral share and other fraud they committed.
6. I had the opportunity to come to know the self-estranged relatives of Dr. Taori and family, and I cannot imagine any of them having the slightest competence to run nor interest in a school or college. Mr. NNN Taori, close buddy of dismissed Mr. PPP and member of the gang 'PPP & Friends', the fiercest adversary of Dr. Taori and also happily "at home" at the ACC Office, is not only

bragging about having the "police in my pocket", but also donning the same shirt on several consecutive days, becoming filthier and smellier by the day. This is not what should be expected from a future "President" of an educational institution, as he is loudly and frequently presenting himself as "future President of XXX".

It goes without saying that the case of XXX has to be viewed from a holistic angle: taking into consideration the timings and strange accusations, the main aim is to drive Dr. Taori and family out of Wardha by defaming, committing all sorts of fraud, and playing the "local power card". Such is the psychology behind the driving forces.

I don't know for sure if your ACC, Smt. YYY, is—consciously or unconsciously —adversely influenced, or if she is merely just not interested in proper performance of her job, or in protecting an institution like XXX and the welfare of the students. What I very well know are the facts as mentioned above, and the logical conclusions out of them: the Charity Commissioner should intensively and thoroughly scrutinise the procedures hitherto and should not allow anyone to dabble with the law out of disinterest, bias, or out of simple boredom of having to manage a position which is not of one's liking.

I personally tried my best to mediate and to give her some ideas from a different angle. There is so much at stake, and I cannot leave a stone unturned if there is a possibility to get things straight and right.

The plot of the adversaries of Dr. Kamal Taori and family to take over the XXX is nothing than the smokescreen to hide much worse criminal acts and, of course, take vengeance on people who in good faith just try to claim what is rightfully theirs.

At present, I am writing a book on case studies of Indian Judiciary System and related issues which involve the necessity of reforming the "Bombay Charitable Trust Act", and the case study of the performance of ACC Wardha would surely be a highlight for the chapters where I am dealing with "Justice done—or Justice done with?", which is the biggest part of the book.

I am convinced that you will take this information into consideration, as we all are trying hard to continuously improve our work, and I express my gratitude for it.

Our international work is already suffering due to the uncertainties having befallen the XXX, and our mutual programmes are stalled as long as it is not clear that the time-proven quality management will continue undisturbed. Thus, our partner institutions abroad are anxiously waiting for the green light, and, in view of the glaring evidence they are informed about, they cannot understand the harm done to a hitherto very much approved institution, and the hesitation of the authorities to protect it.

Looking forward to your reply, sincere regards, and, considering the time of the year, a very happy NEW YEAR,

Yours

Irmel V. Marla (Sociologist/Anthropologist)

P.S. I enclose the copy of the dismissal order of Mr. Pimpelwar, at present having "Power of Attorney" from the resigned members of the Trust, together with the POA document

P.S. I enclose my earlier letter dated 25 July, 2009. Letters of Dr. Taori sent to you in this regard, have been left unanswered as yet.

P.S. I also enclose information on my International Institute and our work.

December 2008/January 2009

Irmel V. Marla (Sociologist/Anthropologist

The Ruling Laws are the Laws of those that are Ruling (Observations on the Normal Practices of the Indian Judiciary System)

> Civilisation is not a cheap commodity. If you are called upon for subtle judgements, you have to make subtle law, and if there are subtle laws then you must make a trade of law in which buying and selling is bound to come in. Therefore, civilised courts naturally become markets for the buying and selling of justice, and those who have no money stand every chance of getting swindled.
>
> *(Rabindranath Tagore: Gora, Tara Press, New Delhi, 2008 (first published in 1909), p.223)*

While reading the novel *Gora* by Rabindranath Tagore, written in 1909 (!) I wondered if anything has changed in India since then; I contemplated on all the various observations, information and complaints I got from all strata of Indian society, coming to the conclusions that on the one hand, we took over the Judicial System from our Colonial Masters, like so many other things the obedient Brown Sahibs were eager to make it their own, on the other hand, no improvement through all the six decades of Independence can be noticed. The following gives some observations and analyses of the very precarious state of condition of our system: fact is that the majority of the Indian people don't have any trust, and those who have a clout on it, widely misuse it.

The Indian Judicial System is based on the Constitution and, while trying to understand and coming to the root causes of the miserable state of condition, we first have to comprehend these basics:

Independent India has given its citizens one of the finest democratic constitutions in the world. As is usual, there have been various amendments through its six decades, and also, there are some flaws due to over- or even misinterpretation, but essentially, it is a very commendable fundament to build a modern society on.

Then, why is there so much dissatisfaction all over the country, why is it possible that we all feel the Constitution is not properly put into practice? We take a close look into one of the most important fields where a democratic country can be analysed and, literally, be judged: its judicial system, its judiciary, the way justice is realised. We have to put basic questions, like 'how can the average citizen gain justice', 'how is the system dealing with crimes, with criminals', 'what is the overall opinion of Indian citizens about their judicial system', 'is there a feeling of security, of trust in the system'? Furthermore, we have to analyse the changes our judicial system underwent during its six decades in existence: is it still up to the rules the constitution demands or else, has it been perverted over the years, and if so, in whose interest?

According to the Indian Constitution, the Judiciary System is the "third power", besides legislative and Government, and, as such, supposed to be an independent force, designed to protect the rights of all citizens and to watch over the Constitution.

Now, let us carefully look at the present condition of our Third Power, its infrastructure, its impact and, most important of all, its independence in practice.

Let us start with the original and, as I see it, not compromisable demands of the Indian Constitution[45] in view of the judiciary system, so that we might not oversee its very strong claims:

The preamble strongly says:

> We, the people of India, having solemnly resolved to constitute India into a sovereign socialist secular democratic republic and to secure to all its citizens:
>
> Justice, social, economic and political;
>
> Liberty of thought, expression, belief, faith and worship;
>
> Equality of status and of opportunity; and to promote among them all
>
> Fraternity assuring the dignity of the individual and the unity and integrity of the Nation;
>
> In our constituent assembly this twenty-sixth day of November, 1949, do hereby adopt, enact and give to ourselves this constitution.
>
> ....
>
> *Part IV. Directive Principles of state policy...*
>
> 38. State to secure a social order for the promotion of welfare of the people.—(1) The State shall strive to promote the welfare of the people by securing and protecting as effectively as it may a social order in which justice, social, economic and political, shall inform all the institutions of the national life.
>
> (2) The State shall, in particular, strive to minimise the inequalities in income, and endeavour to eliminate inequalities in status, facilities and opportunities, not only amongst individuals but also amongst groups of people

residing in different areas or engaged in different vocations.

39. Certain principles of policy to be followed by the State. The State shall, in particular, direct its policy towards securing—

a) that the citizens, men and women equally, have the right to an adequate means of livelihood;

b) that the ownership and control of the material resources of the community are so distributed as best to sub serve the common good;

c) that the operation of the economic system does not result in the concentration of wealth and means of production to the common detriment;

d) that there is equal pay for equal work for both men and women;

e) that the health and strength of workers, men and women, and the tender age of children are not abused and that citizens are not forced by economic necessity to enter avocations unsuited to their age or strength;

f) that children are given opportunities and facilities to develop in a healthy manner and in conditions of freedom and dignity and that childhood and youth are protected against exploitation and against moral and material abandonment.

39A. Equal justice and free legal aid. The State shall secure that the operation of the legal system promotes justice, on a basis of equal opportunity, and shall, in particular, provide free legal aid, by suitable legislation or schemes or in any other way, to ensure that opportunities for securing justice are not denied to any citizen by reason of economic or other disabilities.

45. Provision for free and compulsory education for children. The State shall endeavour to provide, within a period of ten years from the commencement of this Constitution, for free and compulsory education for all children until they complete the age of fourteen years.

48. Organisation of agriculture and animal husbandry. The State shall endeavour to organise agriculture and animal husbandry on modern and scientific lines and

shall, in particular, take steps for preserving and improving the breeds, and prohibiting the slaughter, of cows and calves and other milch and draught cattle.

50. Separation of judiciary from executive. The State shall take steps to separate the judiciary from the executive in the public services of the State.

Part IVA . Fundamental Duties

51A. Fundamental duties. It shall be the duty of every citizen of India—

a) ...

e) to promote harmony and the spirit of common brotherhood amongst all the people of India transcending religious, linguistic and regional or sectional diversities; to renounce practices derogatory to the dignity of women;

...

g) to protect and improve the natural environment including forests, lakes, rivers and wild life, and to have compassion for living creatures;

h) to develop the scientific temper, humanism and the spirit of inquiry and reform;

i) to safeguard public property and to abjure violence;

j) to strive towards excellence in all spheres of individual and collective activity so that the nation constantly rises to higher levels of endeavour and achievement.

(end of the basic quotes)

Let us take some of these basic requirements for a true democratic society as examples for the desolate way in which the Indian citizens have to struggle for their rights and for justice in order to understand what possibly went wrong in all these years, and probably find some ideas for fighting the evil.

Why do the majority of people have no trust in the judicial system? There are a few main reasons:

a) Huge delay in judiciary procedures
b) Lack of alertness in all media to expose those who tamper with the law
c) Leniency on the side of the guardians of the law and on the law enforcers
d) Lack of transparency in judicial procedures

e) Harmful system which tempts lawyers to delay the procedures as it is a matter of money-minting
f) Lack of trust in the representatives of the judiciary, the judges, as people consider the majority of them to be corrupt
g) Lack of accountability of the representatives of the judiciary

The fact that people have to wait for their cases for years and years together and also, that there is no chance for them to put efficient force into speeding up procedures, like time limits for the courts in which they have to decide, or else, forcing the courts to introduce information technology into their procedures, creates an atmosphere of helplessness- and hopelessness. The lawyers themselves are of no help in this matter: they are the ones who benefit from the delays! The worn-out term "Justice delayed is justice denied" comes up every time you discuss the issue, but even judges, lawyers, law-makers are ready to happily agree to that and, if questioned what they are intending to do to fight this evil, they just shrug: "What can you do?"

In this context, we have to highlight the role of our media that could play a decisive role as fourth pillar of power, if only they would come up to expectations, i.e. the expectations of the citizen in a democratic set-up, and not serve a mouthpieces for some power holders who brazenly boast to have the media in their pockets. Fortunately, there are some publishers and some courageous journalists, but, alas, they are exceptions.

Case studies of courageous journalists show clearly that they have to face harassment from authorities, they even risk arrests and worse, to be killed, and they have to face boycotts from publishing houses, and from their own colleagues.

Frequently, there is a big hue and cry about corruption in the judiciary in our media, but it only takes up cases where VIPs are involved in one scandal or the other, sons and daughters of politicians or other influential people get away with almost everything, highly placed administrators are caught in acts of special highhandedness. We observe a type of resignation in the average citizen, like an all-pervading helplessness. Hardly anyone comes forward bold enough to stand the ground against someone supposed to have the opportune connections.

True, there are reports on cases where only the small fry gets caught now and then, but it seems to be used for distracting from the basic problems by making them into scapegoats, hushing up the much bigger frauds which are going on in powerful circles.

Considering the multitude of dishonesty and fraud that is made public, hardly one of the culprits is really forced to step down from his or her position. There is no public outcry—and it is partly the responsibility of the media which are clearly trying to nurse and secure their established bonds with the high and mighty, be it on the all India or on the provincial levels.

As the editor of a fairly big newspaper admitted: "We try to do proper investigation. But we have to find a fine balance, especially when it concerns the judiciary. They could finish us."

Asked about the fact that most cases are hopelessly dragging on, that cases are not closed even after decades, that people are languishing in jails without proper legal aid, he shrugs: "Those who have the means don't have real problems. It is only those who cannot pay who suffer. And our readers are not interested in them. Publishing news is business, not charity."

To this, I quote Rabindranath Tagore (1909!)[46]: "...if, under this government, people have to buy their way out of jail, spending their all to get their bare rights, then I for one will not spend a single penny for the sake of such justice."

In my research for leadership performance, it was necessary to collect case studies on leadership performance at all levels, thus including the Judiciary System, too.

The authentic cases I came across, and also the bleak picture of the Courts, especially the District Courts, led me to try to draw attention at the superior authorities. Below, I give example of a (second) letter I sent to the High Court in Mumbai, after my earlier letter some six months earlier, was only graced with a single sentence of acknowledging that the letter was received.[47]

Excerpts of the Letter to Hon. Chief Justice Mumbai High Court

December, 31st, 2009

To

Hon. Chief Justice Mumbai High Court
XXX

Code of conduct of Judge in XXX District Court

Respected Shri XXX,

Again, I take the freedom approaching you in a matter concerning the code of conduct of an 'honorable' Judge. Unfortunately, I won't pursue the matter I wrote to you last summer, as was suggested by your Assistant, as I don't intend to submit myself to the arbitrary manners of provincial judges, and also, I don't see any sense at present, that a case I might raise would lead to any improvement in the state of conditions in XXX District Court, at least not in my expected lifetime. But, I will definitely use all this authentic material in my book on Indian Judiciary System.

I am not aware that the plea of a lawyer to hear evidence by a judge can be rejected if it concerns a matter of high importance for a case: like in a defamation case, it is of vital importance that the consequences of defamation are taken into consideration. In this case, the judgment as such and also, the damage done to (the complainant) in connection with his voluntary work (XXX) must be a focal point of the judge's understanding of the situation.

My complaint concerns the Chief Judicial Magistrate at XXX District Court who obviously is not aware that citizens seeking justice have to be treated respectfully as it suits an authority in a democratic society, and that high-handedness, arrogance and haughtiness have no place in a modern-day judicial system. From my expertise in psychology and personnel development, having been Head of Dept. of HRD in a German Private Insurance Company for 28 years, I would suspect a massive "burn-out" syndrome in this judge and send him to therapy and/or re-training in issues of code of conduct (if there is any provision for it in the system, otherwise it should be introduced at the earliest). Another possibility of course, which cannot be excluded at present, would be the suspicion that the Judge is biased against the litigant, and this would be worse.

...

... The Judge didn't even look at any (one), spread his newspaper before him, and mentioned that nothing would be heard that day, and that he has no time, and that he is expecting "someone from High Court" (Mumbai, I suppose), and that the cases would be heard in December (!). The lawyer tried to draw his attention, to make him listen, but of no avail. (....) his expression and just not paying attention to anyone, was appalling. His body language said it all: utter contempt of the people around.

I complain especially with the following three points:

1. (xxx—pending case),
2. he high-handedly dismissed fixed dates he himself had given, without any perceivable reason,
3. he preferred to put his attention to the newspaper before him instead of attending to his duties,
4. he would not listen to arguments (xxx—pending case)

The Judge bluntly refused even to hear anything and he rejected (...) to hear (...) arguments. He knew exactly what it was about, and what was at stake, as the lawyer had previously informed him (...), and is it of no value that a senior citizen should have the right to speedy proceedings? Is it of no value that the otherwise good name of Indian Judiciary System is internationally[48] ridiculed through representatives as this Judge? Is he perhaps jealous of the international name and exposure of Dr. Taori and his valuable work (not to forget the various publications of Dr. Taori on issues of sustainable development!)?

Is this the code of conduct of Judges under the supervision of the High Court of Mumbai?

Salient features of as follows:

a) Contemptuous towards people who are, after all, clients of the Court, fellow citizens in a democratic country where civilized behaviour should prevail,

b) Not aware that a Judge should be a role model for decent behaviour, at least paying attention to the persons he called for the date, not to speak of listening properly,

c) Brushing aside polite requests in a very rude manner.

Now, as psychologist, I would advice everyone who is interested in improving conditions in Indian Courts to look after Judges who don't know how to behave. A Judge who is treating people contemptuously, irrespective of the issue(s) at hand, is already punishing them without cause.

I am convinced that, from what I heard about your personality, that you will see to it that the Judges in your responsibility should do their job as efficient, and as decently and efficiently as possible.

I am looking forward to your reply, and, at this time of the year, I wish you a very happy NEW YEAR!

Sincere Regards, yours

Irmel V. Marla

Letter to Chief Minister of U.P. after Election

Present-day remarks: We wrote our letter immediately after the election when we saw some ray of hopes on the horizon for improving conditions in UP. In the meantime, we are convinced that nothing sustainable for the rural poor will be achieved.

It goes without saying that we were not graced with any response.

Respected, dear Bahenji Mayawati,

Kindly accept our heartiest congratulations on your outstanding performance in the recently held elections to the State Assembly of the greatest and the most difficult State of the Indian Union.

It is a fact that your stable rule as Chief Minister for the fourth time must go down in history for one of a people-centred governance. We all realise that the most populous and divergent State which you are heading as the Chief Minister calls for radical, transparent, viable, sustainable policies, which are not mere politic tactics and strategies, but sincere, and practice oriented steps towards improving the overall living conditions, especially in the rural areas.

The set-up of your Party has beautifully brought out various dimensions of the changes required for the State, but the real challenge is those of operationalisation of the necessary plans into action.

We feel compelled to submit a few points of action for consideration at the level of the Planning Commission of the State, as we are committed to operationalise viable planning by a holistic approach (information about our Institute enclosed):

1. Our Open Letter to the Planning Commission, dated January 2007, is self-explanatory and we are convinced that you could examine some of the suggestions for immediate action to bring out the best of the State of UP. (enclosed)
2. There is immediate need to re-structure the training and consultancy services in the State for developing a self-employment-oriented drive of entrepreneurship in this State which requires a basic change of mindset and attitudes. The State Administration is already overstaffed while showing a very poor work culture; the latter is due to the lack of clearly appreciating those who perform. Hence, the real solution can only be to encourage in a big way a sound climate of supporting the building up of rural enterprises by involving all those who matter at the local/grassroots level and establish possibilities for efficiently converge in order to attain improved status in our competitive markets, especially in view of globalisation to which all of us should feel responsible to make the best out of it.
3. The Credit Deposit Ratio of the State is poor, but we can provide turnkey consultancy for the purpose of improving this situation.
4. A big State like UP needs a different approach to planning and, mostly neglected till now, monitoring. But one thing is certain that adequate flexibility and convergence-based leadership has to be encouraged at all

levels of governance without further delay. We specialise and have a network with expert partners to implement this.

5. Bodies like UNICEF have a wide experience in the States. We need their involvement, too, so that mistakes of the past are not continually repeated. They also have the keen urge to supplement efforts of the States for improving the overall living conditions of women and children in the fields of holistic development, with special thrust on the educational sector.
6. There is an urgent need to provide a new, transparent and sustainable type of leadership, and we hope you are in a position to lead this State in that direction by giving the best example for your good governance. Needless to say, that this State would stand to gain immensely if your leadership takes the right steps to improve the overall standard of governance by your Ministers in their departments. Here also, we have tied up with HRD experts who provide training and turnkey consultancy for total quality solutions to the problems of supposed-to-be insurmountable nature.

We are sure that it is the task of the hour to develop and operationalise new sustainable models with *Innovative, implementabe ideas and ideas for India* which we coined as IIIII solutions.

Sincere greetings and best wishes to you and to your uphill tasks, we hope to hear from you soon,

Irmel V. Marla — ***Dr. Kamal Taori***
(Chairperson) — (Hon. Consultant)

IIHRVA in collaboration with *RBHFI*

P.S. Some of the solutions for the above-mentioned problems you might find in our recently published book on: *Operationalising Holistic Human Development—Food for Thought & Ideas for Action in the Rural Context* (information enclosed)

Taori/Marla *Oct., 2007/updated Dec. 2009/Feb. 2010*

Alternative Parliament and Planning Commission India (APPCI)

In view of the overall deterioration of democratic principles and also, of the fact that after six decades of Independence, the plight of the majority of the rural population has become worse than ever. Pockets of backwardness and abject poverty have remained persistently neglected.

Gandhi in *Hind Swaraj* (1908) labelled the British Parliament as "Prostitute", and refused to budge from this term despite objections. We are sharing his opinion, applied to the Parliament of India which is not doing its duty concerning welfare for all.

As we observe the utter lack of accountability for all the decisions and the unaccounted-for squandering of taxpayer's money of Parliament and Government, we suggest to create an alternative parliament, essentially based on "India of my Dreams" and "Gram Swaraj" by Gandhiji, and on the Declaration of Human Rights, as a mass movement.

It is decidedly not meant as anti-Parliament but as a force to show how the interests of the grassroot people can be included into the decision-making.

Basically, we have to ask if this system of relationships, or relationship, is determined or based upon the ability to fulfil greed, consumerism, exploitation, dividing society by privileging some while depriving others, power to those who ruthlessly grab it, supremacy of manipulations in all fields: financial, physical, intellectual, scientific, political, and economical. Other basic questions are:

a) Government for what?

b) Government for whom?

c) By whom?

d) What power?

e) For how long?

f) What is the basis for the democratic "rules of the game"?

g) What we have to analyse and develop alternatives are the roles of:

i) Corruption
ii) Competition ("good governance has to put restrictions in order to keep balance)
iii) Consumer(ism)
iv) Social values, cultural values
v) Religion
vi) Jurisdiction—the common man has no chance to get his right

We have neglected everything which is basic and essential for a civilised country, we are only hankering after the superficial, not-sustainable, and finally, exploitative for the majority of our people.

The infrastructure is in the hands of mafias. Politicians who are not supporting mafias, are mostly just not prepared to do anything against them. Either they are frightened, or they just don't care—in both cases, it is an affront towards the people. Everybody is stuck up in his own place, occupied with his/her own vested interests.

Nothing than excuses: What can I do? My hands are tied.

The basic infrastructure, the basic mindset, the basic governance, basic security, basic laws, and the basic systems have collapsed, in the perception of majority of our people. There is no trust in the "Servants of the People", as they mainly serve themselves. They have lost all credibility and created an atmosphere of loot and greed.

As long as the basic structure, mindset and attitudes, and systems, do not understand the requirements of the basic structures and the issues involved, all planning can only be superficial.

It is necessary to throw some sand into the well-oiled (well-greased) machinery of so-called governance at all levels.

In the present situation, those who are organised, who are ruthless, those who are non-tolerant, who are callous will flourish, they will expand, they will spread their tentacles over all the weak, the simpletons. It is an overall exploitative mechanism which is at work, going hands in gloves with the decision-makers.

Inherent weaknesses of all human beings, greed, fuelled by globalisation, injustices, death of the weak, all deaths, for that matter, whether it is brother, or trees, or water, or cow, anything which is weak, anything which cannot prove its utility and worth, its value, will be finished.

We have enough examples of most serious concern.

So, on the one hand, while we are searching for hope models, for performer's presentations, we cannot neglect the need to take care of the serious developments of fanatism, of whatever nature it may be, religious, ideological, or otherwise. All fundamentalism is against the laws of nature as it is suppressive and restrictive.

All these points require our holistic approach: water quality, health, the termination of the traditional resources, knowledge, feelings, sympathies. All these seem to have disappeared from public concern.

The Alternative Parliament would have basically a constitution based on the Declaration of Human rights. It should be a forum for highlighting the deficiencies and show practicable, implementable ways out of the present abysmal state of affairs.

The deliberations in the Alternative Parliament will be reasoned, scientific, rational, pointed, short discussions, not hours and hours, there will be action-oriented discussions on ministries, bureaucracy, the Panchayati Raj, the Self-Help Groups; all will have a role. And all aims and objectives would be oriented on accountability and cost-efficiency. The thrust will be on cost reduction, and on building up grassroots power infrastructure. The thrust will be on self-reliance, on Gram Swaraj, on transparent, replicable entrepreneurship, on non-exploitative systems of development, on convergence, on hopeful and respectable places for all.

The Alternative Parliament would work precisely on the same models of structured systems. We have a constitution, we have a parliament, we have State Governments, judiciary, executive and civil service. We are not talking of an alternative constitution. Many people have done work on this. But the question will be: are we, as a society, as a state, as a country, as a civilisation, are we really going towards so called "Jungle Raj"[49] or, for that matter, our thrust will be on highlighting the unhighlighted hope models, and providing alternative models for areas of concern, like population growth and other burning issues which are presently tabooised.

The Government has failed miserably. We had 30 crore population at the time of Independence, and now, many people say we have reached about 140 crore. So, there are serious implications and, if it goes on like this, naturally, the trees will be cut, the water will go down, the bio-diversity will disappear, and there will be utter fight for cornering of the scarce resources. The basic instinct of survival would make the living together horrible, and utter violence, cruelty and ruthlessness, and organised loot will be the only outcome. It is so clear. These phenomena we already observe. There is a strong tendency towards it, especially with the role of the middle classes in their majority, the greedy middle classes, they are the same strata of society where the politicians come from. They are not concerned, they don't have the links to the grassroots people, but they decide about them, about their destiny. And, at present, their destiny doesn't look very optimistic.

Operationalising APPCI

Organisational Infrastructure

a) Bottom up: from grassroot level
b) Basic Democracy
c) One village—one delegate
d) Majority vote—preferably unanimity
e) Plenary meeting once a year
f) Speaker: directly elected at the beginning of the plenary meeting and functions till the next plenary meeting which is to be held within the year

   Speaker has only organising/facilitating functions, otherwise he/she is a normal delegate.

A delegate should not have any other elected function, nor can he/she be a government employee (like Sarpanch, Panchayat functionary, or policeperson, collector, etc.).

g) Minimum of bureaucracy: by communication mainly via e-mail

h) Up to 500 delegates: direct plenum (most probably so during the first 2-3 years)

   If more than 500 delegates, the first plenum will decide the options, whether:

— There should be a State APPC.

   i) There should be a regional cluster of (300?) villages with similar problems and infrastructure.

   ii) There will be no honoraries nor perks.

   iii) The villages bear the travel expenses of their delegate.

   iv) The locality of the yearly plenary meeting provides food and accommodation.

One of our main aims is to bring about an overall change of mindset and attitudes, positive visions for an egalitarian society, along the spirit of the famous song by John Lennon, "Imagine":

> Imagine there's no Heaven
> It's easy if you try
> No Hell below us
> Above us only sky
>
> Imagine all the people
> Living for today
>
> Imagine there's no countries
> It isn't hard to do
> Nothing to kill or die for
> And no religion too
>
> Imagine all the people
> Living life in peace.

You may say I am a dreamer
But I'm not the only one
I hope someday you'll join us
And the world will be as one

Imagine no possessions
I wonder if you can
No need for greed or hunger
A brotherhood of man

Imagine all the people
Sharing all the world.

You may say I am a dreamer
But I'm not the only one
I hope someday you'll join us
And the world will be as one

We invite all like-minded citizens to join us in the venture, and we are eagerly waiting for active support and participation. The Alternative Parliament will make use of all modern technology which will enable us to communicate without bureaucratic obstacles, save time and financial resources, and open areas otherwise difficult to access.

Irmel V. Marla
Chairperson IIHRVA
Vice Chairperson RBHFI

Dr. Kamal Taori
(Partner & Advisor IIHRVA
Chairman RBHFI

IIHRVA in collaboration with RBHFI

Irmel V. Marla May, 2007, Lucknow

Article on "Obsessions in Indian Society"

The Problem with the Index Finger

A German proverb says: "If you point your index finger on somebody, three fingers will always point back to you."

Indian society shows various obsessions, distracting people from dealing with things and situations which should be more important for them, like accusing others, or groups of people, of all the miseries, ensuing disasters around them and also, smaller misfortunes. Thus, while pointing the finger on others, they excuse themselves from any responsibility, be it for causing the unpleasantness or else, be it for doing something against.

They never ask themselves what they could do to improve the situation.

By looking for solutions for problems, we have to bother about the fact that problems like overpopulation (mis-population: killing of female foetuses), health issues, environment, etc. are kept under the carpet. Hence, the vital problems and their reasons are not discussed and not acted upon.

What is desperately needed is a change of mindset and attitude, starting with every individual, spreading and actively tackling evils in society.

Let us learn from nature: as a supreme power, it has its own laws. The basic facts are straight and simple. We all come from nature and have to go back to it, irrespective of all the man-made differences of religions, languages, countries, colours, race, age, gender, temperaments, etc. Humans are part of nature, they are completely dependent on a harmonious set-up of all the components nature provides. We are nothing special, we just happen to have the brains and skills to change our environment, to develop into something like "masters of nature" but, to what end? It goes towards destruction of nature and thus, destroying our own sources of life—is this what could be called intelligence?

Hence, as humans are limiting the powers of nature deliberately, narrowing their fields of experiences, nature is only limited by humans. The economy of permanence was written by J.C. Kumarappa, 100 years ago. *Hind Swaraj*, by Mahatma Gandhi, was written in 1908, and deals with fundamental questions of civilisation and environment in a holistic manner.

But, because of all the achievements in modern society, we became more and more compartmentalised which means more and more narrow-minded, limited in our outlooks and thus, more and more obsessed with issues that do not really matter for mankind.

Exemplification of the Practice in Indian Judiciary System: Role and Practices of High Courts (also: District Courts)

To exemplify the desolate state of condition of the judiciary system *in praxi*, we take the role of the average Indian High Court as Indian citizens have to experience.

> Oath of a newly appointed High Court Judge according to the Indian Constitution: (VIII)
>
> Form of oath or affirmation to be made by the Judges of a High Court:
>
> "I, A.B., having been appointed Chief Justice (or a Judge) of the High Court at (or of).. do swear in the name of God that I will bear true faith and allegiance to solemnly affirm the Constitution of India as by law established, that I will uphold the sovereignty and integrity of India, that I will duly and faithfully and to the best of my ability, knowledge and judgment perform the duties of my office without fear or favour, affection or ill-will and that I will uphold the Constitution and the laws."

Considering that every Indian High Court Judge solemnly takes this oath, the average performance is below this standard, more so, that it is nearly impossible for the average citizen to make the non-performing judges, and those who clearly violate their oaths, accountable. An Indian judge seems to be above all accountability, and the citizen is helpless.

If our average judge takes it serious that he has to perform "to the best of my ability, knowledge and judgment", and this "without fear or favour, affection or ill-will", and furthermore, that he "will uphold the Constitution and the laws", then we have to analyse the average performance as daydreaming at best, or, at worst, as deliberately violating everything that he has taken his oath on.

No doubt, there are honest and sincere judges all over India, but they don't shape the image of the Indian judiciary.

They are fighting a hopeless fight, and also, they are fought against by their own colleagues who have their own vested interests at stake.

Case Studies: Interviews

To illustrate the overall image, here are some interviews with well-to-do, socially reputed middle class citizens on their opinions of the judiciary system:

1. Interview

Q: Do you feel safe and secure with the judicial system?

A: Me? Yes, of course. But see, it all depends on what you are prepared to spend.

Q: What do you mean?

A: Well, justice always comes with a price tag. (*laughs heartily*) You have to buy your justice.

Q: You mean bribing judges?

A: I would not phrase it like that. It is like doing favours, just helping the laws onto the right tracks (*laughs again*).

Q: But, the law is supposed to be treating all citizens the same way?

A: Judges have to use their common sense, too. How else would they fit into society? They have to make their living, they have to socialize, it is not so easy for them.

Q: You mean, like George Orwell said, 'All are equal, but some are more equal than others'?

A: Yes, a society has to award its people who are contributing the most.

Q: Did you ever bribe a judge?

A: I would not put it that way (*laughs in an embarrassed way*), but you see, sometimes justice needs a push, I would say.

Q: This is justice?

A: What can you do? You have to adjust to the conditions, do or die. That is my motto.

(End of interview)

2. Interview

Q: *Do you feel safe and secure with the judicial system?*

A: What do you mean? Is there a judiciary system? *(He laughs, I think, he puts the air of a joker, being above trivialities, or else, he wants to show off what he considers humour.)*

Q: *Now, come on, let us take it more serious. You just had a court case, so, you must have direct experiences.*

A: Oh yes, yes. I had to shell out a lot to get my justice.

Q: *What do you mean: 'your' justice? Are there different justices for different people?*

A: Are you naïve? Don't you know that judges also like to make a fast buck? *(I remember that this person has a relative in the US)*

Q: *I think that there are laws in this country to which everyone is subjected to, and that the constitution provides the basics which cannot be compromised.*

A: *(laughing)* Yes, yes. The constitution. Nobody cares. You have to have the right connections and the right bucks to dish out, then you are the king of the law. Then you get your rights, you get your justice.

Q: *Did you ever bribe a judge?*

A: You don't bribe judges, you do them favours.

Q: *What is the difference?*

A: If you don't know by now, you should not live in this country.

(End of interview)

3. Interview

Q: *Do you feel safe and secure with the judicial system?*

A: No, not at all. There is corruption everywhere. And the poor man cannot afford justice in this country.

Q: *What are your personal experiences?*

A: Oh, that. I cannot complain. I always get my justice. I have the means.

Q: *What do you mean?*

A: You see, justice means that you have to fight for your rights. And fight is not always a friendly encounter. You have to find the right lawyer, then, you have to find out about the judge, then you have to speed things up, all these require investments.

Q: *Investments? Did you ever bribe a judge?*

A: Indian judges are not bribed, they just have to be convinced that the right is on your side.

Q: *How do you convince a judge?*

A: Come on, don't be daft. I cannot answer this.

(End of interview)

4.Interview

Q: *You just lost your court case. What is your comment?*

A: I should have listened to my friends and to my lawyers *(laughs bitterly)*

Q: Why? What happened?

A: I thought it is a clear-cut affair. I had all documents, witnesses, everything was in my favour.

Q: *Then, what happened?*

A: Suddenly, my witnesses turned hostile, they contradicted their earlier written statements. Then, the judge dismissed some of the vital documents, and that was that.

Q: *You did not protest?*

A: Oh yes, I did. And I had to suffer several penalty fees for disrespect in court.

Q: *Now, how will you proceed from here?*

A: I have to decide if I go for appeal. But then, I have to invest a lot of money.

Q: *For lawyers?*

A: Oh no, for the judge and for the lawyers, too, of course.

Q: *You mean to say you have to bribe the judge to get your justice?*

A: Yes.

(End of interview)

We all know that there is bias and corruption all over the world, in all countries: where there is money to put hands on, and where there is power to grab, there will be those practices. But, a judiciary system in a democratic country should have effective ways and means to control it, to make its representatives accountable for their performance, to create transparency and evoke trust in its proceedings. The public image of the judiciary in India is insulting the demands laid down in its constitution, and it is the performance of its representatives that is responsible for this.

A Joke from Germany

A gentleman has a court case which is very dubious on his side, and the chances to win are almost nil. He tells his lawyer that he intends to bribe the judge. His lawyer is terribly upset: "Don't you know that this judge has the image of a fighter against all sorts of influencing judges? He is deadly against all corruptive methods! You will achieve quite the contrary, even a harsher verdict than is to be expected!"

At the day of the verdict, the gentleman wins his case with flying colours. On their way out of courtroom, he turns to his lawyer: "You see, bribing a judge pays off in the end." The lawyer is taken aback: "What did you do? Did you really bribe the judge?"—"Oh yes, I did. I sent him money in the name of my adversary."

What is to be done?

There are always at least two options to deal with a situation we find unbearable: either we put up with it, giving in, resign, adjust, make the "best out of it" (meaning supporting a system we should feel responsible to help to improve), or else, we take up the fight, be courageous and try to find a way for the necessary change. The development of a perverted justice is mentioned by Paolo Coelho[50]:

> In the beginning, there was only a small amount of injustice in the world, but everyone who came afterwards added their portion, always thinking it was very small and unimportant, and look where we have ended up today.

Besides the responsibility of every citizen in this country to defend our democratic principles, it is the responsibility of the representatives of the judiciary system, the judges, in the first place to act.

It is not so much the average cowardice, the fear of change, the fear of social ostracism, and the fear of spoiling chances for the individual career, but more the lack of imagination and boldness to create a "network of honesty" for judges. One of the main obstacles is that our judges have no coordinated network where they can share their knowledge and experiences and where they could motivate, and also, put pressure on or expose those of their colleagues who are bluntly violating their oath. Another obstacle lies in the fact that, logically, if such a "network of honesty" would be established, it would mean, at the same time, that dishonesty is existing; most of our judges would shy away from admitting this openly. And this, of course, is again supporting the wrong performance. There are so many pressures: apart from fearing a loss of social reputation (in reality: there is not much to lose any more), it is the fear of pressure from the (old) boy's networks, the (originally British) club-culture. Facades have to be kept shipshape, no matter what is going behind the closed curtains.

It is more than high time that suitable information technology enters the fray, like in all other democratic states. For this, the committed, honest judges should fight, as it would bring about most valuable advantages:

Suitable IT in Courts

a) Would speed up the procedures
b) Would make it much more difficult to tamper with evidence, files, witnesses
c) Would make it easy to communicate with each other
d) Would bring about the necessary transparency for evolving trust and improve the overall image
e) Would make it easy for an "Ombuds"-institution to check performances.

Obviously, the Supreme Court of India cannot take over this role as it is not designed to manage the judicial personnel but to look into verdicts.

To solve the problem in the overall context of all that is happening in India, we must not forget that any reform in isolation would never be sustainable. Hence, the holistic nature of issues must be kept in mind. We have to accept that as humans and as Indian citizens, there is a culture, a personality, traits, patterns, mindset, attitude and also ethical impacts which make it imperative to stress on a change of systems. For this, a huge overhauling of policies and mindset and attitudes has to be achieved, and this cannot be achieved in our infrastructure of compartmentalisation and isolation.

In the context of the judiciary system, it would be worthwhile to reconsider in earnest the ancient system of solving problems within the communities, by self-governance of local institutions, which could understand disputes better and also, solve them to the satisfaction of everyone in a reasonable time.

It all comes down to two major evils plaguing modern civil society of which the judiciary is a very important part:

1. When greed and loot becomes the hallmark of the behaviour pattern of the society, there can be nothing but chaos and grabbing all those who wield power and authority. The weak, the unorganised, the poor and non-assertive have to suffer.
2. Where there is no transparency and accountability, there will be no motivation for either fighting for what is right and just, nor for the authorities to establish an infrastructure which will guarantee justice for all.

We cannot expect improvement overnight; what the Indian citizens deserve and should demand from their judiciary system is the sincere effort to acknowledge and award those who are performing after the spirit of the Indian Constitution, and flush out those who violate it, this in the name of Justice!

We all are looking forward to spot some of the courageous judges who are committed to their profession and who will take up the fight!

Irmel V. Marla

MoU for Cooperation with a State Government for Holistic Action

December 1st, 2008

MoU with Revenue & Disaster Management Department (State XXX)

The International Institute together with its associate, the Rural Business Hub Foundation India, offers its services concerning Disaster Management, on the basis of the paper "Reflections on 'Revenue and Disaster Management—an ideal combination?'" and also in connection with the presentation of Marla/Taori "Holistic Approach to Disaster Management—Constructive Critique".

1) Action-oriented plan for disaster prevention at grassroots level
2) Action-oriented plan for suitable IT for disaster prevention at grassroots level
3) Conducting workshops for Government officers in building up skills and knowledge so that they can function as change agents and facilitators for:
    a) Change of mindset and attitudes towards disaster prevention,
    b) Understanding of challenges and opportunities in disaster prevention,
    c) Creating genuine compulsion for disaster prevention,
    d) Building up commitment for a sound rural economy on 6Ps/9Ps lines
    e) Building up a continuous local Task Force for Disaster Prevention
4) The same way, we are committed to establish and/or intensify efficient cooperation with PRI and the governmental institutions at district and grassroot levels.

We offer our expertise in conducting workshops for Government officers in all matters concerning personnel development, work efficiency and work evaluation, together with turnkey consultancy in view of linking up disaster management with viable enterprises.

Action-oriented, inclusive plans for enhancing efficiency through transparency, awareness and coordination are essential part of our trainings and action plans.

From our paper mentioned above:

> ... all training facilities should be involved in building up the mindset of 6Ps/9Ps entrepreneurial outlook, along our practice-oriented model of SECE (Self Employed (village) Change Entrepreneur). Our Institute offers trainings on these lines and also, train the trainer workshops for creation of Low Cost Practical Consultants (LCPC) to supplement the continuing efforts of the Revenue Department and also, all other departments, so that without losing time, or waiting for extra grants, improvement could be initiated in the existing system.
>
> Another area of our coordinated plan for Disaster Preparedness and Risk Mitigation is involving all the departments like Police, PWD, (watersheds) Agriculture, etc., is to identify areas of their concern or of weak performance, so that we can make an offer along with grassroot bodies, which will be un-conventional, and to the great benefit of all. In the longer run it is in the interest and benefit of all to involve the people at grassroots level and actively do away with secrecy by creating a transparency mode of management of public affairs.
>
> Using the most important task of efficient (un-bureaucratic) Disaster Management as an opportunity to involve the affected masses on a major scale is to look beyond by:
>
> a) Multidisciplinary, cross-departmental result-oriented workshops and brainstorming sessions.
>
> b) Workshops for creating awareness of substituting the hitherto compartmentalised approach by the holistic approach for improving efficiency in the existing system.
>
> c) Setting up a small, pro-active Cell for Holistic Development, with cross-departmental, informal set-up for streamlining coordination necessities.
>
> d) The Revenue Department with its wide connectivities, land related expertise, its traditional contacts with the tillers and also, the developmental programming could take the lead by prioritising suitable schemes/plans to the benefit of all involved.

Essentially, Disaster Management is part of everyday policies and decision-making; it should become a just normal issue which all departments and agencies should keep in mind while doing their routine duties. Thus, a more "normal" approach would evolve, doing away with panic and hectic when emergency situations occur.

We are convinced that our cooperation with the Department of Disaster Management would lead to an enhanced efficiency, transparency and an overall improved system of disaster prevention and management.

Irmel V. Marla
(Chairperson)

Dr. Kamal Taori
(Partner & Advisor)

International Institute for Holistic Research and Voluntary Action (India-Germany)
in collaboration with
Rural Business Hub Foundation India

Marla / Taori
(Excerpts from an as yet unpublished book on Reservation issues)

Excerpts of a Research Paper on Holistic Approach to Sustainable Development[51] by Dr. Kamal Taori

This paper, by Dr. Kamal Taori, which found manifold entrance in our "Models for Replication" and in other conceptual work on our holistic approach for sustainable development in rural areas. We focused on those parts of this research paper which are directly related to our leadership issue.

Our updated remarks are given in cursive script.

Preface

It has been seen that the compartmentalised structure of governance, funding, policy making, technology transfer and even training do not *per se* lead to shift from charity to creativity, capacity and confidence building of the people. The author was entrusted the onerous task of preparing a comprehensive study report on the very vital issue of holistic disaster management and issues relating to empowerment of the people.

Why is Holistic Analysis of the Issues Involved?

With the dwindling resources of the State and lack of confidence in the institutions surrounding the society it is time to take a holistic look. The Joint Secretary system of work distribution may be suited to law and order or regulatory type of system of governance. But when it comes to people-friendly, cost-effective, transparent, right-to-information-oriented convergenistic systems, there is a lot to change. With the rising expectations of the masses and the obvious inability of the system to meet these either immediately or in the near future, there is every possibility that the law and order mechanism would be put to severe stress.

In the light of the developments in the country hitherto, we have to state that these prognoses have more than come true, especially if we consider the terrorist activities and the Maoist threat on Indian soil.

Past, Present and Future

A short analysis based upon discussion, visits, interactions and churning of important policy issues brought out the lessons from Planning Commission, important perceptions about the disaster and the missing linkages, gaps, indifference, insensitivity and on the whole impact of over-dependence on the State. With unavoidable globalisation, the impact and urgency of localisation facilitated drawing of emerging contours on various fronts. The lessons of the past, happenings around the present time and emerging trends brought out the issues of plan of action at different levels of governance and policy making.

Why Strengthen the Grassroots Governance through Panchayats?

During the course of analysis, it has become clear that a holistic, multidimensional plan of action is very essential. The issues of professionalism with social economic reconstruction and volunteering need to be looked into from the angle of employment generation, especially self-employment, emerging viable investment opportunities, role of IT and how policies could strengthen or weaken the capacity of the society to face the challenges posed by disasters. Grassroots governance opens up challenging opportunities, especially after 73rd and 74th Amendments to the Constitution.

The 29 subjects earmarked for Panchayats have also not been effectively transferred. Some States have handed over the functions but the functionaries and the funds are still with the States. The sense of urgency to do justice to the grassroots governance is very much visible but has not been translated into the desired degree of action. The decentralised, non-formal, unorganised, rural-based sectors offer challenging opportunities for facing the multidimensional problems like pollution, poverty, environment degradation and unemployment. However, the urgency of strengthening and galvanising the rural institutions has been widely accepted.

Role of NGOs, Community-based Organisations and Panchayats

Needless to say, the challenges of our time require local resource-based initiatives. Here the role of training, introspection, rewards and incentives have to be practical, affordable and replicable. By neglecting the community-based organisations, tremendous harm is being inflicted on the concept of State and good governance itself.

Twenty-nine Subjects for Panchayats and Problem of Attitude Mindset Accountability and Neglect of Human Resource Development

1. Agriculture including agricultural extension
2. Land improvement, implementation of land reforms, land consolidation and soil conservation
3. Minor irrigation, water management and watershed development.
4. Animal husbandry, dairying and poultry
5. Fisheries
6. Social forestry and farm forestry
7. Minor forest produce
8. Small scale industries, including food-processing industries

9. Khadi, village and cottage industries
10. Rural housing
11. Drinking water
12. Fuel and fodder
13. Roads, culverts, bridges, ferries, waterways and other means of communication
14. Rural electrification, including distribution of electricity
15. Non-conventional energy sources
16. Poverty alleviation programme
17. Education, including primary and secondary schools
18. Technical training and professional education
19. Adult and non-formal education
20. Libraries
21. Cultural activities
22. Markets and fairs
23. Health and sanitation, including hospitals, primary health centres and dispensaries
24. Family welfare
25. Women and child development
26. Social welfare, including welfare of the handicapped and mentally retarded
27. Welfare of the weaker sections, and in particular, of the Scheduled Castes and the Scheduled Tribes
28. Public distribution system
29. Maintenance of community assets

Role of IT and Convergence of Delivery Systems in Rural Areas for Self-employment Disaster Management and Empowerment of Community

Optimum use of information technology can confer tremendous power to the people. The issues of convergence, reliability, transparency, easy affordability, consistency, cost-effective marketing and enhancing viability with infrastructure development could become a reality. The role of policies, whether in funding, pricing, technology transfer or employment, could all be harnessed to bring out the best of the real India.

Operational Guideline and Issues for Action

Even though the exhaustive study brings out in different chapters, areas for action, the levels at which action is required are as follows:

1. International bodies like UNDP, ILO, WHO, etc.
2. Planning Commission
3. Government of India, where 50 ministries with about 100 departments have to research, re-look and rediscover areas of concern.
4. Parliament and other constitutional bodies like CAG, CVC and even Inter-State Council Secretariat.
5. State Government.
6. Panchayati Raj institutions, community-based organisations, training research centres funded by Government and other resources

Since change is a complex process, it would be worth considering the facilitating, simplifying factors and compulsions of our time. These include dwindling resources of the State, massive rising expectations of the masses, capacity of the established institutions to look beyond and on the whole increasing distrust, insensitivity, lack of security along with lack of holistic clarity on viable options. All these make the plan of action an urgent requirement.

How could Rural Development and Panchayati Raj Ministry, Government of India, bring out the Best of Rural Areas?

1. There is need to learn from the lessons of the past, and how, in the last 30 years or so, different programmes meant for rural development or rural employment through training, funding, technology transfer, marketing, NGO support, NRI, grants, rebate subsidies, etc., have failed or succeeded. There is need for involving corporate sector, bankers, trainers, NRIs, press,

politicians and all political parties, both regional and national, to reflect fully upon the lessons of various initiatives launched with big fanfare and publicity.

2. There is need to redefine the role of traditional resources, practices, reservoirs and infrastructures, which were very scientific and sustainable. These have been abandoned because of the so-called practical, sophisticated progressive development policies. The connection is possible only when the local people develop local plans.
3. The role of computers and IT has to be accommodated. Those who use transparency, viability for enhancing the quality of all the programmes must be given all incentives to utilise IT for better programme implementation and formulation.
4. With modern scientific methods of accounting and monitoring, it is possible to give direct resources, funds, and knowledge to rural areas. It need not be routed through the State Government. The State Government must monitor and provide enough incentives to the local bodies to become viable and attractive.
5. The Centre should assist local marketing system so that the rural products and their value addition becomes viable, sustainable, local employment generative, which in turn would bring out the best of the people. This means convergence and fusion of programmes, policies, initiatives and resources at the grassroots level.
6. Centre must not antagonise the States. It must also hand over many programmes, policies and implementation thereof to State Governments, with adequate checks and balances. This will enhance the confidence and capability of the State Government, which in turn will facilitate effective delegation to the Panchayats and local bodies.
7. Administrative and positional skills of Divisional Commissioners (DCs) should be fully utilised to ensure vibrancy and full utilisation of the Panchayati Raj institutions in all the national programmes. This means

regular interaction between Panchayati Raj officials and the DCs.

8. The stakeholders and role players like Commissioners, Panchayati Raj officials etc. must have fixed tenures and clear parameters of judging their performance. This is more important because the fusion and merging of different cultures of 29 departments' subjects could not be an easy task.
9. All these initiatives will require a system for extension and sustainable work culture development. With self-employment this continuity will be ensured.
10. The Panchayati Raj department must have a separate ministry and should concentrate on convergence of 29 subjects.
11. Many feel that the process of democratic responsibility development would require frequency of elections to be increased. For example, at the village level, if every two years or even one year, elections are held, there are chances of better churning, and *amrit* (nectar) may emerge in the end.
12. The role of NGOs, community-based organisations and self-help groups needs to be widened to develop more and more bankable schemes with knowledge-based economy. Panchayats should be rewarded for the investments they bring as a bankable proposition.
13. The Ministry, in its annual report, should bring out State-wise areas of concern and good performance. The list of payments to NGOs could also be appended to this report.
14. There is a need to reduce cost not only of governance but also policing and administration in all respects. Those Panchayats, which are able to construct infrastructure or reduce the cost of development or regulatory system, must be encouraged through better funding and reward systems.
15. Rural entrepreneurs face multifarious problems not only of funds but also of inspectors. If Panchayats could

provide a single window service and also ensure recovery of advances, a low cost practical consultancy could become a big business. Small business development centres at the village or block level could be a big reality by using IT.

16. The more serious problems are of overpopulation, poverty, poor recovery of bank loans, unemployment, neglect of children and women and SC/ST, illiteracy, degraded forest and malnutrition etc. Panchayats could be involved and motivated to take up the challenges with suitable reward systems.
17. Grassroots leadership training and grooming is one of the most challenging areas. NGOs, CBOs, NRIs, retired people etc. could be invited to start rural training centres for entrepreneurship and leadership.
18. All political parties, former MPs, former bureaucrats and even the Secretariat of Rajya Sabha and Lok Sabha should be requested to organise leadership development programmes for all.

Some Focussed Plans of Action

1. Formation of *asarkari* mission or *manch*
2. Rural investment galvanising services
3. Small business development centres
4. Self-employed rural managers cadre
5. Viable bankable investment missions
6. Marketing production training, consultancy clusters
7. Missions for Hidden Investible Potential Power of Organisation (HIPPO), Known Investible Potential Power of Organisation (KIPPO), Threatening Investible Potential Power of Organisation (TIPPO), Frightening Investible Potential Power of Organisation (FIPPO).
8. Missions for Professional Education
9. Missions for eco-friendly development
10. Missions for rewarding the performers

Strengthening and Confidence Building of Panchayati Raj Institutions, Community-based Organisations and NGOs for the Nation-building Process

1. They all must develop skills in areas like financing, training, monitoring and capacity building. This means they need to have specialised bodies to take on the responsibilities without depending only on the Government initiative. This also means they should be able to generate resources and utilise them fruitfully with business-like approach.
2. Good models of replicable nature need to be codified and disseminated so as to serve as role models for others.
3. Youth and women have to be involved in a big way. This means centres of marketing, production, training and consultancies have to be developed as part of low-cost practical consultancies or small business development centres.
4. The role of information technology, communication, self-employment, and rural investment policies need not be emphasised. There is urgent need to involve all professionals.
5. Panchayati Raj and community-based organisations should be brought under a separate ministry so that the constitutional provisions, earmarking of many subjects, special financing systems, etc. are properly attended to.
6. The organisation building requires institutions, financing, policy support and even regular monitoring and guidance. These support systems are totally missing for the unorganised sector. It is high time that volunteers from all services are empanelled for service in decentralised institutions of governance.
7. Disaster management has holistic dimensions. The Panchayati Raj or grassroots strengthening is essential to face holistic disaster on priority. Existing policy and action plans have generally failed in ensuring the full capacity utilisation of the people and villages to meet the challenges. These are also to be linked up with

employment generation, food and water security, capacity to solve local problems by utilising local resources.

8. One may be surprised to know that even in the notorious districts of Azamgarh and Mau of Uttar Pradesh, there are many villages where there are no recorded litigations as per police records in the last 50 years. It needs to be examined how there are so many villages where law and order has not become a serious matter. How do they solve their problems? All these have to be examined with a multi-disciplinary approach.
9. A cadre of low-cost practical consultants or self-employed rural mobilisers would facilitate the extension and mobilisation of rural resources. This can be done at a negligible cost to the Government. Only policy and attitudinal support are required. Massive employment could also be generated.
10. The 29 subjects, earmarked by the Constitution for Panchayati Raj, have not been taken seriously by any department. As a nodal Ministry committed to the cause of strengthening of Panchayati Raj, Rural Development Ministry has to shoulder this responsibility. They must organise meetings and policy research issues with Panchayati Raj Sangathan. It is here that the role of training; financing, monitoring and even performing institutions cannot be underestimated.
11. Regular rewards, incentives and promotions on performance would definitely boost the problem-solving capacity of the people. The innovative, bold, non-conformist approach would facilitate further experimentation at the grassroots level.
12. The village as a cluster has to become the centre of activity. Whether it is rural industries, professional education, local resources, local financing or learning to work together, all these have to be utilised on priority. Due to compartmentalised approach of Government and

poor communication and dialogue, massive resources are being frittered away. This also leads to poor governance and very poor accountability. Only a committed professional team of workers can tackle all these problems.

What would be Success Parameters of Good Leadership and how do They Communicate with the Challenging Time and the People?

We have to explore and define:

a) Natural factors which could facilitate grooming and nurturing of civil society leaders for tomorrow.

b) Role of women in leadership development and women as leaders of tomorrow.

c) Professionalism and leadership.

d) 6Ps system development and the leadership challenges.

e) Grassroots planning and democratic leaderships development.

f) The era of mass communication and IT, and the challenges of change.

g) Role of senior citizens, and grooming and watching of the leaders.

h) Leaders from school and college days in sports, culture, politics, economics, business, society, and the overall grooming through environment of open, transparent, viable and vibrant society.

i) Forces forcing good leadership to emerge… like, right to information act, information technology, media, monitoring and accountability, grooming of the defeated to question and monitor the performance of those in power.

j) The accelerators and decelerators of viable society, and the imperatives of change in a diverse, root-eating greedy society.

k) "Family" as the centre of development and propelling unit to groom leaders in their respective field and leadership, not to be the baby of the few families and monopoly houses.

l) Reservation policies and the problems for leadership issues.

m) Emerging challenges of all seeking position and the mass competition as enabling factors for good leaders to emerge and prove their worth.

n) Decentralisation and imperative of different but efficient leadership styles.

It all comes down to the basic questions:

a) What leaders do we need?

b) How to build up good leadership?

c) How to enhance leadership qualities in politics and administration?

Modern personnel development happens on the job only (not in seminars!). It is not the problem as such that creates difficulties, it is our approach that does it.

It all leads me to analysing holistically the state of condition of governance, obvious corruption, administrative high-handedness, delays, hushing up things inconvenient to some people or only for reasons of avoiding work. It is about the whole unprofessionalism of our highest administrative elite, the failure of the All India Services in general and IAS in particular.

Why is the mindset of accountability and responsibility so abysmally underdeveloped? Why should the "Boss" take decisions (or else, avoid to take decisions which comes logically to failures in decisionmaking), give orders, and all the work is to be done by the subordinates? Really, a very convenient mechanism to always be on the safe side: if anything comes out as failure, it is always the person who acted to blame.

Is it not the very duty of every senior officer to set an example as efficient, competent top professional, or is it just to issue circulars and expect the subordinates to do justice, to function properly? In an atmosphere like this, we can expect nothing from our senior officers who are afraid of stepping out of their AC rooms and see for themselves what is really happening in their fields of decision making? Would they ever consider the risk of a beating or even death as part of true professional commitment and thus a hazard of the occupation for which they are well paid for? Would they ever view their way of functioning in view of their oath to the Constitution? Do they even contemplate their bondage with the Constitution?

Our citizens, the taxpayers, the policy makers, the professionals in all fields, the writers, the media persons and those in permanent Civil Service of our nation have to develop a new way of looking at professionalism in this country, and they have to derive decisive expectations and demands. Perhaps, with this radical change of mindset and attitudes at all levels, we can detect a thin silver line of "India shining", but far, far away!

The following describes the practical necessities for changing from unprofessional, wrong governance—at all levels—to good governance.

It is easy to cry for "Leaders"—we have to learn to lead ourselves first, then we can understand what "good leadership" and "a good leader" means and requires.

The cry for "Leaders" at present just means that others should do the job, and that it is very convenient to be led, by whomsoever, just someone to put the blame on for all failures, and as an excuse for doing nothing.

Ultimately, if one tries to find conclusive answers, there is a big void. After my analyses, there is a structural deficiency in the basic set-up of our public/private enterprises and logically, the subsequent functioning cannot be realised. Hence, it is high time to run them on professional lines, which means:

a) Put professionally skilled personal in charge, so that our "Public Private Enterprises" can function properly as "Public Private Partnerships" where not one side is exploiting the other, and, as is the fact, opens wide vistas for corruption.

b) Change the infrastructure towards transparency, accountability and cost-efficiency which would require proper monitoring and modern controlling mechanisms.

c) Analyse weak points where corruption is flowering and eradicate them.

d) Awareness on organisation development, cost-consciousness, suitable technology, RTI, overall transparency, improving self-confidence in the masses and consequently good leadership.

e) Establish the 'age of change': from corruptive and loot-led systems to fruit-led systems benefiting all citizens

f) System development towards true appreciation of achievers through:

i) Self-correction

ii) Self-determination

iii) Self-responsibility

iv) Self-controlling

v) Self-motivation

to name the most important abilities of a good leader.

A good leader has to continuously keep searching for inclusive, people-based, people-centric, inclusive, environmental-friendly, de-centralised, cost-conscious systems for enhancing self-employment and employability with non-exploitative business orientation.

Instead of the usual talking to the people and telling them what they have to do, a good leader listens to the people in the first place directly, and he needs no middlemen.

To make good use of the media, we first have to build up self-confident, self-reliant media, so that they are not tools in the hands of corrupt, exploitative interests.

At present, we can safely state that the so-called public opinion mirrors nothing than the 'published opinion', artificially created by the slavish, lobbyist-led media of present-day India.

For this, there are good examples for avoiding those dependencies.[52]

Forum of IAS Performers[53]

In view of the overall decisive power in the hands of a few thousand of carefully selected and trained Civil Servants combined with the fact that the infrastructure of administration has hardly undergone any change since the system has been taken over from the colonial powers some 60 years ago, we are of the form opinion that there is a dire need of reforming/overhauling/refining the system.

Remark of an Officer (non-IAS) in a Government Department: "The IAS officers come from lower middle class. Suddenly, they are high officers with high powers. They feel they can do everything to everybody. They like to show their power. They are ruthless."

Remark of a quite average citizen: "You are dependent on their (IAS and IPS) mercy, you have to kowtow all the time. If you don't, they punish you. You have to flatter them if you want anything, they don't serve the people but they serve themselves only."

These remarks which we could continue to quote in extenso, urged us to the final decision to try to bring together people-oriented performers who are committed to their tasks and to improve conditions in this country. Our administration has not yet reached a level to cope with the requirements of modern times and the subsequent changes in society. Also, it has not reached a level where all strata of society are benefiting from the servants who are employed and well paid for their work. We know that there are a lot of good performers in IAS, but their activities are not coordinated as yet; they are literally shrouded in a lonesome fight, most of the time against colleagues and superiors. Some of our thoughts on this are given in the appendix.

Thus, our framework:

We suggest to establish an Electronic Forum for bringing together the most committed brains in the folds of IAS and IPS.

The following shows our basic concept and also the aims and objectives of this Forum.

1. Basic Concept—aims and objectives
2. Parameters of "performance" as precondition for participating
3. Members and membership issues
4. Practical steps—initial activities
5. Appendix—thoughts and analyses

1. Basic Concept—Aims and Objectives

a) We want to avoid any bureaucratic, time-consuming infrastructure. This way, we can take full advantage of modern technology which allows fast communication, and also makes travelling and time-consuming meetings obsolete.

b) The Forum should consist of "performers" only; the parameters we set for this are given below.

c) As a second step, after the IAS Forum has taken up, we want to bridge the existing gap between IAS and IPS by providing a common Forum. The requirements of modern times do not allow the wastage of resources and brainpower because of compartmentalisation and lack of coordination.

d) Communication should be on a task-oriented basis, encompassing:

   i) Exchange of experiences and ideas to improve implementation of policies and/or day-to-day activities.

   ii) Develop practical, action-oriented ideas for citizen-friendly administration and police work.

iii) Share success and failure experiences and suggest remedies for the latter; especially successes should be shared for all to learn from.

iv) The activities of the Forum will be publicised. Therefore, regular media-contacts are of utmost importance. Regularly, a list of our "Performers" together with their achievements will be publicised. This should work as motivating force for others. The same way, malpractices and non-performing will be made public, too.

v) Being a member of this electronic performer's forum should be an honour, and exemplify in action that change is possible, and that it is already taken up by some. It should motivate others to follow suit.

2. Parameters of "Performance" as Precondition for Participating

The parameters are based on practical experiences; they are to develop along specific lines and results of action, and can thus be proven as facts easily. We do not want the evil system of "buddy-dom" creeping in it, and have to scrutinise the fulfilment of the parameters carefully. The parameters consist in the following:

The officer should be/show outstanding performers/ performance:

a) good leadership qualities (role model[54], self-controlled, motivator, inspirator)

b) non-bureaucratic, have a flexible approach, non-biased (be it community- or gender-wise)

c) proofs of sustainable achievements

d) non-conventional, creative, "out-of-the-way", developing and implementing sustainable improvements

e) accessible for "inferiors" and all citizens in all postings

f) outspoken, courageous towards superiors and politicians

g) able to take (personal) risks (for example: career-wise)

h) fight against bureaucracy, corruption, non-performance, and pressure from "powerful" persons and/or pressure groups

i) fight against waste of funds, nepotism, overall negligence, etc.

3. Members and Membership Issues

a) Members of the Forum will be suggested from within and without the IAS/IPS folds. Interested officers can apply on their own.

b) We expect that after having taken off and getting publicity, the Forum will receive suggestions from all over India.

c) All retired and active IAS officers are eligible to participate on a voluntary basis.

d) There will be no formal registration of the Forum comprising chairpersons and other bureaucratic paraphernalia, as the informality ensures utmost flexibility.

e) Coordination of all communication and membership issues will be taken over by the International Institute for Holistic Research and Voluntary Action.

4. Practical Steps—Initial Activities

The International Institute for Holistic Research an Voluntary Action will undertake the first steps by approaching officers known to them as "performers". We will communicate and discuss with them:

a) ideas and suggestions

b) further activities

c) officers to be approached

and act accordingly.

We will also contact media all over India to inform them about our venture and request them to support the cause. They might also be a source of further information about our target group of "performers".

On the issues and problems described in the appendix, we will design a roadmap for our activities. From an insider's view, we cannot describe specific areas of serious concern within the folds of IPS, but we are convinced that we will soon have officers from IPS on our side that will provide the necessary information and analyses.

The Role of Permanent Civil Servants in Our Challenging Time[55] (Excerpt from an Article by the Authors)

They occupy unique positions with lots and lots of security of all types; they are not only placed in these unique and enviable positions, but they should be well aware that implicitly, they also have the professional duty to go beyond their immediate tasks, and also, to contribute effectively in planning, monitoring, involving all resources and all concerned, correcting, and enhancing overall efficiency with cost reduction measures to improve people's confidence in the democratic institutions.

While we all are concerned with issues like civil society, good governance, citizen-friendly bureaucracy and other basic values, here more superficially hyped as "fashionable to mention it in public speeches", it is in their capacity and capability to enhance confidence all around.

When we look at planning issues we feel that this is very one-sidedly done, admittedly not only in India but in most of other countries, too. It is the "top-down" approach which is wrong basically, and calls for a massive reorientation to involve the masses. We deplore the fact that we observe the repetition of the basic mistakes which are causing tremendous loss not only to the public exchequer, but also in view of the loss of confidence in the capability of the state and its representatives. The permanent Civil Service should play a lead role in our turbulent times by acting truly as professionals and leader of the masses.

We tried to analyse the problems and the possibilities for positive change from two angles: within the circle of Civil Service and from an external view, both, outside the Service and also, from outside the country.

The following depicts the main areas of serious concern we analysed[56]:

1. There is a truly poisonous spider net of privileges, allowances, perks, promotions, and the like where we could not find any transparency. At the same time, almost everybody clings to these benefits to the disadvantage of professional work.
2. *Power play:* On the one hand, the Civil Servant enjoys all sorts of privileges and can wield power almost without being seriously questioned, but on the other hand, he is dependent on the "super powers", namely, the politicians who can make or ruin the career. This mainly covers everything in the realm of the active framework a Civil Servant work.
3. *The "All-Rounders":* In previous times, it made some sense to try to select professionals as "fit for everything", and also, transfer them frequently from one position to the other, irrespective of their abilities, qualifications, and knowledge. But in our modern times where there is so much specific expertise required in almost all fields, there are basic requirements for rendering proper work. Decision-making has become much more difficult than it as some decades back, and we have to clearly say that either the Civil Servant has to rely completely, thus being totally dependent, on people around him which is fact at present, or else, the system has to undergo drastic change to meet the necessities of the Twenty-first century.
4. *Frequent postings reduce efficiency:* As already mentioned above, the frequency of different postings is an old-fashioned concept, not adequate to the needs of our times. It is a system which de-motivates and reduces

efficiency of both the officer's and the staff's, finally leading to "harm done" to the society as a whole. The widespread lack of commitment on both the sides is ample proof for this.

5. *Accountability:* There is no real accountability for decisions and actions, and the same applies to the staff concerned. Yes, we have performance reports, but there is not valid system where transparent, qualified tools are applied for improving work and also, assess non-performance. A modern evaluation system provides not only for "right person in the right position", but also gives clear advice for where there is need to qualify more or else, where a person should be given another assignment due to different abilities. At present, nobody really questions a performance report, albeit there are exceptions when there are strings to be pulled and changes in a report have to be done due to other reasons than performance as such.
6. *Beehive of jealousies:* In many cases, we found energies and other resources misused for internal intrigues, squabbles and in-fights. We are of the opinion that the term "Team Spirit" is not on top of the agenda of or Civil Servants. Each of them seems to suspiciously observing the colleagues in case there might be some undue promotion, transfer, or other amenities. Sometimes we even found a pattern of behaviour which we can only consider as (subconsciously) paranoid. This leads to diminishing colleagues at all costs — just "in case", even if it is not directly advantageous or the doer.
7. *Financial framework:* The salary system is not conducive to evoke motivation or stronger commitment as it is not performance-related. Civil Servants and staff alike, complain about this fact by saying that, "Why should I put more energy in the work as long as my colleague who is doing almost nothing receives the same salary?" There are enough good systems of ascertaining performance

and adjust payment according to the results. This could easily be introduced and performance be made part of the salary.

8. *Self-multiplying system:* As in all bureaucratic setups, they tend to mushroom extensively. One reason is that it shows a permanent urge to justify and enhance the importance of one's own work by adding personnel. This is the favourite game of all bureaucrats all over the world, only in many countries, there are already measures taken to clear the Jungle make it transparent and qualified. Why not in India? We are of the firm opinion that roughly 30 percent (or more in certain areas) of Civil Servants and staff are redundant. To tackle this problem will be difficult but it is possible to entangle the web of constantly adding to the lot.
9. *Mindset and attitudes:* Due to some of the above-mentioned reasons (like lack of accountability, lack of proper work evaluation, wrong system of payment), we observe an overall negative mindset, leading to adverse attitudes to work efficiency. "Striving for excellence" is hardly heard of—no wonder, if somebody tries, there will be hostile reactions from colleagues and also, it just "does not pay"! Incentives for efficiency are not heard of, nor is "constructive pressure" felt.
10. *Civil servants: Servants of the people?* We observed an utter lack of "grassroots inclinations" even from officers who should be and stay in close contact to the people they are supposed to serve. There is not much connectivity, interest, or even knowledge about the living conditions and the problems, hopes and fears at grass root level. Even officers who are regularly going to the "field", usually meet only the officials there and from them they get their information. Needless to say that this information is tainted by vested interests. This way, we encounter a vicious circle: filtered informations going into decisions which are—in the worst case—not

conducive to improve conditions for those who need support.

There are some instant remedies[57] which should be included in all trainings and also, made compulsory workshops-cum trainings[58] for Civil Servants already in positions. The following are some suggestions for bringing about change, for setting change into motion by answering the questions individually:

What should be improved?

a) What prevents a continuous improving process?[59]
b) What can immediately and easily be done?
c) What input is necessary? (all resources, preparations, unconventional decisions and the like)
d) What especially difficult problems have to be tackled?
e) How to bring about utmost professional performance?
f) What is to be done towards self-motivation and motivation altogether?
g) What desirable achievements seem to be impossible to gain but would be worth trying?
h) How is my performance as leader displayed and perceived?
i) What is visionary leadership?
j) What is my performance towards taking self-initiative against odds? Or else, self-initiative altogether?
k) What are my priorities in life and profession? How do I balance them?
l) How would I go about taking the lead as change agent?
m) Why should we fight compartmentalism and embrace holistic approach?

While nobody should confuse a "hard line"[60] in the professional role as leadership performance, it must be clearly understood that there are times, when Civil Servants have to rise above their own interests, and take a holistic approach to the work at hand.

With better training, coordination, clarity and conviction it is possible to perform better. The lessons of the past should be taken into consideration actively by avoiding to continuously repeating the same mistakes.

Real self satisfaction and sense of achievement need no recognition from outside.

Leadership grooming areas for the young, and the middle-aged, and use of selected seniors (to draw knowledge from their practical experiences and analyses) should be vital part of all training efforts. The same way, practical steps should be evolved on the fundament of our 6Ps model for developing practical solutions of societal problems.

We all know that the "mantra of decentralisation" cannot solve the problems as long as it is not based on a practical holistic system. The elected grassroot leaders will continue to imitate the "leaders" on higher levels as they perceive them as role models. We have to re-define "leadership" for a future-oriented society and act accordingly. This implies both, leadership for the elected leaders on all levels, and the same for the Civil Servants.

Decentralisation is definitely the answer to most of our developmental problems, but it has to be filled with meaning and determination, with the right mindset and attitudes, genuine commitment and overall meaningful transparency. Modern technology makes it so easy to improve communication patterns which would help establishing real coordination between the different departments and government agencies.

Where there is a will, there is a way!

As long as the whole administrative system is more or less based on greed instead of need, we cannot expect any change for the better to take place.

As Mahatma Gandhi said: "Nature provides for everyone's need, but not for everyone's greed."

References

1. According to our experiences, we prefer to train skilled artisans in teaching methods rather than try to bring teachers into the fold: we met with total lack of comprehension of our concept, and also, with the usual contempt for bridging the gap between 'schooling' and 'working'. *The DSPE is a very convincing model for "earning while learning"*.
2. From our book: *Operationalising Holistic Human Development. Food for Thought and Ideas for Action in the Rural Context*, Concept Publishing Company, New Delhi, 2007, pp 91f.
3. See 6Ps concept in the appendix.
4. In negotiations with selected State Governments Departments of Disaster Management which are interested; we also discussed the concept with a few officers in the Dept. of Disaster Management GoI, but there was no positive response.
5. See SECE-Model for Replication in this Appendix.
6. Working and managing in a *team* has great advantages: it enhances security for the individual, it makes the enterprise more flexible and shared knowledge and skills are always more efficient than the limited ways and means of an individual. Also, from our holistic view, compartmentalisation will be reduced, and the enterprise has more strength in dealing with supporting agents (like Panchayats, etc.) or external agents (for marketing purposes, negotiating, etc.). Assessing of individual potential (and required key potential for the respective venture) and forming efficient teams can be done with the expertise of the International Institute.
7. From our book: *Operationalising Holistic Human Development. Food for Thought and Ideas for Action in the Rural Context*, Concept Publishing Company, New Delhi, 2007, pp 91f.
8. See Appendix I, Overview of Milestone Monitoring System.
9. SECE = *S*elf-Employed **C**hange **E**ntrepreneur.
10. can be applied to all States with Naxal-/Maoist acitivities.
11. See appendix on our alternative concept for *SoEZs*.
12. See Appendix on "SECE".
13. See Appendix on "6Ps".
14. See Appendix on "6Ps".
15. See Appendix on "DSPE."
16. See Appendix on "SECE".
17. See Appendix on SoEZ concept.
18. See Appendix here.
19. See "Hippoo-, Kippoo-…"-Model, Appendix here.
20. See "Dual System of Professional Education", Appendix here.

21. See Appendix: system of "*milestone-monitoring*".
22. See Appendix: 6Ps"-system for holistic sustainable development.
23. See Appendix: Wardha Plan for Action.
24. Kamal Taori: *People's Participation in Sustainable Human Development* (a unified search), Concept Publishing Company, New Delhi, 1998, Kamal Taori: *Sustainable Human Development. Issues and Challenges*, Concept Publishing Company, New Delhi, 2000, Kamal Taori & Surendra Singh: *Rural Industrialisation*, Vikas Publishing House, New Delhi, 1995 (1st ed.).
25. Marla/Taori: *Operationalising Holistic Human Development. Food for Thought and Ideas for Action in the Rural Context*, Concept Publishing Company, New Delhi, 2007.
26. See our Concept: From Ch to CCCC, see Appendix here.
27. See Taori: *People's Participation in Human Development*, loco citato, pp. 14 ff.
28. See our "6Ps"-model, Appendix here.
29. See our Model for analysis "Hippoo, Kippoo...", Appendix here.
30. See "6Ps"-Model.
31. See "Hippoo-, Kippoo-..."-Model.
32. See "Dual System of Professional Education."
33. See details in the respective bio data.
34. See "6Ps"-Model.
35. See our "Milestone"- Model for efficient monitoring, enclosure No. 2.
36. Marla/Taori: *Operationalising Holistic Human Development—Food for Thought and Ideas for Action in the Rural Context* (Concept Publishing Company, New Delhi, 2007), see enclosure No. 3, itinerary of the book.
37. See our model "SECE", enclosure No. 4.
38. See Appendix: "6Ps"-Model.
39. See Appendix: "SECE"-Model.
40. See "Unconventional Approach and Methods for Sustainable Development in Rural India", PPPresentation by Marla/Taori (available at request).
41. See our "Milestone"- Model for efficient monitoring, enclosure No. 2.
42. The same way like there cannot be a thing like "being half pregnant", there cannot be a "diluted", or an "updated" reservation system - the only solution for a healthy, future-oriented, egalitarian society is to abolish the system altogether. What should come in its place to further and strengthen equality and chances for positive development, is elaborated in this article.
43. From *Animal Farm* by George Orwell.

44. We enclose our *Article on the Judiciary System* confidentially. As it is not yet published, the copyright is with us exclusively, albeit copies were already sent to High Courts in different States, Maharashtra foremost, and also to the Supreme Court, Delhi.
45. All quotes from the Indian Constitution are taken from the original, dated November 26, 1949 (updated up to 92nd Amendment Acts), True, there are amendments where we can raise doubts if the legislation has done justice to the Constitution, but here, we have to do with the essential aims and objectives laid down by the mothers and fathers of the constitution. The following quotes are excerpts from the original text of the Indian Constitution (1949) selected to underline the topics in this article.
46. Rabindranath Tagore: Gora, Tara Press, New Delhi, 2008 (first published in 1909), p. 222.
47. As the authentic cases are still pending in the court, I had to delete the contents directly connecting the cases.
48. The complainant in this authentic cases is, in the context of his voluntary work for sustainable rural development, closely connected and networking with international academic and other institutions.
49. 'Jungle Law' is greatly misunderstood: in reality it means 'laws of nature', i.e. a well-systematised set-up, and not the notion of 'anarchy' or 'chaos'. Truly, it also means the survival of the fittest, but it has ingrained lots of protective systems for the weaker. The 'fittest' are those who can protect and who do protect, they are not cruelty-led, like our self-styled leaders, to show power and greed, threatening, inducing fear,and creating a slavish mentality. The laws of nature have an abundance of symbiotic relationships, they are complementarily, and they contain an overall win-win-situation where all can strive according to their abilities. In our 'leadership' system, we find anarchy, disorder, and chaos, all these necessary and valuable tools to avoid transparency and accountability. In our Civil Society, the leaders should follow the natural principle of protection of the weak and weakest is actually perverted, and leadership has to understand that 'Jungle Law' means clear rules of the game, and putting wrong to right, head to feet, fear to freedom, dependency to freedom, irrational to rational, shackles of laws and bureaucracy into freedom, 'hit to fit', hurray to the perverted perception of 'Jungle Law', dire need for opening up, transparency and accountability, from ulta shulta to clear systems.
50. Paolo Coelho, The Devil and Miss Prym, HarperCollins India, 2007, p. 49.
51. From: Summary of Study Report on Holistic Disaster Management and Panchayat Raj Empowerment or Tactics/Strategy for Strengthening Grassroot India, by Kamal Taori.
52. More details are in the chapter on Media.

53. At present in nascent stage; has already got very positive response.
54. We do not consider the example of a certain IAS officer sweeping his office himself with press photographers present, as this is not "performing" after our definition. There are people employed and paid for this task, and everything else is a waste of time.
55. This text is from an unpublished article by the authors, to be included in our book on revamping the civil services.
56. It goes without saying that these analyses apply to the *average* Civil Servant.
57. These remedies might help bringing about some immediate change, but they do not bring about sustainable change—this can only be done by thoroughly overhauling the system and also, only with distinct support from enlightened Civil Servants.
58. to evolve all creative potential of them.
59. The International Institute has developed an easy-to-handle toolkit CIP for which we offer training: see CIP in our Appendix.
60. In contrast to the required clarity, transparency and steadfastness

Bibliography

Jhabvala Ruth Prawer, East into Upper East, Counterpoint (Perseus), Washington, 1998.

Koontz Dean, Twilight Eyes, Headline Publishing Group, 2007.

Limbale Sharankumar, The Outcaste (Akkarmashi), Oxford University Press, New Delhi, 2003.

Marla/Taori, *Operationalising Holistic Human Development—Food for Thought and Ideas for Action in the Rural Context"*, Concept Publishing Company, New Delhi, 2007.

Sibal Nina, The Dogs of Justice, Ravi Dayal Publisher, 1998.

Tully Marc, The Heart of India, Penguin India, New Delhi, 1995.

Weber Max, (21 April 1864—14 June 1920) was a *German sociologist and political economist*, especially worked on issues of power and leadership. and developed "The three types of legitimate rule". see also: Weber, Max (1947) *The Theory of Social and Economic Organization*. Secondary literature in this context: Herbert Spencer (on 'Social Darwinism'), and Noam Chomsky.

Index

Acknowledgements

ent is gratefully given to the magazines where poems in
imes in slightly different versions, first appeared.

o"

"Who"

omic Blue Radio" and "Tree"

v: "The Sea"

xt: "Canvases" and "Skin"

r: "Liar"

"Cafés" and "Reduction"

ander: "Nico"

az Eye"

'Polaroid Land"

terly: "Whole"

s"

ils"

e Flowers" and "Stomach"

laggots"

"

Eggs" and "Flies"

ro Review: "Basil"

AF527450

Echo's Recipe

Theodore Worozbyt

Copyright© 2022 Theodore Worozbyt
ISBN: 978-93-90601-64-6

First Edition: 2022
Rs. 200/-

Cyberwit.net
HIG 45 Kaushambi Kunj, Kalindipuram
Allahabad - 211011 (U.P.) India
http://www.cyberwit.net
Tel: +(91) 9415091004
E-mail: info@cyberwit.net

No part of this book may be reproduced or transmitted in any form or by any means, electronic, mechanical, photocopying, or otherwise, without the express written consent of Theodore Worozbyt.

Printed at VCORE CONNECT LLP.

The mouth has five wo

The recipe is only the e

I cannot imagine a civili

Acknowledgem
this book, somet

751: "Intermezz

Adriot Journal:

Alice Blue: "At

Antioch Revie

Apocryphal Te

Arsenic Lobste

Arts & Letters:

The Bitter Ole

Blinders: "Top

Bombay Gin: "

Carolina Qua

Conte: "Glove

Cranky: "Det

Diode: "Edibl

Epiphany: "M

Flash: "Hello

Glossolalia: "

The Greensb

Horseless Press Review: "Mustard Soup" and "Palaver"

Ink & Ashes: "The World of Onions"

The Iowa Review: "How I Love You"

Light/Water: "Next"

Margie: "A Cat's Life"

MayDay: "Alexandria"

Michigan Quarterly Review: "Hidden" and "Silence"

Mississippi Review: "Shot" and "Violas"

Otoliths: "Bleacher," "The Cart," and "Papers"

Pank: "Mannequin"

Parcel: "A & P" and "Organs"

Phantom Limb: "E"

Poemeleon: "Tapa"

Prime Number: "Your Body"

Quarterly West: "Incarnadine Chameleons" and "Usually a Misreading"

The Route 7 Review: "Ocurrence"

Seneca Review: "O O O"

Sugar House Review: "Again" and "Fugal"

Thin Air: "Apart"

Thin Noon: "Hollandaise" and "Swim"

Tinderbox: "Dear Darling"

Transom: "Whispering"

TriQuarterly Online: "Objectless Fragments"

Contents

Bouche

The Cart

The paths here are curved, some the deer make and some we make with yellow ropes, and also there are paths that I have made only with my anagram, down to the three lakes closest to the powerline, where geese honking scatter and ride the water's edge and all-year birds land on the timbers of the fences, scarlet, gold or brown. The gravel road climbs past a tiny swamp where wild turkeys drink and then ends where we cross the red clay flat, him always first and disappearing unworryingly up though the briars and the long grass grown between the woods where scrub pines have been cut to make the line. In the summer there will be blackberries and no matter how hot the day will be they are cool when you pick them in the dew sun and chew them delicately for the juice, swallowing their seeds.

Atlas

I remember saying what I never said, common prayers beside a long forgotten bed. I won't let the bedbugs bite, I said to the man with silver stars for eyes and a gray enormous head. I put a bit of bitter butter in the better batter in the morning, I whispered to his wife, before he woke. She lifted wide her heavy-lidded eyes; I smelled the feather pillow and she said, *There's more.* Zinnias were strange uncontrollable faces until cut, until arranged, into a throat of watered glass. Recollection has or is a favorite word. *Rigatoni.* Rigmarole. I knew (My my!) of love that it was far away. The sprinkler that he bought at Sears for me to make my corn and radishes grow drew lines of water in the air. Things end with a stroke, then more strokes, glittering, shattering, the same way they begin.

Reduction

Mince two shallots and sauté in clarified butter for thirty seconds. Add ½ small clove of garlic minced or pressed and sauté for thirty more. Add three tablespoons partially crushed Madagascar green peppercorns (preserved in salt brine not vinegar), toss and add ¼ cup good brandy, flame and reduce to a glaze. Add ½ cup dry French vermouth, and reduce again. Add ½ cup mature burgundy. Excess tannin will overpower the reduction. To this add one tablespoon of lightly chopped fresh marjoram, one tablespoon of thyme leaves stripped from their stems, a chopped sprig of French tarragon, and two tablespoons of chopped Italian parsley, leaves only. Reduce to a wet paste, remove from heat. In an oven-proof pan pour a layer of whole black peppercorns. Roast at 400 degrees Fahrenheit until the peppercorns start popping and the smell grows strong in the kitchen. Put the cooled peppercorns on a flat surface and using a small pot or pan with a clean bottom crush the roasted corns, pressing forward and dragging back with the heel of your palm inside the pan. It is important to use only this method for crushing the peppercorns, whose surface and structure grow delicate from roasting. Grinding or pulverizing them will produce dust that will permeate the reduction grittily. Stir into this paste a heavy pinch or two of the roasted pepper. Reserve any leftover pepper; roasted black pepper is delicious. Add this reduction, a tablespoon to a cup or to taste, to hollandaise or mousseline sauce, or a mayonnaise made with extra virgin olive oil, all of which contain the lipids needed to surround and mellow the complex strength of these flavors. This sauce is suitable for any dish where an emulsion sauce is appropriate: fish, poultry, vegetables. It makes a fine variation on Béarnaise or Choron for tournedos or almost any grilled meat.*

* Mousseline is hollandaise lightened with heavy cream whipped to soft peaks and folded in. It is excellent on spring vegetables or any delicate victual. Béarnaise is an unacidulated hollandaise flavored with a reduction of shallots, wine vinegar, and tarragon. Choron is Béarnaise lightly pinked with concassé or paste of tomato. Nice on chicken suprèmes poached in stock and vermouth. Further, death has no flavor.

Basil

Nose isn't bone. Soaked it will soften, an egg on a milk bottle's throat. Black olives in a can are green olives darkened by a can. The night smells late. I step out to pinch basil, the last ingredient. The cedars point slowly at the deepest blue sky. Streetlight drains the wisteria's color but it doesn't matter, it's still there. Snow has been mentioned all day, as if to calm and come. Boys smash glass and mailboxes. Some stars in the sky died long ago. Puget Sound, even where you are, sounds far away.

Violas

Easter Sunday puts a parakeet on Grandpa's glasses. The egg at the bottom of the frozen mug. Look at it. Then the Bud. Grandma says she went to mass today but it was last May she went. Or the one before. She was the cover of a Paris magazine. Calls last a few minutes now. A city name, the Rembrandt coffee service that survived instead in Dresden. In the woods and along the path, violas line up and wither, medals in a dresser. Just one more day with her, is all he'd ask. Ahab, that three-legged chameleon, suns on the feeder's copper roof and then on the red bricks beside the four o'clocks forty years ago, puffing the sail of his vermilion throat at the little brown jobs; the sparrows' dots and dashes.

Cafés

So this is how everything starts itself again, on the sly, in a park, with that light streaming down through a tree captured by someone's camera whom I've known now for how many years that I've forgotten? With valet parking, with *The Robb Report.* In the other room someone is chewing a bone and something is falling apart, the furniture or the music, I can't stop everything on a coin, though I would, if only, well, if only there were not mustard soup under the awning while it showers on the whisper plain. Now comes the part or picture or concentrated scene where the mixed drinks are getting complicated, the blenders and swan-shaped bottles have been dragged out and the pink lights smell of nausea. Soon the dishes ought to be done. Presented glazed and fluttered with truffles or flown away in silver tubs to the pulled down door of the Hobart, the dishwasher guiding racks through greasy steam. And then kissing a girl with long hair behind a door, she was wearing a harlequin costume, and I remember her name and wrote it with a burnt match on a napkin. Someone sneaked the flowers out of the women's restroom during the first service exactly twenty-five years ago tonight, and the next morning the cleaning guy was wearing my shoes. So this is it. Someone, Rheba, orders her baby salmon well done and it poaches in the Gallo for years. I stand at my station and gaze through the copper and stir the dill's pinched lace through a bowl of sauce Dijonaise and the chairs go upside down on the tables. But the chairs never do go upside down on the tables. They are captain's chairs, midnight blue sharkskin suede and darkened oak, and the tables are laid with chargers, candles, and crystal. And that place is still there. The day my father died they fired me.

Gloves

The garden ran along the granite retaining wall. At the far end of the yard where the wall turned and became a sharp, high, cinder-blocked corner grew the climbing squashes that suddenly one morning were infested with beetles that looked like ladybugs until you saw them up close with their black stripes and translucent bodies, that burst with a crisp tiny click when you mashed them. What came out looked exactly like French's prepared mustard, turmeric bright, and it was very unsettling to kill them, picking them off and stepping on them and feeling it under your shoe, the light weight required, though in the very short end they won, chewing every flower and leaf, and there were no vegetables from that part of the garden. Inside the house the ladybugs had massed by the hundreds in the upper corners of the sunroom, and surprised you by biting when you interfered with their movements, so the squash beetles looked like ladybugs to me. The tomatoes were in the middle with the pole beans, and there were hundreds of tomatoes we picked. We ate them sliced with salt and gave them away and there were still too many to eat. When they turned a purplish red they were rotting and if we forgot for a single night to take them out to the compost pile they collapsed on the newspapers and stained the kitchen table and there was that smell like sweetened body odor and the quick circular darting of the fruit flies, like spots at the corners of your eyes, but mostly we remembered to take them out. In front of the wire cages and teepees of oak branches the beans wound their vines around were the sandbox I had built and sanded the corners of and painted the color of sand, and the wading pool, which was blue and decorated on the inner lining with fishes smiling and blowing bubbles. Where the wall tapered to its end there was a shady slope where moss grew and eggplants and cucumbers on a black iron trellis. Our landlord didn't mind this. He was Polish, and still spoke with an accent. There were mineral specimens in that part of the garden, citrines and polished geode slices, one a dark green that I still have a piece of, and quartz crystals the three of us had arranged to catch the afternoon sun that fell on the moss. It was an excellent garden, though too small for corn. Above the retaining wall red and white and pink azaleas had bloomed and faded and were blooming again and some unsuccessful boxwoods filled in the low spaces where the landscaping cloth showed through the pine straw. I kept the Brinkmann smoker beside the slope, and I was cooking a pork roast over coals and basting it with soy sauce and garlic and olive oil while her little girl kept me company with questions. She was three, close to four, I think. It was a summer evening at home when the screen door opened with a slight creak of the spring and her mother stepped out onto the concrete stoop and stopped at the steps that led from the stoop into the yard and held something up, bunched and pale. What are these, she asked. The little girl began shrieking. I looked toward the grill quickly, and then at her where she stood well away with her fists by her side and shrieking. I lifted her. Her tears were on my neck. I looked at her mother. She put them behind her back. It stopped, just like that. Where did you find them, I said.

Cancer

The telephone is wired and prepped to ring. The ring got stolen in the dark in a subway parking lot. The robber held a small gun and said to pretend I talked as the cars went by. We mimed. I could have kicked him in his face when he bent over my case on the street. I think about that moment quite a bit, the kind of shoes I was wearing, requesting trouble. Now I find myself unprepared for how long it will take to deliver my eulogy. It starts like this: Nasturtium seeds always came up from the places I stuck them. I was a boy with a windbreaker of a particular color. My corn was thinner than cigars. Zinnias did something with their faces that saddened me. Daylight didn't go down until nine. The screened porch was full of dull red tiles and webs and bees, and was frightening. I ate charred ribs and loved them, despite the broken tooth. Bobby Kennedy has been shot, I said, watching Hercules cartoons at dawn in my flannels on the leopard chaise lounge. They said, *What?* I made a giant pancake, bet my father I could eat it. A silver quarter. He didn't pay. *If you're sick, you're on your own*, that's a quote, unattributed, having nothing to do with the present situation. No one remembers it. Here comes a black dog on a chain. He is my dog. He lies down. Why does he have fleas, when I have used the proper chemicals? I use the fine steel comb along his tail, snag three. It's difficult to see them, or anything. Those glasses are *bad*, says the girl. More than a chessboard are the eighty-one nuclear seeds Dr. Bone planted in my father prior to the almost certain snip. It looks less and less like I will breed him. When the telephone rings, it's wound on my finger. Tiny diamonds fall like teeth from the setting onto the floor.

Maggots

An odor hangs just outside my door, in my stoop. It comes and goes for years. I got on a gout stool and looked inside the old mailbox. I crawled under the bush beside the window. I sniffed the wall. I found pill bugs and salamanders but not the special tiny clip rendering the lopper useless. The odor seems inside or on top. It was to my mind placed there. It slides along the air into bright pockets smelling round. It is not near the broken plastron of the Turt. The sun did that, not me, but it was my mistake to leave it there, and not put it inside. It's not in garbage or under the floor, and it isn't a catbird in the Norfolk pine. It gathers in the awning but doesn't come in. Peradventure it comes in, lifted from the grass. The wind doesn't matter. It's not my breath. Whether the wind blows or no, it's there, just a little ways away, gathered. It's the possum playing brain in my bed.

Edible Flowers

Gold-winged things shoot from the grass to the line of crepe myrtles too fast for me and the catbirds sing all night their echoes through the pillow wrapped around my head, peck at the dog at dawn, swoop and dive from cables that connect like punctuation or silk knots smeared across membranes, whatever that means. The magnolias drop their brown cups. A sprinkling of water drowns the dust. And there's that slate car again, erasing its roundnesses. These details are especially Sunday. African, you might say, if you thought about our bones. New England, you might say, if there was one. Now it's time for History 232: one face turning into another on the screen. One nasturtium turning summerly into itself, as if ashamed of a love so private it could brook no abrasion of exposure.

E

When they cracked my teeth a sporey smoke dispersed like the musical chairs mild souls choose to play when it rains in a field filled with puffballs. Leyenda on a Ramirez was coming from the rafters, from long, long ago, and the blonde grass rippled and the prawns bled their pigments across the board, and while the surgeon stitched my head he stopped to take a call that put his dog down. I don't know what my eyes looked like, just that they've changed, only not to me. One droops; no one's mentioned it. When they carved onto my face the barely recognizable name of my mistakes I posed supine so insensately I was left for alive. What I wanted then was not love or fame or even a lobster bib at Chasen's or hobo steaks with Ronald Reagan cooked in a pound of butter, just a drag on my former brand and to remember—thumb on E— how my fingers moved.

Flies

The old woman who may have been the owner of Ruan knelt and prayed a moment before the plates left on the table opposite ours on the porch where the scarab-colored bottle flies lit at the plate edges, rubbed their forelegs and flew away. Food was left on some of the plates and I wondered whether she was praying for the sin of wasted food or whether she was happy to have had a full table of customers. I was happier then that she had the business. The ashtray was a slice of tree. There was a counting of white cells, their white rings. I said steal it. The rain ends, but you haven't noticed. But you aren't facing the window as you should, your face also gray. The waiters flicked the switches and brought out the brooms.

Missing music is the eighth circle of melancholy, no one said. Some things are on twenty-four hours, like news of forever and the commercials for it, just beyond the plaster and the lathe straps of the wall. Signal noises crawl around like rats from the Netherlands. And you can't sleep to them. How happy, by contrast, Denmark's statistics are reported to be. It seems the day is an alphabet with buzzing ends.

Mustard Soup

Périgourdine truffles pox a Lyon chicken, the blue tagged feet gripping up at the air. I can't wrap a sheep's head in cheesecloth despite its imploring eyes and I don't eat much offal behind the softly clicked door, from my tray. My address?: Baudelaire, my liver has been bored, once removed. *C'est ca, Tuscaloosa.* No one truly likes the gamey crisp of cornichons better than a kosher dill nor the webby fat cauling rabbit breasts and thighs chopped *à la campagne*, shaped in a paste, more than Normandy butter on pumpernickel triangles. And that clear cooled bone gel. No one really likes loving that. But living is recipes. We agree to eat something above the grass. I spent four seconds drinking sirloin roast juice from a plate in the dead man's house with my face. Then I turned red and lowered my cheek to the table and would not say a word.

But what has happened to that girl in her strawberry dress, her books tangled like hay in her hair?

Intermezzo

How thin the world is some mornings, how suddenly the landscape reappears without itself to depend upon, the silver scraped from the mirror like the sun on the frost, and it seems you could put a finger to the light and tear it like a tissue. Looking out the louvered blinds becomes then a subterfuge of impersonations, and suddenly the soap you've used for years leaves a sickly smell. The pea soup, it's too salty or not salty enough; peevish, soon to be sickly, one can't decide. For twenty years I wondered about the name of that tree I saw from my window after a disappointment I never got over but can't quite recall, heavy with golden velvet. I filled a brass teapot with soft antleresque cuttings. The arborist told me Chinaberry twice and then I saw them everywhere. One can be lonely for death just as one can be lonely for conversations with a dog, a thing that can't happen but. My desk is clean, but I overblended the soup and honestly my desk is far from clean. It is far. My grandfather, as I have, gave up smoking. I recall him smiling faintly from the table's head at the end of a big meal when I was a boy, a teen I think, it could not have been much later, and saying quietly, or tiredly jokingly, and it seemed, even though he wasn't looking my way, that he was talking straight at me across the length of the double-leafed table—*Maybe I should celebrate by having a cigar.* It had been years though, many years, since he'd smoked a Tampa Nugget, I'm sure of that, and he didn't have one, and I wonder now why he thought he could.

The World of Onions

A World of Onions

Onions are those roses which outlast the winter, becoming sweeter, until they finally succumb to their own succulence by releasing reseda sprouts. The world assumes the shape of a Copra onion, a slight swell at its equator. Onions, to my mind, are the truly heroic vegetables. No battle in the kitchen can be won without them, yet they make no claims for themselves, wage no wars, and require no decoration. Celery and carrots and turnips can be safely done without, but no soldier will enjoy an onionless chow in the mess. Onions are without cares; it is we in our carelessness who weep over onions, as it is we who make the mess, wage the wars, and require decoration. Like wish-dreams, onions are stored best in a dark place, cool and dry.

Without a gas mask handy, all so called remedies for onion tears are useless. When the clear blood of onions grows warm, tears will naturally follow. A highly volatile, sulphurous, and acidic gas is released from the northern and southern hemispheres (and this is the most peaceful way to divide an onion; East and West are in most cases more aggressive directions, perhaps because this is the direction of the planet's turning). This gas attacks the mucous membranes of the unprotected eye. If you have no root cellar—and who is lucky enough in these times to have one not converted into a bomb shelter—use refrigeration to retard the release of noxious molecules into the mist, and leave the root end attached while you work. Learn to cut at the proper moment, with a quick stroking blade, and you will seldom shed a tear at the dismemberment of even the most vital and powerful rubine globe. Organic onions are the most powerfully equipped to cause pain, a reminder of our place in the schemes of things, and should be approached only from behind.

The onion's outer skin, or flesh, is rosy or yellow or the palest vellum-white. We call especially thin and delicate paper Onion Skin, and we type upon it, or we used to. Nietzsche, that great philologist after whom all philosophy is a form of resignation, might have enjoyed peeling back the Latin of the English word: "unity, union, a kind of large pearl," the *OED* discloses. On and On and Is, graphemes made into onions. Onions, I like to think, are an under-code, crisp and cipherous. Perhaps they are, instead of the nerve stimuli in the mind which produces the initial image, the truly first metaphor, since they arise from soil, not the etymologic folds of the loamy brain.

Ancient Egyptians worshipped onions, and regarded their concentric structure as emblematic of eternity. King Ramses IV, who died in 1160 B.C., was entombed with onions in his eye sockets. Other mummies have been found with onions standing in for the genitals and the feet. Egyptian slaves, doomed to die moving massive tombstones and knowing it, refused to work without their allotment of beer and onions. Now, as I write this, I am cooking onions in my electric oven, drinking an icy beer, and thinking what a reluctant mover of stones I would be, since I already have my beer and onions.

I might well be baking onions in the round, for pure worldly love, but I am not: my meal tonight is a domestic camper's vegetable packet wrapped in tin foil, a heaping of carrots and celery and red-skinned potatoes and garlic and *fleur de sel* and butter and Vidalia slices, the onion of my home state, Georgia, which I miss, and where in the township of Pocataligo it is illegal to partake of onions while "lounging on bakery shelves." Libyans, who recently reentered the world's eye when Mommar Khadafi opened Libya to inspection for Weapons of Mass Destruction, eat the most onions, consuming 66.8 pounds of onions per person each year. I miss Libya as well, though I have never been there. Khadafi, presumably, misses his son.

Onions are melting with a brown sugary smell into the other vegetables and the kitchen air. My reaction or response to this aroma is profound; I experience not nostalgia for the steaming plates of my childhood at my grandmother's table but immortal longings for the plains and vales and monuments of an ancient land whose name I do not know. This is the true historical being of the onion, the steaming primaveral taste that stems deeply into the collected chambers of the human mind. In all likelihood, our ancestors consumed onions before they caught the lightning's tail. Mussolini is said, apocryphally, to have remarked that bombs dropped from great altitudes seemed to him the images of beautiful roses. Closer to the mark are onions. Great lashes of power have brought down whole cities, nuclear blooms that resemble quite strikingly the flowers that give rise to onions.

The very best onions, I must say it, are not those watered with bottles of *Vichy*, but they *are* French, and this is fitting, since the onion achieved its present royal status only after Stanislaus I, the former King of Poland (twice abdicated) and later Duke of *Lorraine*, popularized French Onion soup. Antonin Carême, the great chef for whom the process of caramelization is named, recorded first this delicious outpouring of sugars not from ripe berries or fruits or canes, but from the onions roasted by peasants over hearth fire. From these onions came the bursting drippings of sugary juices that blazed the coals, sweetened the humble room, and inflamed the imagination of the maestro.

Onions are for me the common binder of those clashing loves that friends and lovers alike feel towards one another, and perhaps for each other as well. Onions, like any marriage of soil and air, are a daily office. Julia Child and I, before time took her to the onion fields where Paul waited so long with his basket, were perfect strangers on a street, but I share still in the secret of her queenly *soubise*. If you and I were to meet, our mutual strangeness might be unperfected, but let us hope it's not in Blue Hill, Nebraska, where any woman wearing a "hat which would scare a timid person" is forbidden by law to consume onions in public. Nor would I wish to break bread in Wakefield, Rhode Island, where sharing one's onions with a friend over a café luncheon is strictly verboten. (Put away your spoon in Okanogan, Washington if you are onion-hungry: that utensil will land you in the clink.) A better turf on which to assess the civilizing effects of onions is Bourbon, Mississippi, where local codes require that each glass of water served in a restaurant be accompanied, discreetly, by "a small onion."

The enormous Sago palm maggot, which in some parts of the world is both a staple and a delicacy, is usually fried in coconut fat, and eaten from a bowl made of a leaf; you and I most likely will not have eaten it before we die. But those who have and do, they eat the universal onion. Planets mimic stars, and stars are as atoms against the vast and immeasurable deeps of the cosmos. Scientists tell us that pondering the newest view of the past captured by the Hubble telescope, the Ultra-Deep Field an image of immensity so unfathomable that it inspires not even wonder or vertigo but simply a rushing blast of astonishment that pondering this map of the beginning is akin to looking at the sky through an eight foot drinking straw. Smaller still are onions than the stars, but no less vitally in their fields of soil do they agitate and swell. At the core of some onions we find a bright curlicue of green, a comma, a comet's spiraling cone. Garlic is old when we see this in a clove, but in the onion! It may well be that its hidden green is fresh from the sun, burgeoning, gorged on its own sugars.

Every part and parcel of the onion is useful, including its fibrous roots, whose flavor is unpleasantly bitter and should not be infused into a liquid, but are fine fodder for the compost heap, where all of us one day unwillingly, soldier and statesman alike, will go. Any other casting from the knife is sheer flavor, the outer skins of yellow onions being particularly good for developing rich color in strictly vegetable stocks. I do believe, too, that their relative proximity to the soil is expressed in a mineral flavor that one does not find in the crisp interior, which is younger, and therefore less complexly composed. The greens of spring onions brighten to true emerald when exposed to the slightest heat, but lose all color and flavor when cooked for more than a few seconds. A sprinkling of fine scallion rings over Basmati rice perfumes and flavors the dish equally well in India or Pakistan. Never murder an onion by boiling it.

The fullest flavor of the onion can only achieve declension through the slowest and most methodical methods of cooking. Slivers attain their perfection through a long stirring and observance. A delicious soup, if you persist in patience with your cookery, may be made of nothing but onions and water and a knob of butter, a grinding of salt and pepper. To make a soup of onions, slice them evenly thin, and simmer in the fat and rendered juices for at least forty minutes. The best plan is to spend an equitable hour, staring and stirring until a deep nutty brown is achieved. Satie is a fine accompaniment to this meditative process, and of course a quiet bell, a *glas*, of dark red wine. A glug into your onions deglazes the crystals from the pan and adds richness both of hue and taste. Serve with hot bread and a green salad tossed with the best olive oil. But don't get caught in Peewee, West Virginia eating onions while sitting in the cemetery. To eat them legally there, you have to lie down.

Missing Ingredients

Objectless Fragments

I bent coins with my teeth, and they broke. That's what currency can't reconcile, green stacks and time, its escapements, the gleaming plates, the missing letter. A bicycle comes down from the attic in time but in time for what? Love spun in the mouth? The set-up, the derailleur oil, the grandmar legged in the crystal snifter, the sea pulled along like blue ribbons at the grips? Forgive my objectless fragments. I'm a fraud. Joints crack and burn, swifts sweeping every day into new chimney aches, a flea in the ear, a moon in a tree, a molten spot hidden under black fur, the light gold disc thrown too far toward the curve in the road. Broken eyes and a heart on the street. What list is clear? Citrine eyes: if only we could look with them long enough to see what worlds they make of us, their shepherds handy with chains. If only brindle didn't silver. The past is black and white, the smirk of daguerreotypes, the future other shades, another pair of colors seeping like clay along the edges of the house, the nervures of leaves on the pavement.

Atomic Blue Radio

I listen to its tuned sounds crack in the dark against a pillow near the Post and the heavy Army blanket static and pretend the pine trees are still standing in the yard where sunlight flowed into a gut hollow, and then there is the picture of the silver cat on a shoulder named after yours melting into the picture of the black and white face of the mannequin staring down and to the left as is proper from the insides of an international magazine and that used to be practiced for fun in the den on the wine dark carpet by the owner of that face, to my horror, the slug still lost in the bedroom ceiling, the supplies still canned and filmed with greasy dust in the cupboard, short parades in the dark, the jar there where roaches bred their ticking hisses. Look at me, the mouth said and then death had a face with warm clear skin that I would find with my almost yelling but not quite by then loving mouth, almost yelling by then but not quite yelling, *Stop that,* as if there were any stopping that and as if my tongue could stop it.

Next

Mondays they lift a star out of my mouth. Fridays the knife slips past gas refused, a cluster of deading needles, a dribble or two, some white packing and arms that swing trails of sussurizing OK?s, one hoverer asking a question that seems to me a matter of love, though I have impedimentary tonguelessnesses and cold silverings stick a question mark finger with metrical holes down my throat. My tongue hugs at stitched syllables. The music I prefer takes a long time to be tuned, not that I've asked for any love, and whited out girls pretend to run around, and the static tastes cold, and I am cash-heavy, the money is freezing a hole in my flat-assed pocket parakeet parabola hmmm umma gumma oh pink careful with that axe Eugene Oregon but when it comes as I lie on my back it is Poncé on a C3 Ramirez and so blood graft and carving whiz become remote and serene, and I could have told them, yes I *could*, but their language was absolute and technical and remote from the beautiful icily detached love I was seemingly feeling, that it was all the same to me what they did with their delicate nails so softly.

Billets

I am sending them one by one. Only some of the interest will ever be paid. Nothing can be read to its conclusion. I pick up a gray weight with a number. I draw it toward my chest, as many times as I can, eight ideally, toward the tip of my nose, and lower, more slowly. Then I tremble pleasantly. I am made of water, the oxygen boiling away. When I meditate, which is never, I arrive only at how cruel and mistaken I have always been. Who can think of lunch at a time like this? It turns out to be me. The past comes forward, forming a chain, like baby teeth under pillows, or the long bloodline of dogs bloodying their mouths on moving tires, or simply a hand relaxing, lifted through the air, wishing for wind, asking please for a check.

Palaver

Though I mopped, the grit lies underfoot. The live-forever pot got kicked over by some community college boys. It kept growing, like a cigarette. The spider shrinks blacker on the white oven as it dries. The rat in the wall discovered my food was all in tubs with gaskets. This desk machine emits a scratchy palaver, not those claws, and the scent in the premature grass makes my dog howl only in his sleep. Poor him, how he trembles, mistaking me for what he wants, and how I throw him to one side of my life, a blue couch. The taxes that I pay up this morning are Zeno's rush into the night. Under the building my mother burned down with chicken fat balls I shimmy along the dirt and the webs. I look back at the square of brilliant sunlight and the face of the caretaker, who yellows my last warning before he closes and latches the crawlspace door.

O O O

Poems, ugh. On no one's tongue. They come out and across in little pieces like newspaper puzzles. What do they mean? What do they mean to mean? Who can finish them without a hunky dictionary and who can be bothered with such a wicket of lyrical honey? Scrabble beats them to a pulp. Poker played by stars is even better. Poems are, as my last friend called my ejecta, a ghastly ochre. Poems are mashed grapes, impersonating tears. "O O O" could be a whole poem, if I said so. What's up with that? My mother is a poem, so one poem goes. Whither hast thou gone, Pater? moans another bleakly. When I was in the gymnasium and smoked, runs a transgressive one. Plenty about love's genitalia in this pantoum, but no fucking. Stepped-on snowflakes, straight-eye for the queer guy, incredulously boring, and filled with the white space one would expect from ancient hegemonies, poems can simply go away now. Go away, poems! Let the work of savant contractors continue: gutter running, cutting in, fabricating, soiling the doilies on graves.

Polaroid Land

Some assemblage of details that passes for an afternoon (cheese impregnated with bits of spicy peppers, a bathing suit the color of an inexpensive but dependable burgundy, the musty pressures of grape skins, something else, too) lets me remember how better to ignore the low-frequency explosions taking place, the noise beyond the wall, to my left and of course out of sight. The violence is blasé. I want to be agreeable, I never complain anymore, I want to improve my home with supplies from the home center and make time for the needed adjustments to my vision but it is too late for the politesse of obligation and the specter of its bludgeoning cudgel to stand successfully in, gleaming with mail, for the sleek powder of my nerves against your nerves, the vibrations that color eyes and render up the sound of a watermelon being sliced open, a pink cool cough. Lunch is more than enough. Thoughts of tomorrow are not so limpid as they once were, delicious coffee in a black mug with cream on the balcony, being surrounded by begonias and me gazing eye to eye with a hovering bumblebee for what must have been hours on end, cutting a shape of outdoor carpet, all so rich as cinema that one wants to weep in synch with the availability of…what? Some contract with the past seems to have been violated or vacated, a flower or an instrument of going, and the flashbulbs pop precisely through which I fall, feeling brightness, the softened glass fibers, smelling their darkened strands. My flexed wrists, I smile at them. They are thin.

Incarnadine Chameleons

Rose wears a short sleeved sweater. Her sweater is two colors of blue and she is not tall. It must be cool out. Rose seems tall until I hold her again and again. May I please present Ms. Rambler Peace Tropicana Lincoln is how I think I might introduce her to my grandmother who suddenly can stand and is saying for the first time Oh my, Roses, pressing a white-gloved fingertip to her cheek. Shalimar is in the air. My right arm holds Rose at my side. Her waist under my pulse is flat but not narrow. She kisses me in full sun. There is a flavor of cucumber water on my lips, a green forgiveness. There is a simple and witty reason she has just come in at the break of morning with a slightly abstracted smile. And the glasses my grandfather wears are wireless octagons, even thicker than when he last wore a suit. He's thinner, shorter, staring elsewhere. His face seems too familiar. His black pinstripe is baggy. He isn't talking. I understand Rose's last name now; it's what the sun meant to say in Amsterdam when it wore red shoes. Rose has that skin, an apricot falling through water. Rose says she'd like to watch that, the fruit of herself in a tear, the rain across the window of a blue boat, but she can't, and I am left here in this quiet as she was left, thinking of the four o'clocks she grew, home to puffing chameleons.

Chargers

Shot

My glasses went flying with a red grunt. The color drained from your lips, but your eyes stayed shiny. The ceiling was full of holes and it was winter, but we climbed under the covers and felt better when you laid your head on my chest and your hair fell. Lying there, I could see through one corner the night sky. A cold echo rippled my ribs and I felt the rat's yellow teeth run into my fingertips. I touched my gums and then my eyes with the tips of my fingers. This white-haired sanitary thing I hold into the light by its pink tail, it wriggles a little and then just hangs there, waiting. It is what we wished for, twisting our bodies. It's Halloween today. The guns wear costumes. The candy is plentiful, I passed it out in your absence, I shouldn't have answered your phone. The stars seen sideways throw needles, drawing time like blood. A dead cat keeps jumping on the window unit, his eyes pressed open just in case. Mister Cardinal wakes, wakes, wakes, wakes, just beyond the window.

Occurrence

The owl in the flashing beam is not the one that loosed a feather in the river path, that spelled the scarcely hidden summons in the trees. My hand concatenates a swirl in the dust, I nuzzle dark birds that will not leave my shoulders. At the river in the morning I feed the granite boulder with an apple core, my eyes pour out their salty light. At the top of the path where mountain mint was, and the berries feeding grouse, Ambrose stood and knotted the round-headed snake in the night. He pointed its head toward the yellow walls, the soft sleeping truncheons of your marrow. Then he was gone.

Skin

Few coddle an egg. Fewer bake an English muffin from scratch. Not that I do any frigging thing myself, but I have the feeling if I had contained an egg things might have gotten better. I wouldn't mind the return of my hair nor how swimming pools might clear up and put on a sunny face and it wouldn't sting to open my eyes when I pulled myself to the bottom and fingernailed the quarter's bezel. The rubber mask smell would only mean I'd spit in my round glass and washed it so it wouldn't steam, as Jacques Cousteau would be saying, handing my grandfather a slice of wine sausage cut with his personal dining knife. I'd have coddlers with stencils of songbirds, one red, one blue, on their outsides and silver lids, and a chance to add a butter curl and a burp of cream to the cup before I scrubbed my face with rye toast.

Canvases

I like to keep this apart from that. Old things smell fresh when you burn and inhale them. Crazyhorse is one word if you "hide spelling errors." In the canvases of Beatriz Milhazes, often a blue fish eye stares, unless it is a sun in full eclipse painted through a filter admitting cerulean. Sleep in cartoons is represented by a line of z's. Stereolab was like that, colorful bicycle tires laid over and over each other, like rain on a pond. *I will write no more forever*, I wrote on the test, and got an A. It never occurred to me I wouldn't. I wasn't jealous of the light when you closed the shades. *Jalousies*, is the word I thought of saying. Pince-nez. But I never found the bullet in the rafters, because I never looked. I only knew the ceiling didn't leak. Or at least the floor remained dry. For some reason in the other room I was carefully holding my glasses, and slung them when the pistol went off and my voice cracked open some new can of cream of mushroom sound. I bought a green glass pen and green ink, just to see what you would do with them.

Stomach

A dog ate a turtle from a tub of turtles, cracking its shell in many places but swallowing it whole. The little girl who cared for them noticed. The doctor put the dog under with a shot and opened its stomach and removed the turtle, which lived, as did the dog, which would have died. She'd insisted. She was right. Cut it open, she'd said!

Every Second

People die excruciatingly every second. I have a wart. Crayolas, please, the number of a chessboard. I've noticed how hard it is to do anything, even to prepare to do anything. To sit up straight or sharpen Midnight Blue, travel again toward love's frontier. When the solar eclipse came, I was on the plaza. Things slowed down, were submerged in the faraway shadows of the sun. I was young. I still can notice myself there, as if I were moving the pieces around, as if that place I still dream of was a bezel I could spin clicking around my unusual hands. A pigeon landed in my hair, confused. I was drinking bourbon with John and Calvin over crushed ice. A Spanish girl walked by so beautiful they named a language after her.

Papers

You can never be positive so I killed it. I didn't want to. I didn't enjoy it, as some do. But you can't be sure in a shadow so I went ahead and I killed it. It was black and slightly shiny. It had a white shape. Can't you see that I had no choice? I blunted its abdomen with the stock and cleaned up the mess with some papers. I still have a scar on my left hip that looks just like that thing.

Organs

The monkeys came to say hello. Some looked like intelligent spiders and some looked like funerals with red hats. Others paused in the shadows, gazing. I agreed they all were interesting, all of them saying noises. One of them squatted. And then several. I wasn't sure about the monkeys then. Truly I was never sure about seeing the monkeys. It seemed too much like a visit, part of a plan made without my saying first what I felt most about monkeys, especially monkeys there, in that particular place, with its air of impassionate and collected domesticity, that they were not my children, that my kinship to their wild stupidity and violence, their tendency to nibble things they found on each other's scalps, the swelling unruliness of their reddened backsides combined with the ungovernable screaming at the sight of the wrong blue-headed bird; that and their failure to embrace the peace that surpasses understanding, all made me nauseated by the smell and leaping sight of them, those monkeys you included in plans made without me and that you apparently loved so well, without any of the reservations I felt deeply inside my organs. I wanted to ask you, it feels certain now that I wanted to ask, how it was you decided to bring us there, and why, among these monkeys and their hideous fleas, but I could not form the questions in my mind. I was too busy watching how the monkeys came at us with such muscular and scurry-limbed curiosity. I rubbed the back of my neck, as if to feel the welts their brown-toothed bites would soon leave. I felt a queasy sleepiness arrive at my senses; the scent of rotted fruit and scattered feces and orange urine clouded my nose, my deviated septa. The sun became oppressive, as it does at that time of day. I have to sit down, I said, I have lost all my appetite. But you only danced away, flapping your arms and twirling in the tall grass, singing a wordless song.

Late Intermezzo

Water

When I woke and wanted water I found the bag in the living room. Though to say I found it is not quite true. I *saw* it, and moved around it to avoid it, at least as much as was possible given the size of the room and the arrangements of the low furniture. The bag was black and shiny, it seemed a kind of plastic or oilcloth, and was large, almost too large for a man to carry. I still could not say what the bag contained, only that it had appeared while I slept, or at least that I do not remember it having appeared before I slept, and that it seemed to envelop objects of various sizes and shapes, some angular and protruding against the interior surfaces of the bag, stretching them taut to the point of breaking, some soft and sagging, like wads of yarn, that had settled to the bottom. Someone has put it there, was my conclusion in the dark. And perhaps with a smile to himself. It was not tied or sealed, its top was lightly folded over, almost slumped one might say, and so had I decided to walk toward it, instead of making my path around the island, I could easily with the merest touch of my hand have pushed the bag open and divulged to myself its contents. But I was afraid, afraid of touching it. My sense of the bag was that its purpose was aimed at *me*, and I was disturbed by that intimation. And this may seem odd to you, but the identity of the man who left the bag did not immediately concern me. It was enough to know that he had come for a purpose, with the bag, and left it, himself. It was only later, when I had begun to recount the events in an orderly way, that certain facts came to light and my curiosity was further aroused as to the *character* of such a man. But to return to the story. I made a path around the island and took a bottle of well water from the refrigerator and drank it standing in the light cast from the open door. It was delicious in the way that only ice-cold well water in the middle of the night can be, and I drank it all without stopping. Thirst, not hunger, is what time is made of. Refreshed, I looked back at the bag. I say looked back because in my thirst I had disregarded for a moment the presence of the bag, turning my back on it so to speak, watching and I suppose preferring the cold interior light of the refrigerator, even though the purpose behind the bag seemed to be a malevolent or at least not a beneficent one. The bag had not moved or shifted, though it did appear, since I had more fully awakened, to shine more brightly in the darkness, and more imposingly.——It has long been my practice not to lock my front door at night. It is my belief that burglars will invariably break a window or use the cover of shadow in the back of a house to obtain entry, and that by leaving the front door unlocked I afford myself a method of swift uncomplicated and instinctive escape, should I need it. Experience has proved this. So the apparent fact of the bag's having been carried through the front door (I found no broken window and the back latch was secure) and deposited in its particular subtle position, bulked in the room toward its center but nearer to the front door than the island, suggested that who brought the bag was neither fearful nor incautious. Perhaps it is too much to infer that he was *bold*, since I was and remain unaware of his purpose or any agency behind his purpose. I admit I was intensely curious, I am still curious, about its contents, despite the many years that have passed since the razing of that house by the skillful manipulations of the courts of eminent domain, an ending that left me bitter for a time, even though I was compensated for my troubles. But in those rare moments when I am able to abstract or remove myself from the latent dreads and terrors of that event, to experience no trembling at what might have been the aim of the man with the bag, I feel as if the sea had suddenly been revealed to me in the shape of my dilated eye, or my hand had become a spider whose spinnerets wove linens around stars. But just as quickly these feelings pass into a kind of dulled indifference to the weight of my memories; and the vault of my senses seems only to surround a deep fatigue; and I cannot bear to think of who he might have been, or what the bag contained, or why it was put there.

The Carvery

Whole

After losing the arm I lay sleeping for days and then I went down to the river. To wash my body seeing my dog run and the spittle glitter on his muzzle. A row of thin stakes I had pulled from the grass and hidden well had been replaced with freshly numbered markers. The ribbons scarving trees were pink. X's were painted on the fountains. There was no point in touching them. We crouched, his flank warm, behind a huge illuminated gazebo roofed with crimson tin. Too many fags using the old one, a man with a heavy beard had said at a party. A yellow caterpillar shrieked and swallowed bluebirds whole. It scooped up turtle tracks and industrious colonies and then it started in on the bank. A small crowd of men stood silent, nomadic, sipping steam as it chewed at roots. When I felt the wood beetle crawl onto me I looked down to stroke the glossy back, to pick up wings by the sheaths and feel the tug of barbed legs as they clung. My dog sank his muzzle onto my thigh. My knee cracked, giving us away.

Irises

Here are platinum irises that mean to be a summer spelling stone by stone the light. This is the plan: O! The honey raw on your berries and seeds, it too silvers the yoghurt and its three unmentionable names. No one mentions the mail either, and just as well. We do so well in silence. I will not have forgotten the scent of your kisses, a metaphor of nothing else. There is nothing else but the raspberries that fall in languor into my lips, your body a stream of light impersonated by water, passing over time.

Again

The moon too has a smile far away and a pair of wedded scars. Late in the afternights, when through the window platinum laid bars of itself over the bed, I understood twin calculi of distances, why they traveled in ships foiled with stained gold a pencil tip could make black and a vacuum. The moon, long away to long for in the hours deepening gravity; and the lilies on the table falling, petal by petal, with a sound pink as the cheek of the woman whose name scrys other destinations. This is not a fable for children or men who know only desire in the night, but a story that belongs to a way time has of becoming only the thing it measures. If I look at you, the wave you were becomes the moment of my beholding. If you look at me, then all these particles of sand, whiteness all around you, hold just still, and wait for what you were when I saw you first in the shadow's green penumbra, your right hand lifted nearly to your brow, the glasses dark and the smile waiting in the photograph for me to take it, as if I were the one who would take it.

Tester

My best arm scar lies along the green silk bag filled with beads intended long ago to soothe my eyes. Today I watched it being watched. Just now I am content with the part of the song, that it lies beyond reading, that it goes palm up and feels better. I substitute tomorrow for myself; there is no hypo I won't flow through or remark, just as a needle comes to its own point eventually, maybe asymptotically, even yet in a harborless town with a river writing away and brown as a melted crayon, residue I scraped from water wrinkled paper with my nail and left in an ashtray broken forty years ago against a hearth of granite loaves with "Secret Agent Man" playing on the console, my windbreaker crisp and dangerous as I threw myself across that sunken living room like a harpoon and a cardinal smashed through the opened glass of the sliding door and stained the drapes with thrashing. And there are white letters left on that paper. That's how it works. First we put the colors on, then we paint them black. What we take away is writing. So far I have one more chance, and that's a motto. I keep cutting, it feels good, who knows how much more will be left out of this when I am done.

How I Love You

The dust in the throat of the flower the breath inside the water the invisible hiss of rosewater breaking from the yellow petal the spot of radioactive paint hidden in the red box the beaker bubbling with elixir the star blown lavender bar in the dish the clock against the wall that looks unbroken the honey spilled into every cup the puffs of cotton in the dark the way Kora puts cheese on fine green spinach the little essay by Coleridge that no one else will ever have the ten thousand tender weeds the nearness of the sound the chocolate crumbles on the stair the old folks by the shore the squash in their baskets the teeth in the leopard skins of my shoes the coat in hiding the bed with its numbers the kitty kat the whole sky on my fingers the smell of the sun where you stand the smell of bones borne away the dresses black and white the gloves with hands within and without the bucket that carries the breathing into the water.

Michel Deguy's Dessert

I hug wool in front of this screen because the room with the chair in it is chilled and looking up spins and my body seems to prefer to spin. Michel Deguy is enjoying dessert with friends my nausea ignores. The crème brulee, a simple thing I failed to make, cracks brown as a fig in the tree where the birds devour brown summer tears. My vitals sit hollowed, and a giant feather falls and belongs to no one. I watched a commercial. A monk with glasses turned over a baby turtle, dropped a spider onto a plant from a page, and then was forgiven when he sneezed.

Eggs

Under the canvas tent, I browned some scrambled eggs with the mess kit. Bobby Ryan ate them, who was smaller than me. He was very small. It was dawn and the dew was heavy, it had turned colder and the dawn fog came to the top of the hill. I propped a dead blue jay in a maple crotch and shot him. I planted thorns in the hollow yellow rose. There was a...what I noticed most often was that my memories, or their claims, were not streams of continual action, but were like a series of still photographs or clips strung together. Everything I could remember filled up only a few hours of my time. Then I knew that the habitual categories of memory were like the patterns of stars we see in the night. I can still taste what then...eggs?

Bleacher

In a windbreaker on the bleachers. In a bleacher, the game going on, I remember the wind. It was hot and smelled ironish. The ball was soft, and valium. In the midnight blue truck, the bottles lay iced. There were Heinekens. The bats were red metal, like those glasses from the fifties. I did not like the sound they made against the ball. Soon the players would quit. It would storm. In the rain the catfish bit, driven up I guess. The string on a chain cut through my poncho and cut my back, wriggling. They did not want to die.

Liar

My grandmother died today. I thought not of her but of you. My dog drowned your mother. You glowered. You gathered to attack. I was not afraid I was repentant. I pulled back the paper wrapping that covered the body. The package was too small to be remains. A silver salmon lay inside, broken into statuary shards, its length intact. Its dorsal and ventral parts were thrown outward, in fragments. I covered it back, ashamed of my growling, swelling belly with a tick on it.

Tree

No light was meant to touch a beating heart. *Do not, don't,* Doctor, press your fingers to my throat. That is the color of his flanks as he hurls and hauls his body up the hill from the water, blackly brindle-striped. His teeth stream the river, his tongue slaps air with pink silent laughter. Here is the clear stone held to the lamp, the bronchial tree of the ant.

Façon

Swim

Nico is four, his father is teaching him to swim. An island of pines rides high above the grass, hulled by a wall of mortared granite, and the tall thin trunks point toward cirrus clouds like the masts of a ship getting ready to sail under good weather. Nico has a ship book in his room. It is impolite to point, even at yourself. Ice-water from an orange plastic cup made to look like an orange with its hat cut off and stamped with a design of dimples and leafy vines makes a thick thunkle when he jiggles it back and forth; sweat beads of condensation drip on his thighs. His father's shadow crosses over his horn-rimmed glasses. He looks up. Nico is smiling in the shadow his father casts. He is looking up at his father. His father is darkly tanned, his hair is black, the hair on his chest is very black and tightly curled, his eyes are clear and green as chips of Coke glass, his teeth are brilliant. He scoops Nico up in a smooth motion. The pool is the color of the August sky, and the waving water throws a net of light onto the bottom. When the water rises *whash* around him a ringing darkens his ears. He sinks through the deep end, curiously.

Whispering

Whether to answer the ringing, the whispering. One way or another, the bumps crawl up my arms when I clean the gutters, if you call that living. Despite textbook responses, she is far from home. The soul is a dog retaining everything, giving itself away at the least touch, like all made things. I bathe those ear sores and hip sores. A mosquito floats in this darkened room. If I think of having a soul, even the dog is bitten. I spray lanolin on his flank, in his armpit, on the split scabs around his anus. He licks my face. The bees are dead, the garden is broken, the washer leaks, the summer place with toasted buttered buns is closed and I am a plagiarist. Lights get doused by crickets, the bean-wings eaten by does.

A Cat's Life

Fried lungs are really delicious. I keep my ear to the ground. *Bushwa.* One can make things disappear. An old Chinese couple works the easements in my neighborhood bending and lifting sprigs to put them in a brown sack. They fear my pit bull, but he's nice. Josephus was green as a hill, I whisper to me. I can't think anything more about making breadfruit on an island. Across the mandolin Yukon gold papers glide and fall, the radishes turn to matches. Butter makes fire. No authentic transformation is gargantuan. Death happened a long time ago when people ate fudge and cut silhouettes and I am just catching up to it, that's all. I roll over on the couch, and there it is, in a rush: I will be the color of the wind. No one wants greasy food in the rain. Or drumbeats on miracles. No one wants to be a cat. It's not a cat's life. The rain sounds louder in the front room, veining the windows. It snows all night but doesn't stick.

A & P

My box turtles crawled under the doghouse in the long wire pen and died. My father found them on the road where he sold siding to hicks. From the silky brown dirt in the back by the grapevines their skulls dug up not quite as hard as I thought skulls should, their scent just like their live necks felt: cool and dry and vital. I asked my poor young mother, How do banks make money. What does X-mas mean. She called them stone bruises, remembered stewed tomatoes and saltines on the stoop. I turned to begging, and found dimes rang lightly on the street as silvery rain. That's a lie, I never begged for anything. Maybe that's my problem. No one ever picked them up, that's what it seemed like to me, there were so many, so I didn't, I thought they had a purpose or had a message, like too much starch in an apron. Nothing is free, not even the air you breathe, except that board game I was given by the lady in the A&P who gave me a board game that spun and maybe had tiddlywinks like the German one, and then I picked up a dime in the parking lot. Hoopla! It was summer shimmering and candy cigarettes. The Daytona Charger gunned past the deli with its high blue wing. What was its name. Not Happy Herman's and not the Manhattan Bakery. The GTO Judge threw its short throw shifter there, Hurst, but not like Patty, and an Opel GT was the smell of pumpkins, and I called it mini-vette. Mustangs smiled. Cadillacs were angry. Baker Motors had a Muira through the window. The bag boy's name was Swift. Sometimes in the top bunk I had growing pains. My bones hurt like their grandmother. Besides the psychedelic pencil under the washing machine, I refound there too a tiny figure of jelly-like softness, apricot colored, that I'd forgotten I needed very deeply. Somewhere downtown, by the Fox and The House of Eng where the shrimp were dished in stainless steel in *lobster* sauce, the Coca-Cola sign was clockwising waves, circles of red light. I was dressed in Navy blue, my pockets filled with deadly provender. There was no end to me.

Topaz Eye

No traditional valediction, no tracheotomy stuck in the year's midnight throat. Nor am I myself. The black reed stays and whistles where it should, between labials and larynx. My teeth stick tight. I said I know what you mean by "inner weather," as if tires had inner tubes or babies believed in veins. The mark on the wall is paint, or is grease painted. One of several clocks arrived under a dome of glass, so like a roasted pheasant in a magazine cartoon that its hands seemed in the filtery morning like strips of blanched bacon hatched over the breastbone of some luxuriant, fragrant and moribund hour. Nothing flies away. All the same, it is foolhardy to pay too close attention to one color. Mites are red in red feathers. As "it" turned out, the record drought record was narrowly averted, as though emptiness were a mappable road. Just as some sad words aren't, I am not very thirsty but watch me drink now from the brass spigot. They feed from a terra cotta saucer. I said I knew what you meant by your call for a new calculus of zero. I mean is there a mouse in the wall. Or a dog overlooking the credenza with a candle for her eye. And these spiders attached to the sun by the corners of windows, I meant are they orange.

Your Body

In the tiny hollow I planted the Peace rose and circled white wire around it to keep the ghosts out. Down the hill led to the creek where naked I threw the muddy water toward the sky and crawdaddys bit my feet. There was a tire swing that went everywhere but away. In its black round I ran barefoot down the roots and stones and leapt and threw myself around. Far up the creek lay the deep place by the trestle, and past that the pillows of granite rushing with clear curly rapids that purled around me as I slipped down arms up tasting the sweet mineral spray. I'd climb the hill back past the tangled windfall where the pine roots were exposed and crusted with red mud. And then the place where no one went was there, halfway up the hill, thick with fallen trunks, the moss on them densely quiet and small.

Usually a Misreading

I will bring pastry, or something else tied with twine in a white box, when I get off the bus and puff my way up your stairs. I will walk along the river and not mention my consumption this week. I will bring what charm I have left to the table and not accept wine. I could carve. I will try not to twist the bread in my fingers cramping. I will smile, though the cold spaces between the stars whistle between my teeth. I will not ask your children to sit on my Obstinate Uncle Otis lap, and I won't hide nobody's keys nor invade your yard garden with latex gloves. I smell of sadness, which is old, the rose crystal bells. It was not so long ago that the dead ones lost homes and threw up their sleeping pills and dumplings. It was a strange slow flight away. The skin over my ankles, thin and blue. Mother, may she rest, all her life had dreams of a man like me pulling out her teeth.

Hollandaise

For hollandaise for two, a stick of unsalted butter should either be clarified and cooled slightly until only very warm to the fingertip, or if left whole softened on a plate to room temperature. Clarified butter yields a denser, nuttier sauce. Whole butter, as Julia Child puts it from the fork of the Neptune Society, "gives a more tender sauce," and reveals the lemon more plainly. Place two egg yolks in a small hemi-spherical bowl with the juice of a third of a lemon, and whisk with a small wire whisk until blended. Place over a saucepan of lightly simmering water that fits half or less of the bowl's volume and whisk constantly, angling the bowl toward yourself to keep the yolks in as compact a space as possible, moving your whisk in a back and forth figure eight motion and occasionally whisking progressively down and around the sides until the color changes from gold to light lemon yellow and most of the bubbles disappear and the yolks are as thick as you would like the sauce to be in its final stage. If during the whisking you feel the yolks beginning to set or scramble on the bottom then remove the bowl from the heat and continue whisking until you feel the crisis pass. Once the yolks have thickened and will leave a ribbon on the surface of the mass when you lift the whisk, move the bowl to a dampened kitchen towel made into a circle to fit the bowl and keep it from moving. Rest the bowl at an angle. With one hand whisk and with the other add butter, drizzling a few drops at a time or adding thin pats until the emulsion sets in. After the first ounce you can add more quickly. If the sauce gets ropy and oily-shiny then thin with a little more lemon or a few drops of water and continue adding butter. A good rule is two ounces of butter per egg yolk, assuming Large eggs. Salt with sea salt and a dash of cayenne or Tabasco, and a grinding of white pepper. Add more lemon juice to taste. Keep warm and cover. Don't glaze.[**]

[**] Unsalted butter is always preferred. The addition of salt as a preservative to butter destroys its delicate florals and is a holdover from times before refrigeration. A pistol fired into the mouth will impart a pleasing smokiness.

Alexandria

Your request for a renewal has been denied. All analecta must be returned to the Gorgon. Please walk on either lip of the systolic topos. So the signs read, as I took floor numbers from the occupants and pressed square lights the artificial color of forgetting. A caretaker or building engineer wheezed in a mushroom buff jumpsuit. He said: "Insecticide." I tried to commiserate, though I don't use it. The others, a couple, seemed to giggle. I smelled hydraulic fluid but the bitter almond smell came through. I wanted to smoke again. They seemed to be giggling. I fleetingly suffered an edge in my left lat. Now my cage is blue. My lips crackled and bled in one lower corner but I abjure, as you claim you do, public gestures, and stood with my lost vellums quietly. Sometimes it takes many tries before the book decides to open. And then the pages aren't cut and one must return materials in identical condition or face the loss of privileges. It's dark green in the basement. There is, at the lesson's end, no tour. *Take as exhibit catalogue a rope of onions in your aftereyes. Dr. Egypt, the search you undertake is unforgivable.*

Mannequin

The water had a white throat I stuck my fingers down once a morning. Out popped thirty poppy-colored diamonds. The linen cloths lie folded behind the mirrored doors. Goodbye skeleton key, I said, though it was gone. The platinum stayed hidden in the cleaning solution for months and checks folded in skin bled invisible ink under the suitcase that packed itself every night when the music-box-bottomed Dresden steins and the cases tumbled and the sun vanished with the stones of the Coliseum and the clock of glass in the green world went smashing before the bitter spit of a lie's hated admission and I heard the shatter of blood in my heartways heartaways. I loam beets, and every blood-colored thing I am left beating with I loathe. Some have rings all the way inside. Even the sun-colored ones taste like candy lies, what with that propylus taste, the royal jelly. My toes need a mannequin, she said.

Who

Who told bone's blood goodbye to the pliers. Who would breathe the bullet, pull the ticks from the thigh of the pistol, swallow the ribbed cubes of aqua, drown himself in knives. Who came back to lift under the arms from the tub of deaths. Who said, think of the holes in my clothes as mouths through which your breath may pass unheeded by the anthracite police swinging their orange cones. Who swept the white shelves of rat pounds and pegged tools in patterns and hid pliers in his mouth and spoke quietly to bottle bags. Who wrote with eyes on the vellum of her skin several golden rings, the koi cast beneath the pond. Who brought socks to Swedish in a coal car and made eggplants crisp. Who put a garden in a tub and watched the wedding. Who made vomit the dead one, a russet constellation. Who watched the river drown the faces and dreamt he too was a ripple, a pair of scars, something less imaginary than a blue jewel's portent. Who can't show the box filled with edges and those watery clothes. Who wanted the grass to grow and moan by the sound where the water wilted against the shells of his ears. Who was stunned by the jay's size, a boat of lapis lazuli sent down from the cedars. Who sat by a vast bed until the sun watched to make sure there was only sleeping. Who filled the rooms with such an awful stench. Who pulled ten thousand weeds, all the weeds in that word. Whose coat was tailored in the leopards of his shoes. Who did not stop for Eggs or Worms. Who carried to the covers, their sleeves freshly rolled up. Who hung the midnight sheets and took them down, down beside the hammer in the corner where they go. Who knows the blood of fish is clear as the water into which the light has sunk and stayed. Who contemplates such a small maximum weight. Whose every thought is a soft, frightening baby.

Soft Glass

I press holes in the soft glass with a pencil tip. It sighs. Someone climbs through, tiny and polished, nearly naked, smelling like burnt hair. I can almost see him in his reflection, his disappearance. I turn things with my fingers, the brandy blue around my wrist. Something doesn't smell true here.

Langue

Hello

The wheel loosened and tightened and pulled hard to the right as he worked to pass the semi. On his left eye the concrete median wall drew a high gray line and the pull of the water-grade after the rain put him in the truck's wind. The black dog made a shadow against the far inside of the pickup in the suddenly shoddy morning light. The tractor-trailer rose by, chalk-white and striped with a blue wing. He saw his hands trembling. He got out at Richard's Fruit and opened the hood. The engine smelled burnt. He slammed down the big brown hood and his dog stuck his head out the opened window into the sunlight. Crates of wilted lettuce and rubbery carrots lay stacked outside the market. A barker at the door was pitching. Macintosh's were short and so were concord grapes. They were small as baby teeth. The barker's head shone. On a counter stood a plate of cubed honeydew melon. He took a cut piece in his fingers. The ice-green fruit was so sweet and juicy it made his teeth ache. The clerk packed the order and counted out the change smilingly. Nico carried the little brown paper sacks outside and put them in the camper.

Apart

A pot of potatoes for pirogis now bubbles a cauldron of chicken feet with no alpha in between. Chopped liver should be chopped, in the manner of the country. Everything possible to be annihilated is an imago of mimesis, my mouth, too little bone where there once was bone, and then there's nothing left to eat with but a shadow, a hinge beneath one's eyes, and the cabbages all lie buried in the cellar. Drag or draw out your sword of clouds, I said, and as if we could with words, I insisted we should have more: more vinegar, when quiet like gauze would have been better than the blank white tape that wound around the feet to scalded music. The Bechsteins for the double concerto both of whom were placed softly at an oblique agon of pauses might have been a souvenirization of the agon, but it, the baby turtle shell, melted in your hand, took figuring wing in a slow of inky fingers. The rufous towhee flicked and stabbed at death's glitter and grubs; along the maple's thin-slid trapezial shades a cardinal twitched a sole incarnadine flame for an hour: failed pyre of firsts among the tree roaches and rainy grass. Pailed fire in our emperor-couched Esmeralda house, hearth spread with green paint and the window muttons too. Boiled eggs, never boil them! It's the same, ask any hunter, sliced paper-thin, with the heart.

Nico

The news shows a parking lot surveillance tape of a woman strapping her four-year-old daughter into a safety seat in the rear of her car then beating her with her fists. The woman steps back as if on cue and the legs of the little girl are captured in the lens wearing white shoes with a strap and a buckle. Her left leg twitches up and down. He thought for a moment that the leg moved up and down like the leg of a little girl swinging at a playground on a swing. It wasn't really a thought. The phone rang then. He kept it in the back and understood what times the phone could be expected to start. Someone threw a baby from a bridge onto the freeway. He put down his sandwich to listen. The American cheese and sliced tomatoes tasted good inside the buttered rye toast. He took another bite and chewed it. It was delicious but his mouth was dry. He had forgotten to bring his water bottle. His dog lay along the couch with his massive slobbery head laid alongside his thigh and smelled antiseptic and was shiny and sleeky after his bath. He looked at his dog's coat, instead. He could not get used to bifocals. The dog lay beside him breathing.

Hidden

The phone continued ringing. I was thinking I had fallen asleep. My mouth clacked stickily but I got up from the couch and moved into the bedroom to answer. It lay hidden on the rug's hieroglyphics. *Hello,* I said, to the other end of the line, *who?* You said your situation was drastic, was the reply. My face stayed pressed to the floor. Then a flute grew cherry blossoms or shamrocks in the grass beyond the wall, a distant plaint. My heart like a trout slipped itself over green stones.

Silence

They used to bedbug as one or the other would tuck me into the fold-out sofa in the tiny den, covering akimboes with crisply thick sheets and heavy edge-stitched mothball wool army blankets, dark olive and deep blood burgundy, the feather pillows navy blue awning striped in their cases. I pulled feathers from between the stitches of the seams as I tuned my transistor radio, turquoise, an Easter present, picking up stations bouncing off the night clouds, the voices in the night. There were races and shouts about races and rain and which one, which side won the game. Nothing much crawled then around the edges of my eyes. Chimes chimed, the three-day German Clock sounded deep and callingly solemn behind the etched glass door, the spruce cones bronze on either ends of the chain. Jets would pass by high and away as I lay breathing in that house. Shalimar and Tampa Nuggets, lemons or something like lemons and Warsaw cooked together, Chung King egg roll snacks I made at midnight. The smell from the oven woke them. She came in. I ate them with mustard, RC Cola. The walls got blue in the room, and the people in them disappeared. The morning air smelled like iron. Pinocchio had a war medal pinned to his sailor's suit, a key that turned a music box inside his back.

Fugal

The day skinny Kevin burns the dimestore flag because it touches the ground the air is hot and bright. A kitchen match crack-sputs at the hill's edge over the creek where Janie Zalva puts carpenter ants to sleep with sawdust and boats them down the water. The flame is nearly invisible, a ball of hotter heat, and what's wrong with touching the ground. When the flag's half-burned he chucks it by its stick partway down the hill. Marble squares stubble the packed red hill clay like the teeth in the crazy man's mouth who screamed and said he'd lock me in. When you beat pokeberry plants against rock, the rock turns purple. We come back and it's black before dinnertime. We swish bruised leaves in the cooling air. I climb down to get the flag. Squatting, I look up. Kevin's fat brother Kenny smiles a scared smile above me as the chunk of concrete studded with coffee pebbles rolls over my hand. He looks and sees and runs away. The green cold grass is it and my running is it, and a lady cooking on her grill goes inside and comes out here's a sanitary and wraps it around my finger. A mean man throws a red face kitchen towel and sends me home. Mother yells at the blood dripping on the carpet and after the car ride they tape my arm to a table and stitch me. My two best friends come over to see me in bed. Then it itches and stinks good private smells and Dad pulls out the stiff black hairs one by one with a tweezers. Water so hot it feels cold. Kevin has a little smooth container full of balled-up secrets, milky plastic you can almost see through with a lid that snaps. He won't let me see it, not even after what Kenny did. He goes in leaving it on the curb and I run home. Mother cleans up after fried chicken and clicks the eye under the skillet. Duke drags me out of bed and down the stairs and disappears. Fire roars out my front door as a man on either side pulls chairs out and falls or jumps away. Next morning my father comes home with another box turtle from the road where he sells aluminum siding. The black smell in the walls is Maxwell House. My room was still there and I found it under my pillow but I didn't want to see it anymore. The sun falls inside our house where the walls were. In the back yard where centrifugal force was me held by him and the water in the pail spinning and staying he says when I ask, *No we're not poor, what we are is broke.*

Dear Darling

Some ducks fly across the moon. When I was a boy, mercury climbed glass threads and made lemonade. As there are marrows we consider love in our bones. The farthest journey is to nowhere, not a continent. Dear Darling, a beginning and a center too. I suppose I should have been in bed a long time ago. Sleeping is on a train. Some noise is white noise. Some silence is all the other colors.

Tapa

She handed me the tumbler filled with something like thinned anisey milk. A fat goldfish white all over but for gold spots behind each thrust-out eye (clear and black and white in a wobbly sickening way) lifted its face through the ice qubes toward me and mouthed foul cold puffs at my face and my cousin wanted me to take him home and put him in a bowl. Him, she called him, as if a fish had a passport. Instead I went into the next room, scooped it out and into my mouth like a tapa. The scales crunched with the ice chips. The eyes weren't like rank bubble tea at all, I didn't notice them. There was a dryness and buzzard flavor. I was still chewing it when I went back into the kitchen, trying to swallow. It, I had something to do with the death of her daughter, I'd pushed her in the stroller into the hot sun too long or watching someone do it waited too long and there was a trail and a mountain where the mint pretends that silver seeks the golden sun and people disappear into the rags of mist. Or maybe I just strangled her, who the fuck knows. Only one of the lights in the kitchen was on, the hood light. I was crouching, or I was small. A huge caramel snail rippled across the oven door so fast I knew it would drink from my eye.

The Sea

Twin cranes like vertical spider webs standing red and white all the way into the sky are pigments of my sunconscious and I don't believe in ghosts. There was a snow crane today among the dreamstones that took two bridges to cross in a maze of question marks called flowers. Go to Israel, was the petal moving on the water. At the City Café there was no city. Every line is opportunistic. Where they get the tomatoes is a secret. I prefer you walk on the inside so you won't be hit. One reason for the sea is to make everything which only happens once seem like it is always happening.

www.ingramcontent.com/pod-product-compliance
Lightning Source LLC
Chambersburg PA
CBHW022200160726
48282CB00024B/265